PAL Series
Program-Assisted Learning

Dennis P. Curtin
Kim Foley
Kunal Sen
Cathleen Morin

Windows® 95 PAL

Microsoft® Word for Windows® 95 (Version 7.0) PAL

Microsoft® Excel for Windows® 95 (Version 7.0) PAL

Microsoft® Access for Windows® 95 (Version 7.0) PAL

MICROSOFT® WORD FOR WINDOWS® 95 PAL: PROGRAM-ASSISTED LEARNING

VERSION 7.0

Dennis P. Curtin

Kunal Sen

Cathleen Morin

Prentice Hall, Upper Saddle River, New Jersey 07458

Library of Congress Cataloging-in-Publication Data:
Curtin, Dennis P.
        Microsoft Word for Windows 95 PAL [computer file] : program-
assisted learning [for] version 7.0 / Dennis P. Curtin, Kunal Sen,
Cathleen Morin.
        1 computer laser optical disc : sd., col. : 4 3/4 in. + 1 manual.
        Computer program.
        System requirements: 486 PC or better: 8MB RAM (16MB recommended);
Windows 95; Microsoft Word for Windows 95; SVGA with 256 colors
(640x480 minimum, 800x600 recommended); sound card and speakers
(optional); printer (optional); hard drive with 10MB free; 3½ in.
high density floppy disk drive; mouse; CD-ROM player.
        Title from manual t.p.
        Summary: Program-assisted instruction program for learning
Microsoft Word for Windows 95 (version 7.0). Displays interactive
animations, graphics, movies, and step-by-step instructions.
Includes concepts, tutorials, and drills.
        ISBN 0-13-237041-7
        1. Microsoft Word for Windows—Computer-assisted instruction—
Software. 2. Word processing—Computer-assisted instruction—
Software. I. Sen, Kunal. II. Morin, Cathleen.

Z52.5 <1996 00468> <MRC>
652—DC12   96-11147
                                                           CIP
                                                           Rev

Microsoft, MS, Windows, and Wingdings are registered trademarks of Microsoft Corporation
in the USA and other countries.

Acquisitions editor: Carolyn Henderson
Marketing manager: Nancy Evans
Director of production and manufacturing: Joanne Jay
Production manager: Lorraine Patsco
Illustrator: Warren Fischbach
Design director: Patricia Wosczyk
Senior manufacturing supervisor: Paul Smolenski
Editorial assistant: Lori Cardillo
Production coordinator: Renée Pelletier
Project manager: Cecil Yarbrough

Interior design by Kenny Beck
Additional design by Christy Mahon
Cover art by Marjory Dressler
Cover design by Ginidir Marshall
Screen shots by Cathleen Morin

 ©1997 by Prentice Hall, Inc.
A Simon & Schuster Company
Upper Saddle River, New Jersey 07458

ISBN 0-13-237041-7

Printed in the United States of America
9 8 7 6 5 4 3 2 1

Prentice-Hall International (UK) Limited, *London*
Prentice-Hall of Australia Pty. Limited, *Sydney*
Prentice-Hall of Canada Inc., *Toronto*
Prentice-Hall Hispanoamericana, S.A., *Mexico*
Prentice-Hall of India Private Limited, *New Delhi*
Prentice-Hall of Japan, Inc., *Tokyo*
Simon & Schuster Asia Ptd. Ltd., *Singapore*
Editora Prentice-Hall do Brasil, Ltda., *Rio de Janeiro*

CONTENTS

QUICKSTEPS BOXES

  QUICKSTEPS BOXES

P R E F A C E

Word processing is probably the most common application of computers. The ease with which you can draft and revise memos, letters, reports, and other documents with a word processing program like Microsoft Word increases both the speed and quality of your writing. You can enter, edit, change, reorganize, format, and print text without having to retype all of it each time you make a change. This ease of use encourages you to revise and reorganize your material more frequently so that you can express your ideas more clearly and prepare more professional-looking documents.

The applications of programs such as Word are almost endless, ranging from the same tasks that can be done on a typewriter, such as writing memos, letters, and reports, to entirely new kinds of tasks that aren't possible without the power of the computer. For example, you can prepare a form letter that you can then use over and over again, with just a name or phrase changed here and there. Contracts, sales letters, and collection notices are typical form documents. You can even desktop-publish documents because Word can change fonts, print in columns, and print graphics along with text. These features open up a new world of opportunities since you can now inexpensively desktop-publish catalogs, advertising circulars, reports, articles, and even books. You can even use a Word document to store Internet World Wide Web addresses so you can go to them just by double-clicking an icon in the document.

This text, *Microsoft Word for Windows 95 (Version 7.0) PAL: Program-Assisted Learning,* is an outline and guide to the accompanying interactive multimedia program *PAL,* our system of *Program-Assisted Learning.* This learning system assumes only basic Windows experience such as pointing, clicking, and dragging. Everything else you need to know to become a proficient user of Microsoft Word for Windows 95 is presented here.

PAL—PROGRAM-ASSISTED LEARNING

PAL—*Program-Assisted Learning*—is designed to guide you through learning Word for Windows 95 while you use the actual program. It does this by displaying interactive animations, graphics, movies, and step-by-step instructions on top of the Word screen display. PAL is an intuitive, easy-to-use system that makes learning Word not only more efficient, but more enjoyable. When you use it with this text, it lets you master the most frequently used Word features more quickly.

1. PAL's setup procedure copies to your computer's hard drive the PAL program and a database containing the program's text components. The graphic, movie, and sound files on the PAL CD are not copied to the hard drive, so you must have the CD in your computer's CD-ROM drive when you use the program. The PAL CD also contains the files you copy to your own 3.5-inch floppy disks when you make your *Word Student Resource Disks,* described later in this preface.

2. When you start PAL, an interactive multimedia window opens on top of the Word screen to guide you through interactive concepts, tutorials, drills,

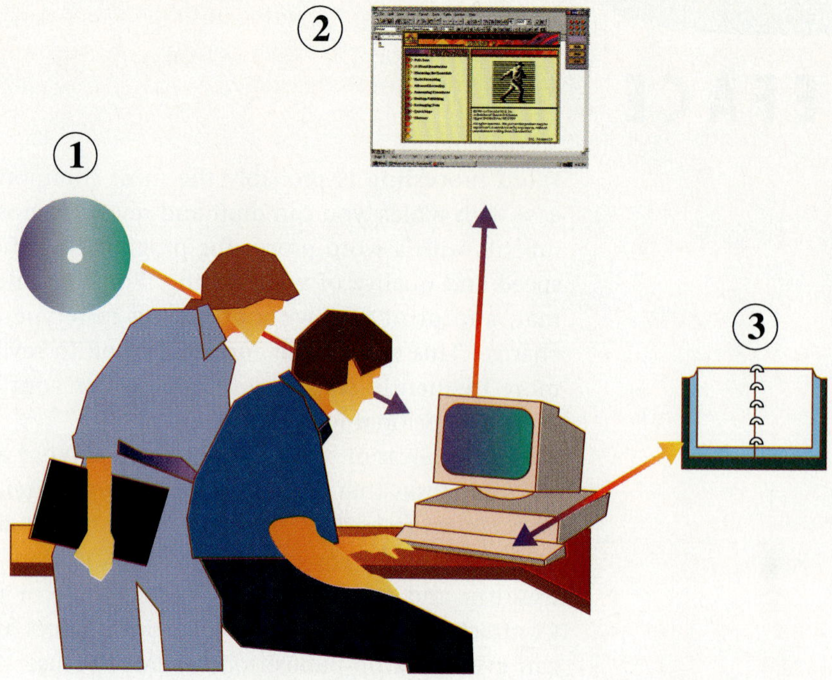

The PAL System. The PAL system uses on-screen interactive multimedia and printed text material working together: (1) the PAL CD; (2) the PAL window on top of the Word screen; (3) the PAL text.

and review questions. As you study Word, you have immediate on-line access to illustrated glossary terms, demonstration videos, and step-by-step procedures.

3. This book, a guide to using the PAL system, provides the context for your studies with concepts, examples, exercises, reference material, and a checklist of on-line activities.

T I P
Also Available at a Computer Screen Near You

Microsoft Word for Windows 95 PAL (Version 7.0): Program-Assisted Learning is one of a series of texts that use a highly visual, interactive multimedia approach to learning Windows 95 and its application programs. Similar texts are available on Windows 95 itself and on the Microsoft Office applications Excel and Access.

PAL—The Advantages of Its Approach

There is a big difference between a static textbook and a dynamic, interactive multimedia presentation. Here are just some of the advantages of using PAL:

▶ Basic concepts are presented interactively so they are more interesting and understandable than those presented in a text.

▶ You do not have to refer back and forth between the book and screen. Many resources are just a mouse click away, ready for instant access. Click a blue word or phrase to see an illustrated definition. Click a **QuickSteps** button for a step-by-step guide to a procedure. Click a **Graphic** button for an illustration. Click a **Demo** button to see a movie of a key step demonstrated on screen. Click a **Loudspeaker** button to hear a word pronounced.

▶ The on-screen instructions and animations of concepts are immediate and understandable demonstrations of the computer's usefulness that will help motivate you to learn.

▶ Review questions—both multiple choice and true-false—are more interactive than in a textbook. They provide immediate feedback and directions. You are immediately told if you answered correctly or incorrectly and, if incorrect, you are directed back to the section where the material was covered.

LAB ACTIVITIES—FIVE STEPS TO MASTERY

Learning operating systems and application programs takes time and practice. There really aren't any shortcuts. This text recognizes that no one masters procedures the first time through. It takes repetition and practice—and yes, even mistakes. Our approach uses five steps to mastery: concepts, tutorials, drills, exercises, and projects. As you proceed through these five steps in the order shown, you are given less and less guidance and have more and more room to make mistakes. You are also required to use more and more procedures to perform combined tasks.

1. *On-line concepts* provide you with a step-by-step interactive introduction to, and a walk-through of, the procedure you are studying. Your actions are controlled so you cannot make a mistake.

2. *On-line tutorials* provide you with step-by-step guidance as you explore a procedure for the first time using the actual Word for Windows program. If you follow the steps, you can't go wrong.

3. *On-line drills*, which you complete after finishing a matching tutorial, are very narrow in focus and drill you on a single procedure. The purpose of these drills is to allow you to repeat a procedure until you have mastered it. For example, you may format several documents instead of the one you formatted in the tutorial.

4. *Text-based exercises*, which you complete after the drills, are more challenging than drills and usually require an understanding of more than one procedure. Procedures are not spelled out for you. You either have to recall

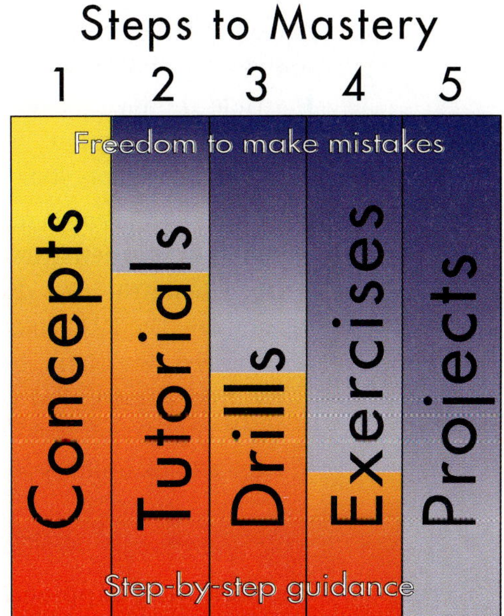

them or look them up. These activities are much like the real world, where you are told what to do but not how to do it.

5. *Text-based projects* state a problem or provide a situation and tell you what should be done about it but provide no instructions on how to do it.

WORD FOR WINDOWS 95 PAL'S ORGANIZATION

Word for Windows 95 PAL is organized into pictorial tutorials called *PicTorials*.

PicTorial T takes you on a simulated tour of PAL and its elements. You'll see how to explore concepts, complete tutorials and drills, and answer review questions.

PicTorial 1 introduces Word and shows you how to get around the program's screens. You create, edit, save, and print a simple document and explore Word's extensive Help system.

PicTorial 2 teaches you the procedures you absolutely must know in order to begin to get value from Word.

PicTorials 3 and 4 explore the ways in which you can enhance the appearance of your documents with character, paragraph, and section formatting.

PicTorial 5 shows you how to use Word's Mail Merge feature to prepare form letters and labels, and introduces other time-saving features of the program.

PicTorial 6 introduces more advanced features applicable to desktop publishing, such a formatting in columns, creating and editing tables, and using graphics in your documents.

PicTorial 7 shows you how to use Word's ability to exchange data with other application programs, linking and embedding objects such as line drawings, photographs, sounds, and video in your Word documents.

PAL—WHAT'S NEEDED TO USE IT

The complete PAL learning system contains the following components:

▶ This text is your guide to using PAL. It contains conceptual and reference material, an outline of your on-line activities, exercises, and projects.

▶ Inside the back cover of the book is packaged the CD which contains the entire PAL program. Printed on the flap of the back cover are instructions for installing PAL on your system and for making the *Word Student Resource Disks*.

▶ The *Word Student Resource Disks* contains all of the files needed to complete the computer activities in this text. You cannot run PAL past PicTorial 1 without having the first disk in the floppy drive of your computer (though you can view the PAL Tour and PicTorial 1 without it). To make these disks, you will need two blank, formatted 3.5-inch high-density (1.44MB capacity) floppy disks and the PAL Identification Number (PIN) printed on the outside of the CD package. Note that it is illegal to use the PAL Identification Number from a book unless you are the rightful owner of the book/CD package.

Supplements

The following supplements to this text have been made available by the publisher:

▶ An *Instructor's Manual with Tests* contains suggested course outlines for a variety of course lengths and formats, teaching tips and a list of competencies to be attained for each PicTorial, solutions and answers to all computer activities, and a complete test bank of over 200 questions.

▶ A Windows-based computerized testing program, *Prentice Hall Custom Test*, features user-friendly test creation as well as the ability to administer tests traditionally or on-line, evaluate and track students' results, and analyze the success of each exam—all with a simple click of the mouse.

Sending Your Opinions and Feedback

We are happy to hear from users or potential users of this program. It's through such exchanges that improvements are made. If you have any comments or questions, send them to one of us at the Internet e-mail address listed at the end of this preface.

Acknowledgments

We would like to thank all of those people who have worked hard to make this the best possible program.

On the academic end have been the following reviewers of the text or the PAL program:

▶ Kathryn M. Baalman, St. Charles Community College

▶ Susan Blackman, Fort Lewis College

▶ Kate Crawford, Edison Community College

▶ Edward Eill, Delaware County Community College

▶ Michael A. Feiler, Merritt College

▶ Lisa E. Gueldenzoph, Bowling Green State University

▶ Matthew Hightower, Bakersfield College

▶ RobertA. Hogue, Youngstown State University

▶ Lester W. Horn, Pensacola Junior College

▶ Barbara Hotta, Leeward Community College

▶ Rajeev Kaula, Southwest Missouri State University

▶ William Kornegay, Miami-Date Community College

▶ Hao Lou, Ohio University

▶ Philip McCauley, ITT Technical Institute

▶ Mike Miller, Kansas State University

▶ Lou Price, DeVry Institute of Technology (Columbus, Ohio)

▶ Fred M. Schwartz, Business Solutions Unlimited

▶ Dennis D. Shafer, Cuyahoga Community College

▶ Randy Stolze, Marist College

▶ Frederick L. Wells, DeKalb College

▶ Donald C. Westlake, Computer Learning Center (Los Angeles)

▶ Marlys Willard, Iowa Western Community College, Council Bluffs

At the publisher's end Cecil Yarbrough continued with his efforts to improve our texts. His guidance and leadership are always most welcome. Supporting the production at the publisher have been Suzanne Behnke, Warren Fischbach, Joanne Jay, Christy Mahon, John Nestor, Lorraine Patsco, Paul Smolenski, and Patricia Wosczyk.

All of these people, each and every one, took a personal interest in this text, and that interest shows in the work you are now holding. Any shortcomings that remain are our responsibility.

DENNIS P. CURTIN Dennis_Curtin@msn.com
KUNAL SEN 76625,2444@compuserve.com
CATHLEEN MORIN 102662,237@compuserve.com
KIM FOLEY 74071,2240@compuserve.com

A PAL TOUR

PAL stands for *Program-Assisted Learning*; it is an interactive multimedia series consisting of textbooks and accompanying computer programs. PAL guides you through learning Windows 95 and its Microsoft Office application programs by displaying animations, graphics, and step-by-step instructions on top of each program's own screen display. You'll find that PAL is an intuitive, easy-to-use system that makes learning Windows 95 and its applications more efficient and more enjoyable. ▶

Installing PAL and Making the Student Resource Disks

The PAL program must be installed on your computer or network before you can run it, and to do more than view the PAL Tour and the first PicTorial you must also have made your own *Student Resource Disks* using the *MakeSRD* program that comes on the CD, together with the PAL Identification Number, or PIN, that is included on the inside back cover of your book/CD package. Instructions for these steps are included on the back cover flap of this book.

Once PAL is installed on your system, you are ready to learn how to start it—also called *opening*, *running*, or *launching* it—and how to close or exit it. To use PAL you first turn on your computer to start Windows 95. Then follow the steps in the QuickSteps box "Starting PAL." (If you will be running PAL on a network, your lab instructor may give you special instructions for starting PAL.)

Q U I C K S T E P S

Starting PAL

1. Insert the CD into your computer's CD-ROM drive.

2. Insert the *Student Resource Disk* with the PAL Identification Number, or PIN, into your computer's floppy drive.

3. With Windows on the screen, use the mouse to point to the **Start** button at the left of the taskbar at the bottom of the Windows screen, and click the left mouse button to display the Start menu.

4. Using the mouse, point to the word **Programs** on the menu to display a submenu listing the programs on your system.

5. Point to the words **PAL Systems** on the menu to display another submenu listing the PAL programs on your system.

6. Click the name of the PAL program you are studying. PAL opens with an animation, and then the *Contents* window appears.

C O M M O N   W R O N G   T U R N S

No Student Resource Disk?

If you start PAL without the proper *Student Resource Disk* in your computer's floppy drive, a dialog box will appear asking you to insert the disk.

▸ If you have the disk, insert it into your floppy drive, then click the drop-down arrow in the lower-left corner of the window to display a list of the drives on your system. Click the drive into which you inserted the disk, then click the **OK** button to continue.

▸ If you don't have a disk, click the **Demo** button and you can explore the PAL Tour and PicTorial 1. Or click the **Cancel** button to leave PAL.

The PAL *Contents* window is much like the table of contents in a book. When you select a PicTorial (chapter) from the list on the left, the sections in that PicTorial are displayed on the right. Just by selecting one PicTorial after another you can easily scan the entire contents of the program. When you select one of the sections on the right, the *Section Introduction* window appears. From this window you can explore the section's concepts or begin a step-by-step tutorial or drill. And PAL's Remote Control is always available to help you move around in the program. The illustration "PAL's Organization" shows a sample of each of these screens.

PAL's Organization. PAL Is organized into a series of related windows, each of which is described in this introduction.

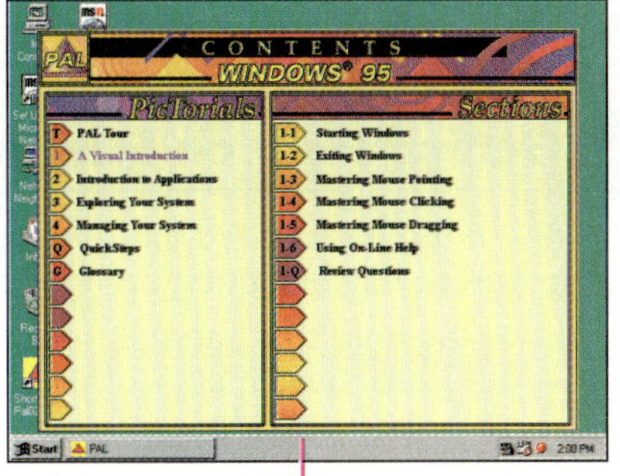

The *Contents* Window

When you start PAL, the *Contents* window appears. Clicking a PicTorial on the left side of the window displays a list of its sections on the right side.

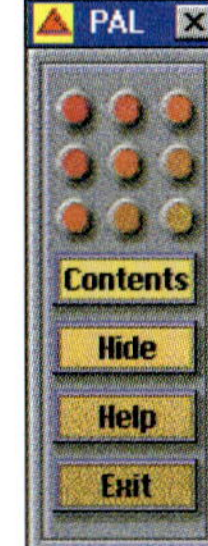

The Remote Control. The Remote Control is always on the screen when PAL is open.

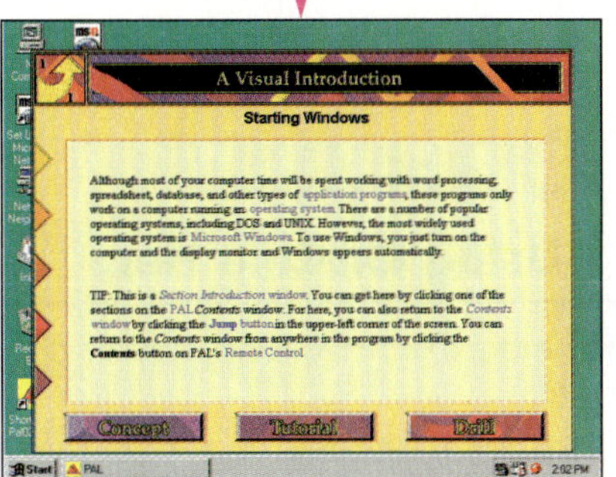

The *Section Introduction* Window

Clicking one of the sections on the *Contents window* displays the *Section Introduction* window. This window is your gateway to learning about a topic by exploring concepts, a tutorial, and a drill step by step.

The *Concepts* Window

Clicking the **Concept** button on the *Section Introduction* window displays a step-by-step introduction to the topic you are studying.

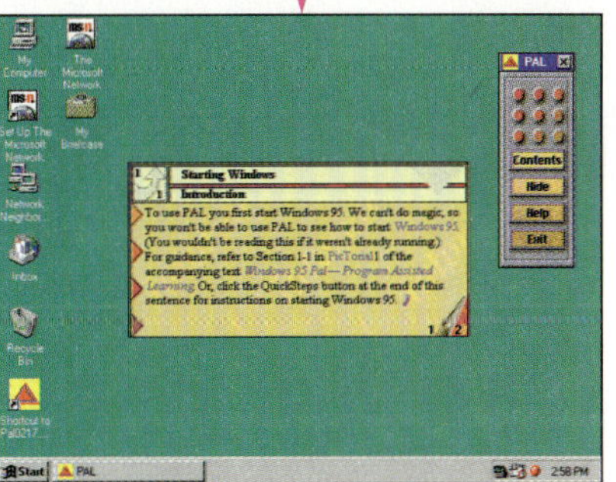

The *Tutorial* Window

Clicking the **Tutorial** button on the *Section Introduction* window displays a smaller *Tutorial* window that leads you step by step through a procedure.

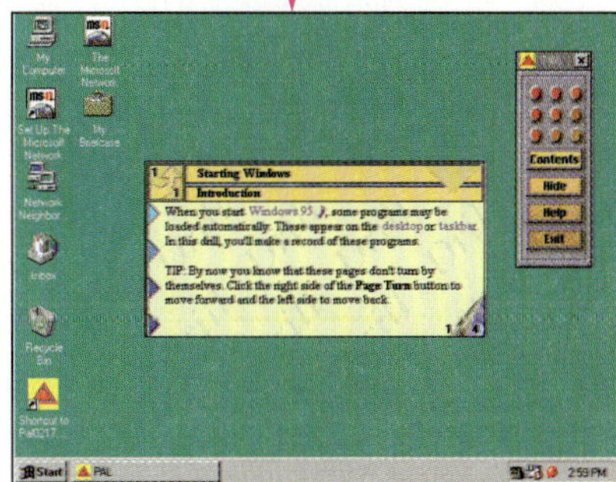

The *Drill* Window

Clicking the **Drill** button on the *Section Introduction* window displays a smaller *Drill* window that leads you through a procedure so you can master it.

T I P

Stopping the Opening Animation

PAL begins with an opening animation. If you don't want to watch it, you can click anywhere in this animation with the left mouse button and go directly to the PAL *Contents* window.

Getting On-Line Help

You can use the **Help** button on PAL's Remote Control to display Help at any time. Clicking It once with the left mouse button displays help on things you point to. Clicking it twice takes you into the on-line Help system.

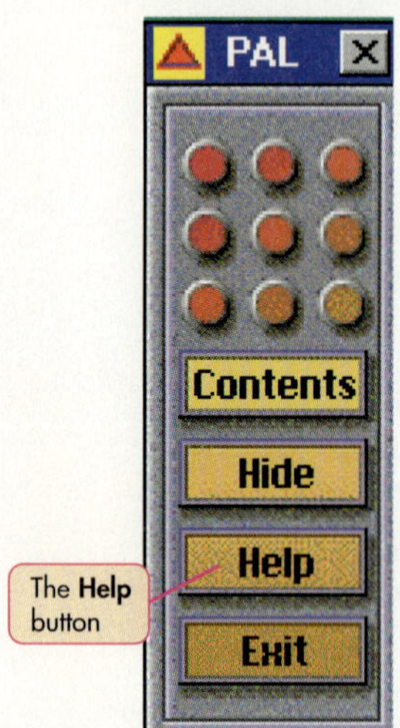

The Help Button. Clicking the **Help** button on the Remote Control adds a question mark to the mouse pointer. When you then point to any PAL object on the screen, a description of that object is displayed.

QUICKSTEPS

Getting Help on Screen Objects

1. To find out what any PAL button, window, or other object does, click the **Help** button to add a question mark to the mouse pointer.
2. Point to the object in question to display its description in a window that slides out from the Remote Control.
3. To close the Help window and remove the question mark from the pointer, click the **Help** button again. (You can also click anywhere on a clear area of PAL, but be careful. Clicking buttons or glossary terms activates them.)

QUICKSTEPS

Using On-Line Help

1. For more extensive Help, double-click the **Help** button to enter PAL's Help system.
2. Click any Help topic button on the left side of the Help window to display Help on that topic on the right.
3. Use the scroll bar to scroll through Help text on the right, or click the **Done** button to close Help. Within any Help text, you can also click a **Graphic** button (📷) to display a pop-up graphic, a **Demo** button (🖥) to display an animated demonstration, or a **Loudspeaker** button to hear a word pronounced.

Hiding and Restoring PAL

If a PAL window or the Remote Control covers a part of the screen you want to see, or if you want to put PAL away for awhile, you can hide it by clicking the **Hide** button on the Remote Control. This reduces the PAL program ("minimizes it") to a button on Windows' taskbar. It is still running but not taking up space on your screen. When you want to see it again, click the PAL button on the taskbar to restore it. (If you cannot see the Remote Control, clicking the PAL button on the taskbar moves it in front of all other windows.)

Closing PAL

When finished with PAL, you can close it. This removes it from your computer's memory and the screen. To use it again, you have to restart it from Windows' Start menu. To close PAL, you would normally use the left mouse button to click the **Exit** button on PAL's Remote Control, but you can use any of the procedures listed in the QuickSteps box "Closing PAL and Setting a Bookmark."

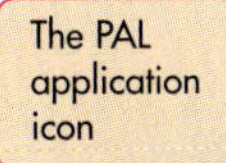

Closing PAL. One of the quickest ways to close PAL is to click the **Exit** button on the Remote Control.

Closing PAL and Setting a Bookmark

To close PAL and display the PAL Bookmark dialog box:

▶ With the left mouse button, click the **Exit** button on PAL's Remote Control.

You can also do any of the following:

▶ With the left mouse button click the **Close** button (⊠) on the Remote Control's title bar.

▶ With the left mouse button, click the PAL application icon on the Remote Control's title bar to display a shortcut menu, then use the left mouse button to click the shortcut menu's **Close** command.

▶ With the right mouse button, click the Remote Control's title bar to display a shortcut menu, then use the left mouse button to click the shortcut menu's **Close** command.

▶ With the right mouse button, click PAL's button on the taskbar (at the bottom of the Windows screen), then click the shortcut menu's **Close** command.

When the PAL Bookmark dialog box asks whether you want to mark your place:

▶ Click the **Yes** button, and the next time you start PAL, the PicTorial and section that you have just finished will be highlighted in the Contents window..

▶ Click the **No** button to close PAL without setting a bookmark.

PAL ACTIVITIES CHECKLIST

☐ **T-1 PAL TOUR.** In this section, you begin to explore the PAL system of learning.

1. Follow the steps listed in the text-based tutorial that follows to display PAL's *Contents* window.

2. Click the **Exit** button on PAL's Remote Control to close PAL. (If you can't see the Remote Control, click the PAL button on Windows' taskbar.)

☐ **TOURING PAL ON YOUR OWN.** In this section, you explore starting and closing PAL on your own.

1. Start PAL and this time click anywhere on the opening animation to stop it before it finishes.

2. Click the **Help** button on the Remote Control and then point to objects on the screen to see what they do. (If you can't see the Remote Control, click the PAL button on Windows' taskbar.) When finished, click the **Help** button again to turn off Help.

3. Double-click the **Help** button on the Remote Control (that is, click it twice very rapidly) to display the Help window. Click Help topics on the left and read about them. When finished, click the **Done** button.

4. Close PAL using any of the procedures described in the QuickSteps box "Closing PAL."

5. Start PAL again and continue to the next section.

In this tutorial you turn on your system so it starts Windows 95 and then start PAL. On some systems, additional steps may be required. If this is the case with your system, your instructor will supply you with the information you need.

LOOKING AHEAD
Pointing and Clicking

To perform many actions with the computer, you use the mouse to move the mouse pointer on the screen so that it points to a button or a menu command, and then you press and release the left mouse button. This is called pointing and clicking, and you will become expert at it as you use PAL. Here is a tip in advance: Always hold the mouse so that it is perpendicular to the face of the monitor. That way, when you move the mouse left or right, the mouse pointer will move in the same direction on the screen. When the mouse pointer is over the button you want to click, press the left mouse button gently so you don't move the mouse at the same time.

Getting Ready

1. Open the door to floppy drive A or eject any disk from that drive.

Starting Windows 95

2. To start Windows, turn on the computer and the display monitor. If you can't find the on/off switches, ask someone where they are. When you turn on the computer, the computer first runs a diagnostic program to be sure the system is operating correctly. Then the Windows loading sequence begins. At some point in the process, you may be prompted to log onto Windows or a network.

3. When the Windows desktop and taskbar are displayed, you can begin work. If a *Welcome to Windows 95* screen appears on the desktop, point to the **Close** button in the lower-right corner of its window and click the left mouse button. There also may be other windows that appear on your screen automatically.

Starting PAL

4. Insert the CD into your computer's CD-ROM drive.

5. Insert the *Student Resource Disk* with the PAL Identification Number (PIN) into one of your computer's floppy drives.

6. Using the mouse, point to the **Start** button on the taskbar and click the left mouse button to display the Start menu. (Your menu may look different from the one shown here.)

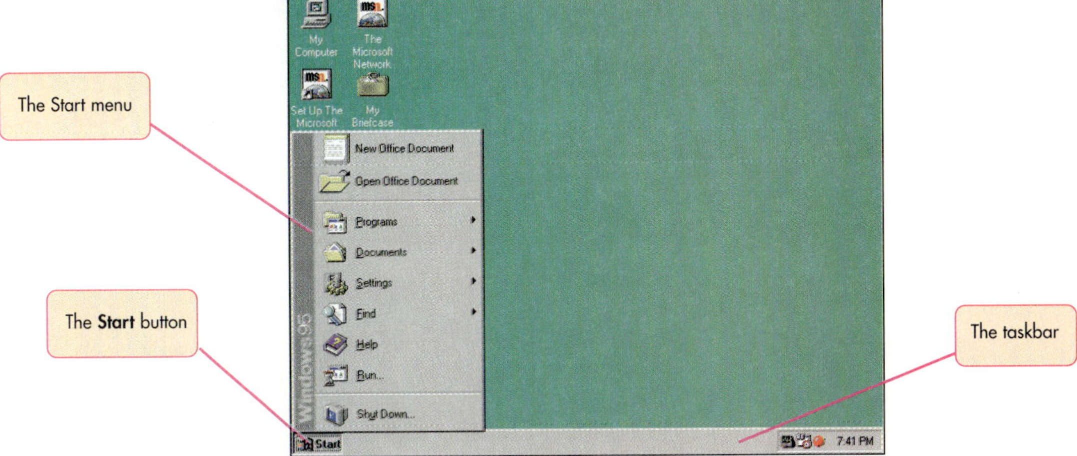

7. Point to the menu's **Programs** folder so it cascades and displays a submenu. (Your submenu may look different from the one shown here.)

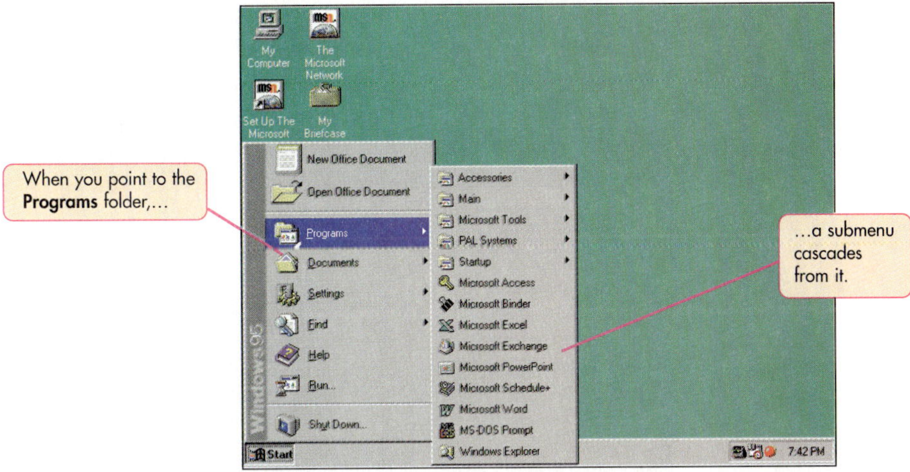

8. Point to the menu's **PAL Systems** folder so it cascades and displays a list of the PAL programs on your system. (Your submenu may look different from the one shown here.)

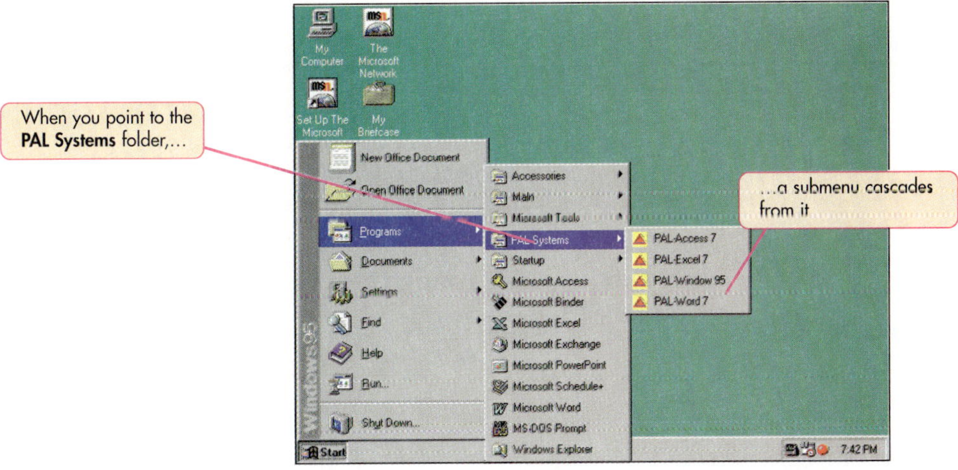

9. On the PAL submenu, click the name of the PAL program you are studying. This starts PAL and displays an opening screen and an animation.

10. With the left mouse button, click anywhere in the animation screen, or just wait for the animation to end, and the *Contents* windows appears, listing the PicTorials (chapters) in the course. Notice how a button for PAL appears on the taskbar (at the bottom of the Windows screen) and the PAL Remote Control appears at the top right of the screen.

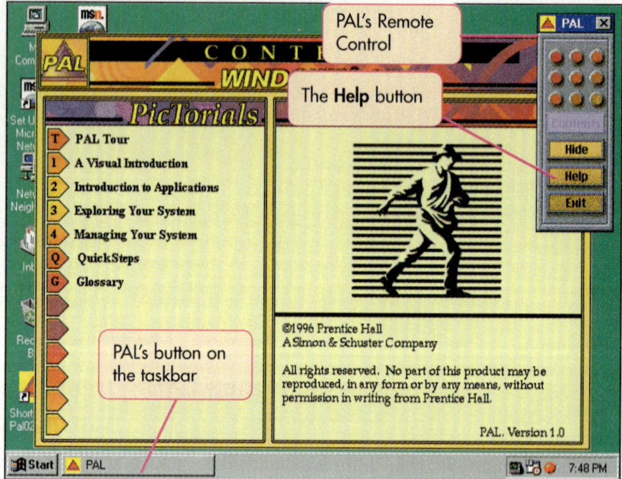

Exploring Help

11. Click the **Help** button on the Remote Control to add a question mark to the mouse pointer. (If the Remote Control is hidden, just click the PAL button on the taskbar to move it on top of other windows.)

12. Point to PAL objects on the screen to display a description of them in a window that slides out from the Remote Control. When finished, click any clear area of a PAL window to close the Help window. (To avoid clicking command buttons and activating them by mistake, just click the **Help** button on the Remote Control again.)

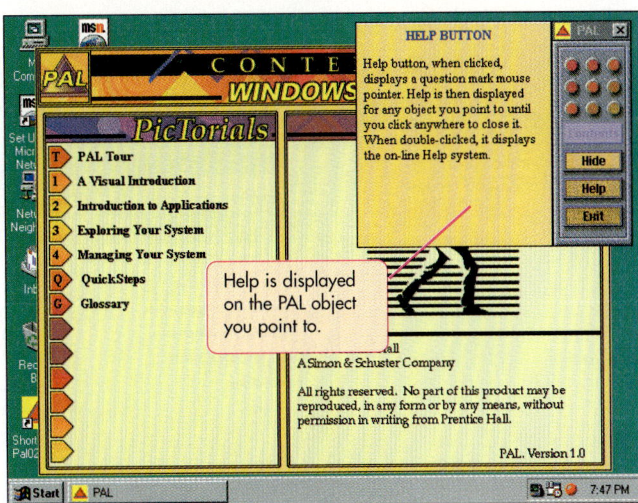

13. Double-click the **Help** button on the Remote Control to open the main Help window.

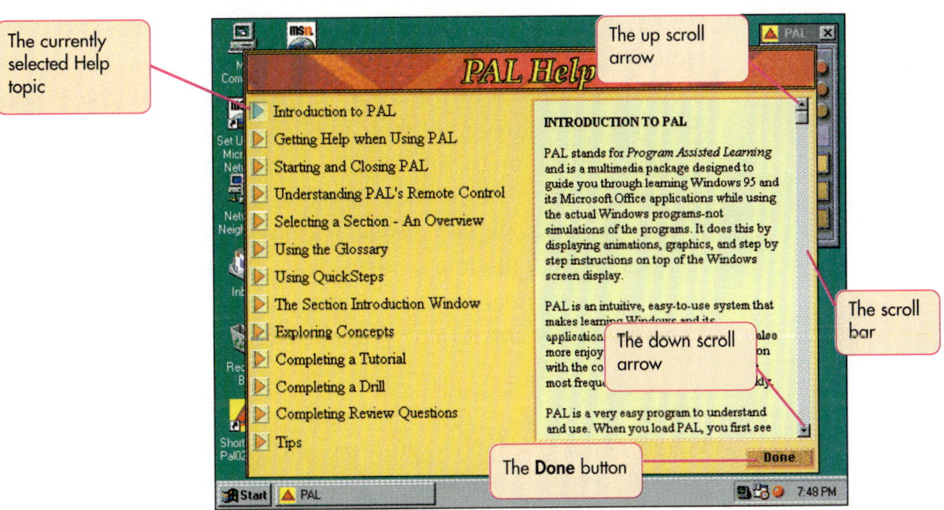

14. Click any Help button or topic on the left side of the window to display Help on that topic. Sometimes, the Help text on the right side of the screen is too long to fit on one screen. To scroll through it, click the up and down scroll arrows on the scroll bar.

15. When finished exploring Help, click the Help window's **Done** button.

Finishing Up

16. Continue to the next section to learn more about PAL. If you have to quit now, click the **Exit** button on the Remote Control to close PAL. (If the Remote Control is hidden, click the PAL button on Windows' taskbar to move it in front of other open windows.)

T-2 PAL—GETTING STARTED

Starting PAL displays its *Contents* window and Remote Control. Both of these are used extensively when navigating and studying with PAL.

PAL'S Contents Window

When you start PAL, the first window you see after the animation is the *Contents* window, which is organized like the table of contents in a book.

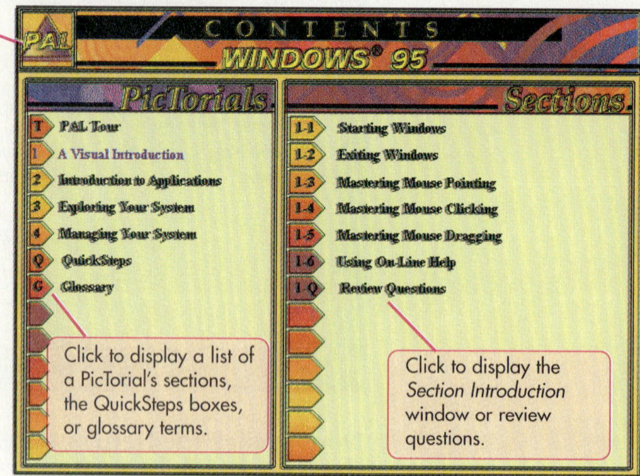

The PAL *Contents* Window. To study a section click the PicTorial on the left side of the window and then click a section that appears on the right side. You can also click **Glossary**, **QuickSteps**, or **Review Questions** to move to those sections of the program. You can click the PAL logo in the upper-left corner to display ordering and version number information. You can then click the **Credits** button to see a list of the people who developed this program, or click the **Done** button to return to the *Contents* window.

To begin study, first select a PicTorial from the list on the left side of the *Contents* window by clicking its name or number. When you do so, a list of sections or topics in that PicTorial is displayed on the right side of the window. (Sections are hidden by a logo when you first load PAL.) You can click one PicTorial after another to quickly skim through the contents of the entire program. When you find the section you want to study, click its name or number on the right side of the window to display its *Section Introduction* window. When finished with all of the sections in a PicTorial, click **Review Questions** on the *Sections* list to display a set of questions that test your understanding of the selected PicTorial. You would normally answer these questions only after completing all of the sections in the PicTorial.

PAL'S Remote Control

When PAL is open, the Remote Control is always on the screen. Like the remote control for your television or stereo, the buttons on PAL's Remote Control enable you to control the PAL program. If the Remote Control gets hidden by other PAL windows, click the PAL button on Windows' taskbar to bring it to the front. If it gets in your way, you can drag it to a new position.

LOOKING AHEAD
Dragging

If the Remote Control gets in your way, you can move it to a new position. Point to a clear area of its title bar, hold down the left mouse button, and move the mouse in the direction you want to move the Remote Control. As you do so, an outline of the Remote Control moves on the screen. Release the mouse button, and the Remote Control moves to fill the outline. This is called dragging, and you will become expert at it as you proceed through this PAL.

The Remote Control. The Remote Control is always on the screen when PAL is open.

▶ **Zip** buttons, arranged in a grid, immediately move any PAL window to one of nine preset positions on the screen to get the window out of your way. For example, if you click the upper-right **Zip** button, the PAL window will zip to the upper-right corner of the screen. You'll find these buttons a quick way to see what's under the PAL window.

▶ **Contents** button returns you to the opening *Contents* window where you can select a new PicTorial or section to study, display questions for any PicTorial, or display lists of QuickSteps and glossary terms. The PicTorial and section that you last worked on are highlighted when you return.

▶ **Hide** button acts like a Windows **Minimize** button. Clicking it reduces PAL and all open PAL windows to just a button on the taskbar. This is useful whenever any of PAL's windows get in your way. To display PAL again, click the PAL button on the taskbar.

▶ **Help** button displays Help on the PAL program. Clicking it once lets you point to PAL objects to display a brief description of them. Clicking the **Help** button again turns pointer help off. Double-clicking the **Help** button displays the full Help system.

▶ **Exit** button closes PAL and removes it from your system's memory. To use it again, you have to restart it from Windows' Start menu.

Like all Windows applications, the Remote Control has a title bar. You can point to a clear area on this title bar, hold down the left mouse button, and drag it to a new position on the screen.

▶ **Application icon** at the left end of the title bar displays a shortcut menu when you click it.

▶ **Close** button (⊠) at the right end of the title bar is the standard Windows 95 button used to close an application. Clicking this button removes PAL from your computer's memory and the screen. To use it again, you have to restart if from Windows' Start menu.

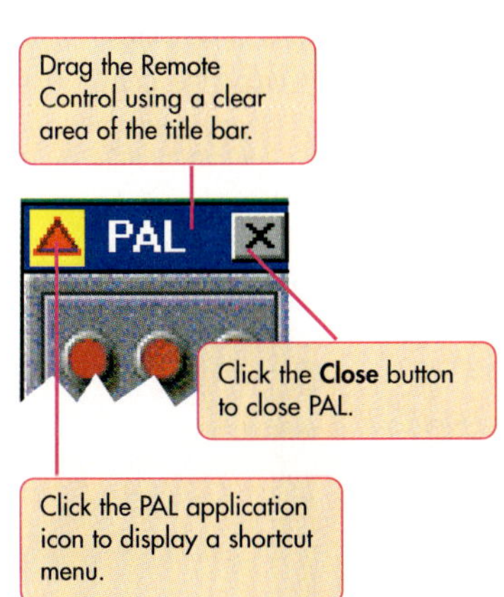

The Remote Control's Title Bar. The Remote Control's title bar can be used to drag the Remote Control, display a shortcut menu, or close PAL.

PAL ACTIVITIES CHECKLIST

☐ **T-2 PAL TOUR.** In this section, you start PAL and use it to explore PAL's Remote Control and a few basic ways to navigate through the PAL program.

1. Start PAL or click the **Contents** button on the Remote Control to return to the *Contents* window.

2. On the *PicTorials* list, click the letter **T** or the name **PAL Tour**. This displays a list of the sections in the tour.

3. On the *Sections* list, click T-2, **PAL—Getting Started** to display the first screen of the tour.

4. Follow the instructions that appear on the screen. If nothing seems to happen, click the **Page Turn** button in the lower-right corner of PAL's window. Clicking the left side of this button moves you back one step and clicking the right side moves you forward.

☐ **TOURING PAL ON YOUR OWN.** In this section, you explore PAL's Remote Control and a few basic ways to navigate through the PAL program.

1. Click each of the PicTorials on the *PicTorials* list to see their sections in the *Sections* list. Don't click **QuickSteps** or **Glossary** yet. If you do, click the **Done** button in the windows that appears to return to the *Contents* window.

2. Click PAL's button on the taskbar to move the Remote Control in front of other windows.

3. Practice clicking the **Hide** button on the Remote Control, then clicking PAL's button on the taskbar. Repeat this until you understand exactly what is happening.

Selecting a PicTorial on the *Contents* window displays a list of the sections in that PicTorial on the right side of the *Contents* window. Clicking any of those sections (other than **Review Questions**) displays the *Section Introduction* window. This window contains a brief introduction to the section and it is your gateway to exploring a procedure. The window displays three buttons—**Concept**, **Tutorial**, and **Drill**—which you would normally click in that sequence to explore the concepts and procedures covered in the section.

The *Section Introduction* Window. The *Section Introduction* window introduces a procedure and allows you to display an interactive concept, a step-by-step tutorial, or a procedure-mastery drill.

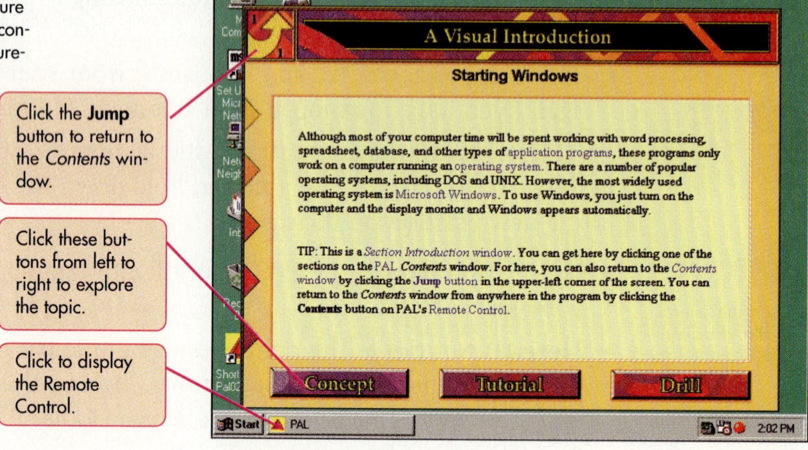

Click the **Jump** button to return to the *Contents* window.

Click these buttons from left to right to explore the topic.

Click to display the Remote Control.

UNDERSTANDING
Hot Spots—Items to Click for More Information

While working with PAL there are many clickable "hot spots" in the windows that display additional information.

▶ Click any term highlighted in blue to display a pop-up glossary definition, many of which are illustrated. After reading the definition, click the pop-up's **Done** button to close it. If you display a glossary term, and then click a glossary term within it, click the **Back** button to return to the previously displayed glossary term.

▶ Click a **Graphic** button ( ) in any of the steps or glossary windows to display a pop-up graphic of the procedure described in that step. When finished looking at the graphic, click the **Done** button.

▶ Click a **Demo** button ( ) in any of the steps or glossary windows to display an animated demonstration of the procedure described in that step.

▶ Click a **QuickSteps** button ( ) to display the *QuickSteps* window. (These buttons appear primarily in drills.) This window lists the steps that you follow to complete the procedure. To move through the sequence of steps, use the scroll bar. When finished, click the **Done** button to return to where you were.

▶ Click a **Loudspeaker** button to hear a word pronounced.

Understanding Navigation

To navigate PAL, you click buttons in the windows on the screen.

▶ The **Jump** button in the upper-left corner of many windows has two numbers on it. The left number indicates the PicTorial you are in and the right number indicates the section within that PicTorial. Clicking the button backs you up one level. For example, if the *Section Introduction* window is on the screen, clicking it returns you to the *Contents* window. If a *Tutorial* or *Drill* window is on the screen, clicking it returns you to the *Section Introduction* window. One of the fastest ways to navigate the system is to click other buttons to move forward and then click this one to move back.

▸ The **Page Turn** button in the lower-right corner of many windows moves you forward and back through the steps or pages. This button also has two numbers on it. The left number indicates the step you are currently on. The right number indicates the total number of steps in the concept, tutorial, or drill.

▸ When you display the last step in a concept, tutorial, or drill, a window tells you that you have finished. You can then click any of the listed *jump terms* to go to the indicated places. (You can also click the **Jump** button one or more times to back up and go down another branch.)

Exploring Concepts

Clicking the **Concept** button on the *Section Introduction* window displays a section illustrating and describing the key concepts underlying the procedures you are studying in the section. To move through the concepts, follow the instructions that appear in the window or click the right or left side of the **Page Turn** button to move forward or back.

Concepts. *Concept* windows vary somewhat but display an interactive introduction to the procedure you are studying.

Completing a Tutorial

Tutorials are designed to guide you step by step through specific procedures using the actual Windows program that you are studying. When you click the **Tutorial** button on the *Section Introduction* window, a smaller *Tutorial* window appears with an introduction to the tutorial. As you proceed through the steps, you are told what to do with the actual program you are studying. For example, a step may tell you to pull down a menu and click a command. If you carefully follow the instructions, you will be introduced to the actual procedure without ever getting lost.

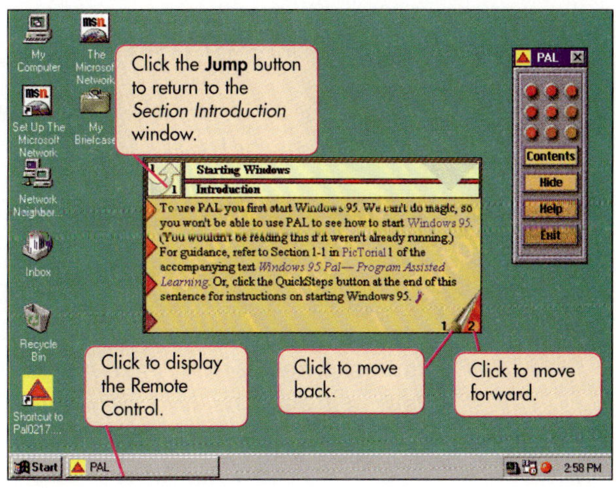

The *Tutorial* Window. The *Tutorial* window displays the steps that you follow to complete a tutorial. Clicking the **Page Turn** buttons in the lower-right corner move you forward and back through the steps. Clicking the **Jump** button in the upper-left corner returns you to the *Section Introduction* window.

Completing a Drill

Drills are designed to let you practice the procedures to which you were introduced in the tutorial. They reinforce your understanding of these procedures and improve your skill in implementing them.

When you click the **Drill** button on the *Section Introduction* window, a smaller *Drill* window appears with an introduction to the drill. This window is identical to the *Tutorial* window.

☐ **T-3 PAL TOUR.** In this section, you explore the sequence you follow to explore a section—first the concept, then the tutorial, then the drill.

1. Start PAL or click the **Contents** button on the Remote Control to return to the *Contents* window.

2. On the *PicTorials* list, click the letter **T** or the name **PAL Tour**. This displays a list of the sections in the tour.

3. On the *Sections* list, click **T-3, Exploring a Section** to display the first screen of the tour.

4. Follow the instructions that appear on the screen. If nothing seems to happen, click the **Page Turn** button in the lower-right corner of the window. Clicking the left side of this button moves you back one step and clicking the right side moves you forward.

☐ **TOURING PAL ON YOUR OWN.** In this section, you explore PAL's organization until you become familiar with it.

1. Click any PicTorial on the *PicTorials* list (other than **QuickSteps** or **Glossary**) and then click any section in the *Sections* list (other than *Review Questions*). This displays a *Section Introduction* window.

2. Click each of the three buttons at the bottom of the *Section Introduction* window to see what happens. When a new window appears, click the **Page Turn** buttons in its lower-right corner to see how they work. Click the **Jump** button in the upper-left corner of the window to return to the *Section Introduction* window.

3. Repeat Steps 1 and 2 until you feel comfortable navigating through the program. If you get lost at any time, click PAL's button on the taskbar to move the Remote Control in front, then click its **Contents** button.

T-4 COMPLETING REVIEW QUESTIONS

Review questions are designed to test your understanding of the procedures discussed in the PicTorial.

Displaying Questions

There are two ways to display questions. At any time, you can click the **Contents** button on the Remote Control to display the PAL *Contents* window. You can then select the PicTorial on which you want to be tested. Click the **Review Questions** button at the bottom of the *Sections* list on the right side of PAL's *Contents* window to display the *Review Questions* window. Also, as you complete a PicTorial, the last window in the last drill lets you jump directly to the *Review Questions* window.

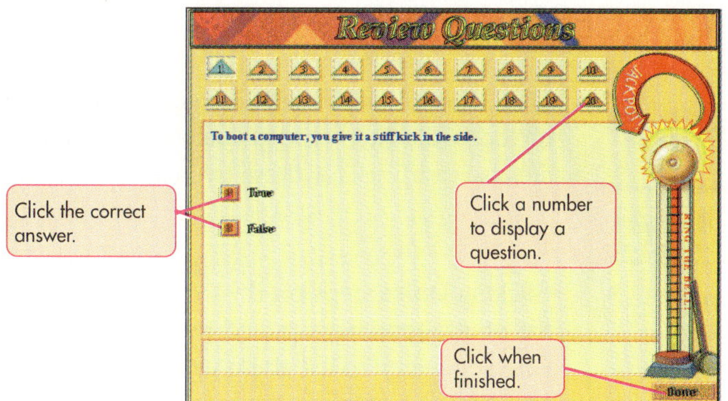

The *Review Questions* Window. The *Review Questions* window allows you to test your understanding of the material you covered in the PicTorial. Clicking any numbered button on one of the two rows of buttons at the top of the window displays a question.

Answering Questions

With the *Review Questions* window displayed, click any numbered **Question** button to display a question and then click to answer it. When you answer a question, you are told immediately whenever you got it right and your current score is indicated on the score meter.

When finished answering all questions, click the **Done** button to display the *Question Summary* window. Here your results are summarized and for those questions you got wrong, you are referred to sections in the accompanying text for more study. You can click the **Print** button to print the summary, click the **Continue** button to return to the questions (if you haven't finished answering them all), or click the **Done** button to exit questions and return to the *Contents* window.

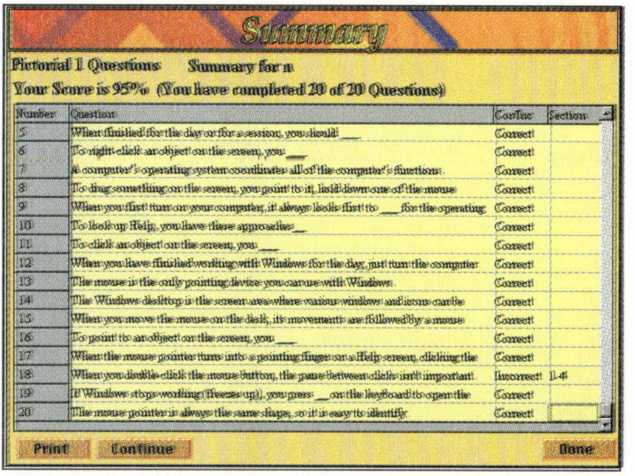

The *Question Summary* Window. The *Question Summary* window displays your results and suggests what to review in the text for those questions that you answered incorrectly.

PAL ON-LINE ACTIVITIES CHECKLIST

☐ **T-4 PAL TOUR.** In this section, you explore PAL's review questions.

1. Start PAL or click the **Contents** button on the Remote Control to return to the *Contents* window.

2. On the *PicTorials* list, click the letter **T** or the name **PAL Tour**. This displays a list of the sections in the tour.

3. On the *Sections* list, click T-4, **Completing Review Questions** to display the first screen of the tour.

4. Follow the instructions that appear on the screen. If nothing seems to happen, click the **Page Turn** button in the lower right corner of the window. Clicking the left side of this button moves you back one step and clicking the right side moves you forward.

Throughout PAL you will encounter many items that are accessible in context. These include QuickSteps and glossary terms. On the *Contents* window's *PicTorials* list, there are also headings for these two elements that let you access them directly.

QUICKSTEPS

Clicking **QuickSteps** on the *Contents* window's *PicTorials* list displays an alphabetical list of all QuickSteps pulled together for you in one place. This is especially useful when you want to use them when working on your own documents. You can use the scroll bar to locate any procedure, and click it to display the steps you follow to complete it. You can even click the **Print** button to print it out for future reference. When finished with a QuickStep, click the **Done** button to close the QuickSteps window.

GLOSSARY

Clicking **Glossary** on the *Contents* window's *PicTorials* list displays an alphabetical list of all glossary terms. Each of the terms on this list can be accessed in context by clicking highlighted words or phrases in other PAL windows, but here the entire glossary is pulled together for you in one place. You can use the scroll bar to locate any term, and click it to display a definition. When you are finished reading a definition, click the **Done** button to close the definition window and return to where you were. However, if you click a glossary term within a glossary definition, first click the **Back** button to return to the previously displayed glossary term.

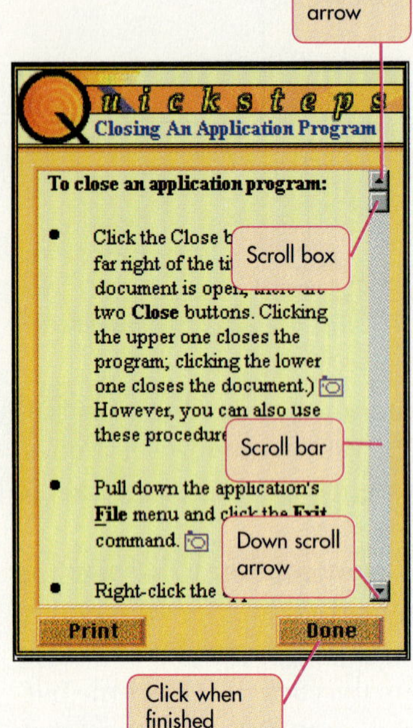

The *QuickSteps* Window. The *QuickSteps* window lists the steps you follow for a procedure. The scroll bar allows you to scroll through the steps if they don't all fit in the window. To use the scroll bar to scroll through the text, click the up and down scroll arrows or drag the scroll box.

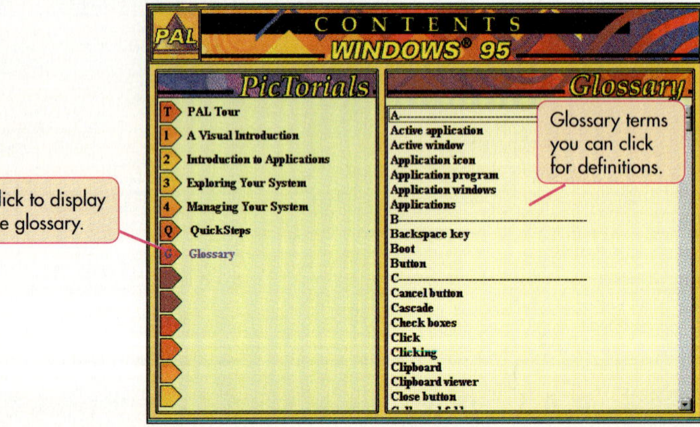

The *Glossary* Window. Clicking the **Glossary** choice on the PAL *Contents* window displays an alphabetical list of glossary terms. Use the scroll bar to locate any term, click it to display a definition, then click the **Done** button to close the definition window.

PAL ON-LINE ACTIVITIES CHECKLIST

☐ **T-5 PAL TOUR.** In this section, you explore the direct-access listings of QuickSteps and glossary terms from the *Contents* window.

1. Start PAL or click the **Contents** button on the Remote Control to return to the *Contents* window.

2. On the *PicTorials* list, click the letter T or the name **PAL Tour**. This displays a list of the sections in the tour.

3. On the *Sections* list, click T-5, **Directly Accessing Embedded Items** to display the first screen of the tour.

4. Follow the instructions that appear on the screen. If nothing seems to happen, click the **Page Turn** button in the lower-right corner of the window. Clicking the left side of this button moves you back one step and clicking the right side moves you forward.

WORD—A VISUAL INTRODUCTION

After completing this PicTorial, you will be able to:

- **Start and close Word**
- **Describe the parts of the Word screen display**
- **Open, save, and close documents**
- **Enter and edit a simple document**
- **Move around documents on the screen**
- **Use the toolbars to execute commands**
- **Use Word's on-line Help system to get help on procedures**
- **Manage folders and documents from within Word**

To PERFORM useful work on your computer, you use *application programs* such as word processors, spreadsheets, and databases. Different kinds of programs do different kinds of tasks. For example, you use spreadsheet programs to work with numbers and word processing programs, such as Word for Windows, to work with text. ▶

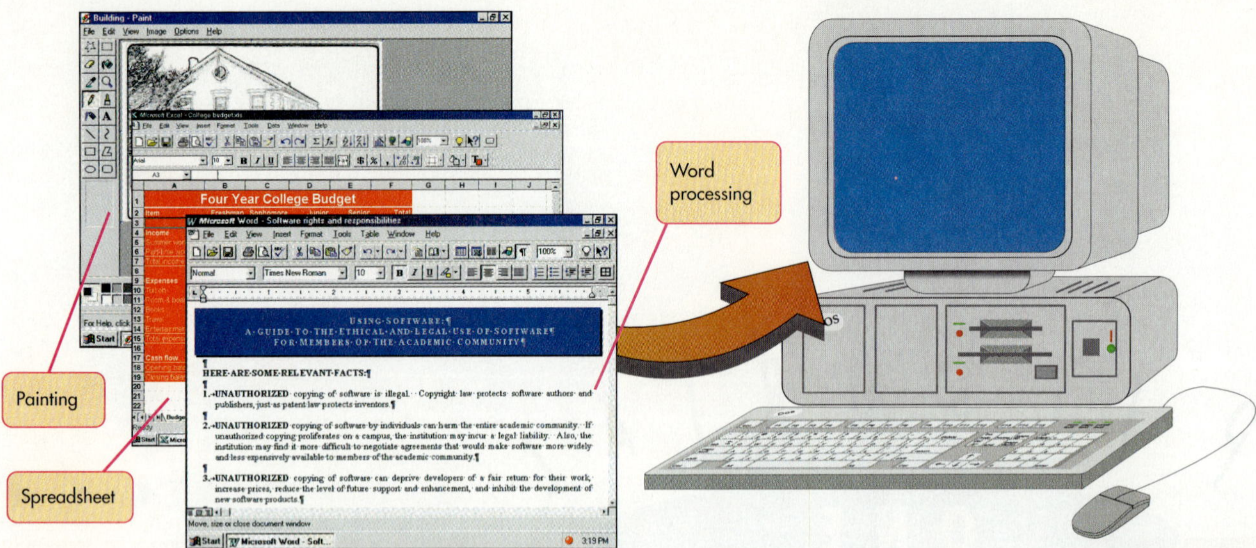

Learning how to use a new application program is much like learning how to drive. To drive well, you have to learn the rules of the road and how the car should be maintained for safety and reliability, but you can't wait to get behind the wheel. Once you have taken at least a spin around the block, you have a feel for driving that makes you want to learn more. In this PicTorial, you take Word for Windows for a spin around the block. Just as an experienced driver sat next to you and told you everything to do on your first drive, we'll sit beside you and guide you through this first lesson. The goal here is to master some of Word's most basic features—starting and exiting Word; opening, saving, and closing documents; getting around a document; and using Help. You should relax as you explore these procedures and get a feeling for the program.

1-1 STARTING AND CLOSING WORD

To use an application program such as Word, you must first know how to start it—variously called *starting*, *opening*, *running*, or *launching* it—and how to exit it. How you start Word is illustrated below and described on the next page.

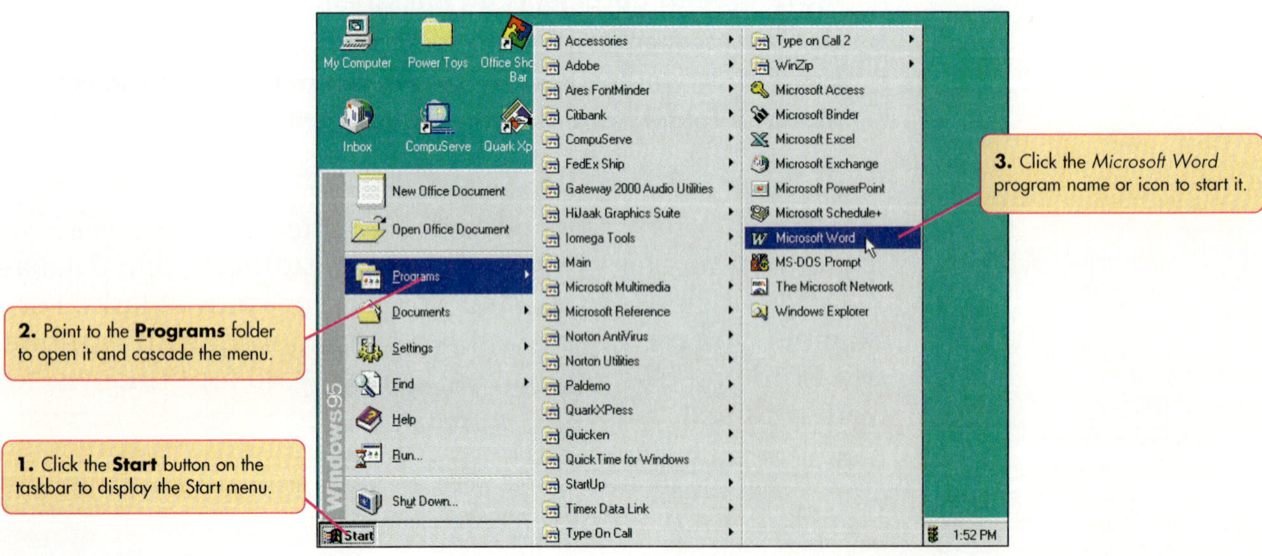

Starting Application Programs

There are a number of ways to start Windows 95 programs, but the most common is using the Start menu. When you use the mouse to click the **Start** button on the taskbar at the bottom of the Windows 95 screen, the *Start menu* appears. When you highlight any name on this menu with an arrowhead next to it (▶) and pause or click, a submenu cascades out from the first menu. Once you locate the icon and name of the program you want to run, you click it to start it.

When you start a program, its button is displayed on the taskbar. When more than one program is running at the same time, you can quickly switch between them by clicking the taskbar button of the one you want to use.

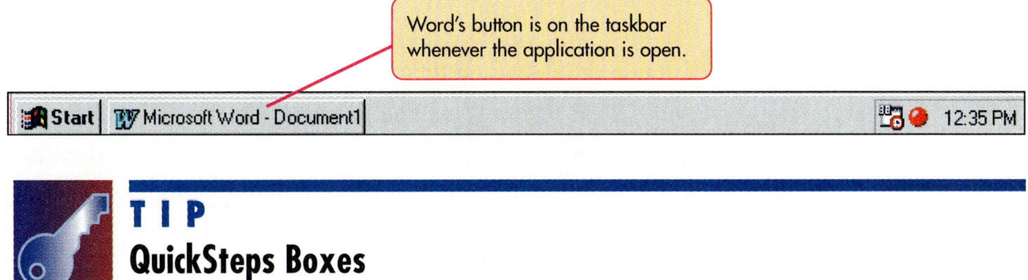

T I P
QuickSteps Boxes

QuickSteps boxes summarize the steps you follow to complete Word procedures. These boxes can be found throughout this text and serve two purposes:

▶ On your first pass through a section, they give you an advance look at the steps you must follow to complete the procedure. Don't actually execute the commands this time around. If you do so, you may not know how to recover from any mistakes you might make.

▶ Later on, when you want to refresh your memory about a procedure, they make it easy to find and review the steps you must follow. At this stage, you can use them as a quick reference guide.

Q U I C K S T E P S
Starting Word

1. Click the **Start** button on Windows' taskbar to display the Start menu.
2. Point to the **Programs** folder on the Start menu to cascade the menu.
3. Click the **Microsoft Word** program name or icon to start it.

Closing Application Programs

When you are finished with a program such as Word, you exit or close it. This removes it from the computer's memory and removes its window from the desktop and its button from the taskbar.

It is important to quit Word using the commands designed for this purpose. Word creates temporary files on the disk while you are working, and these are deleted only if you exit correctly. If you quit incorrectly, your document may be left damaged.

You can close almost any window simply by clicking the **Close** button at the far right of the title bar. This and other methods are described in the QuickSteps box "Closing Word."

Closing Word

To close Word:

▶ Click the **Close** button at the far right of Word's title bar. (If a document is open, there are two **Close** buttons. Clicking the upper one closes Word; clicking the lower one closes the document.)

You can also use any of these procedures:

▶ Pull down Word's **File** menu and click the **Exit** command.

▶ Right-click Word's button on the taskbar, then click the shortcut menu's **Close** command.

▶ Double-click Word's icon at the left of the title bar, or click the icon to display a shortcut menu, and then click the **Close** command.

▶ Right-click the title bar, then click the shortcut menu's **Close** command.

▶ Hold down [Alt] and press [F4] when Word is the active window.

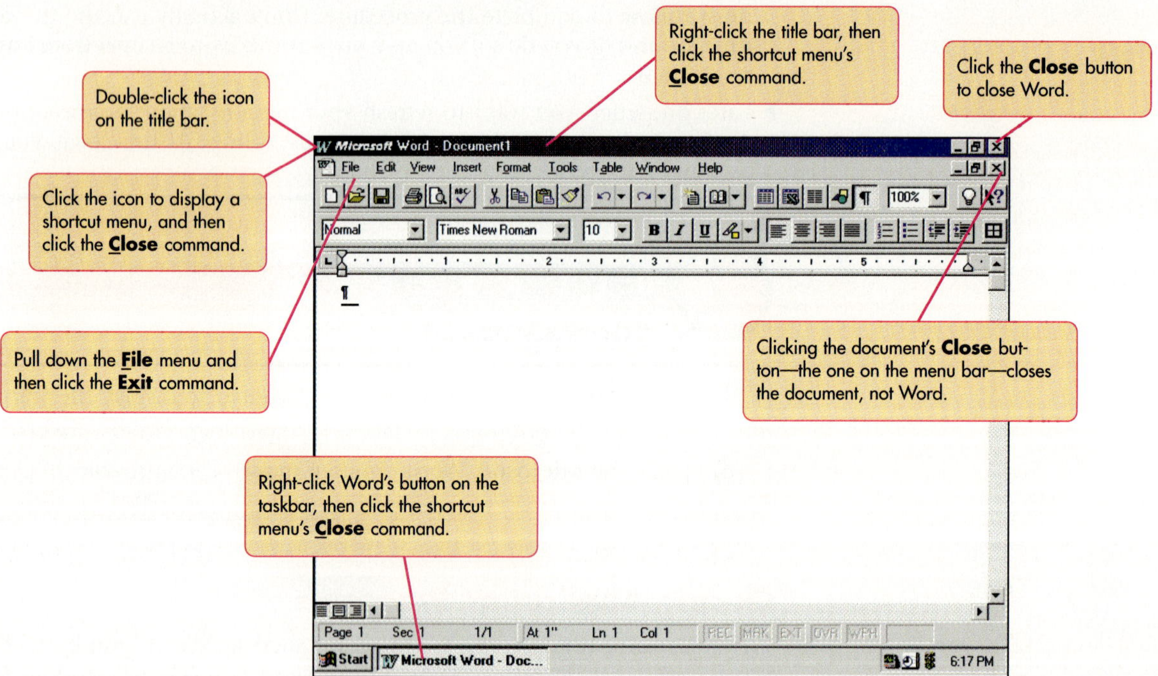

If you close Word without saving changes to any open documents, a dialog box asks if you want to save the changes.

▶ To save the document, click the **Yes** button.

▶ To abandon the document, click the **No** button.

▶ To cancel the command and return to the document instead of closing it, click the **Cancel** command button.

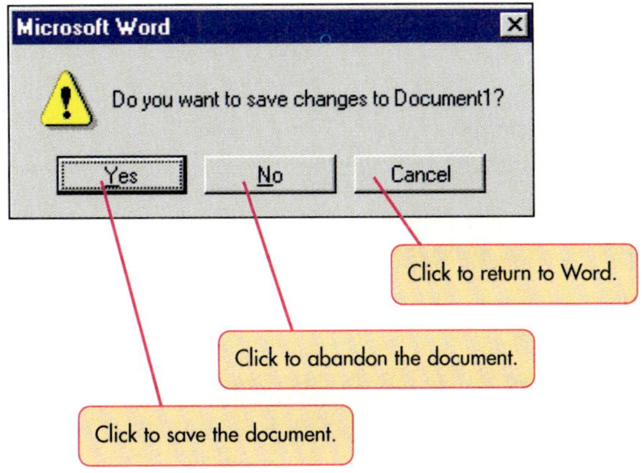

PAL ON-LINE ACTIVITIES CHECKLIST

☐ **1-1 CONCEPTS.** To do any useful work on a computer you must first start an application program. In this on-line concepts section, you are introduced to starting Word using the **Start** button and the Start menu. The concepts you learn here apply to all Windows applications.

☐ **1-1 TUTORIAL.** In this tutorial you explore starting Word using the **Start** button on the taskbar and then closing it.

☐ **1-1 DRILL.** In this drill you continue to explore starting Word using the **Start** button on the taskbar and then closing it.

The Word screen actually contains two windows: the program's window and a document's window. The program's window displays a number of elements that make the program fast and efficient to work with. You should become familiar with the names of these elements.

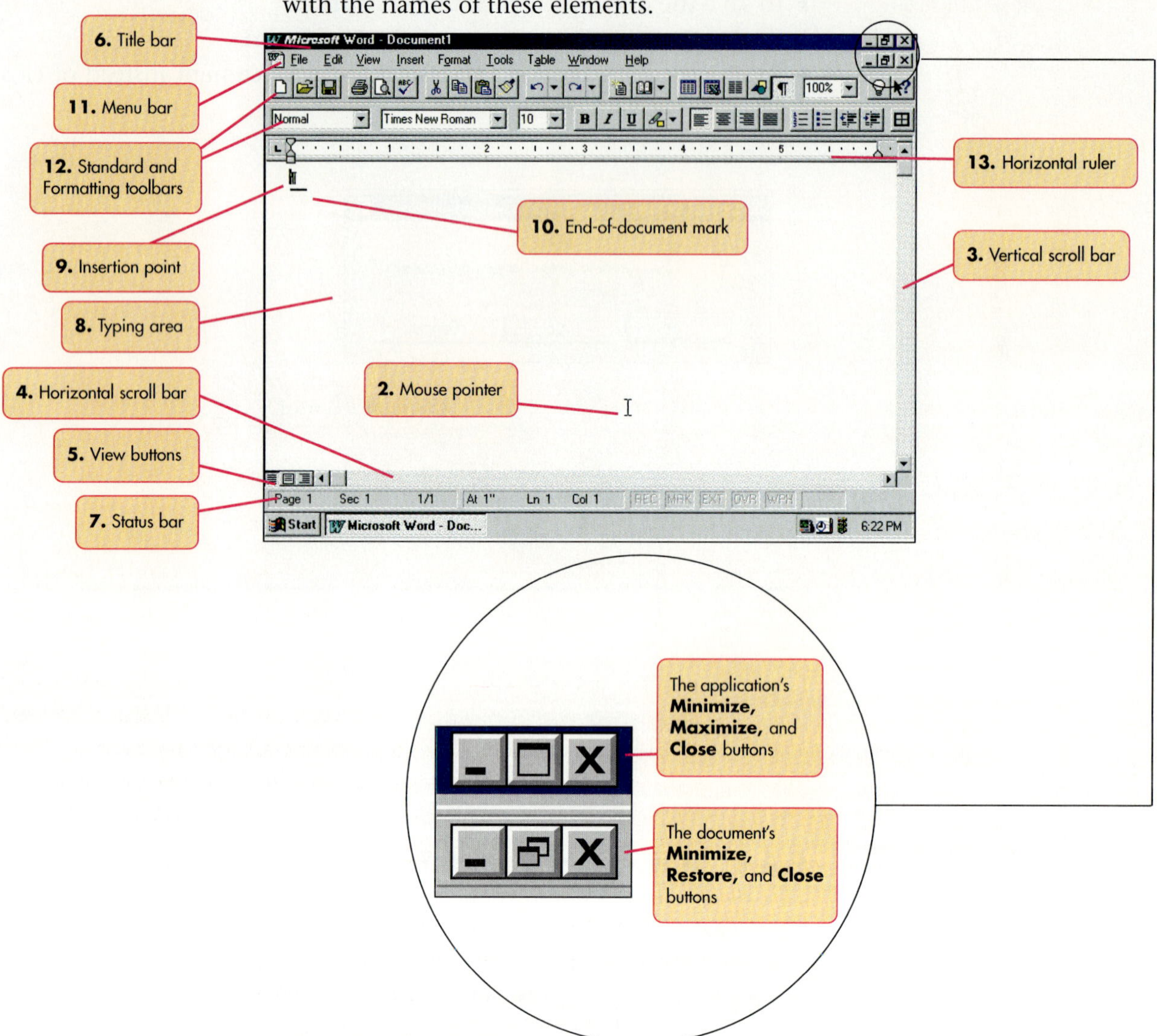

Sizing Elements

1. When you first start Word, its window is displayed at the size it was when last closed, and the document window is maximized so it fills Word's window. Each window can be independently maximized by clicking the **Maximize** button, minimized by clicking the **Minimize** button, and restored by clicking the **Restore** button. The **Close** button is used to close the application.

Navigation and Display Elements

2. The *mouse pointer* moves when you move the mouse so you can point to things on the screen and click to select them. It changes shape when you move it about the screen. All of the shapes it might take are shown in the figure "The Mouse Pointer."

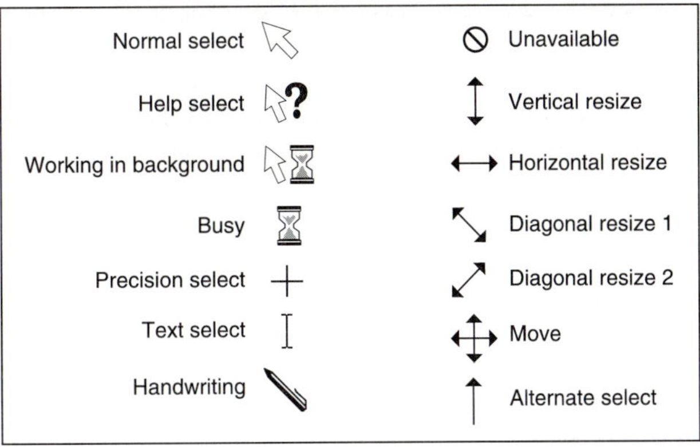

The Mouse Pointer

3. The *vertical scroll bar* scrolls the document up and down in the window.

4. The *horizontal scroll bar* scrolls the document side to side in the window.

5. Three *view buttons* at the left end of the horizontal scroll bar display the document in normal view, page layout view, or outline view. You usually work in normal view and then switch to page layout view when you want to see how the document will look when printed.

Status Elements

6. The *title bar* lists the name of the program and any open document. It also displays an icon at the left end that you can click to display a shortcut menu, or double-click to close the application. At the right end are the **Minimize**, **Maximize** or **Restore**, and **Close** buttons that affect the application's window.

7. The *status bar* displays information about your document and the program. The first section indicates which page is displayed on the screen and the second section indicates the position of the insertion point in the document. Items displayed in the third section are described in the box "Understanding the Status Bar."

Editing and Formatting Elements

8. The *typing area* is the area of the screen where you enter text. Initially the only things in this area are the flashing insertion point and the end-of-document mark.

9. The *insertion point* in the text area indicates where the next character you type will appear.

10. The *end-of-document mark* indicates the last line in the document.

11. The *menu bar* lists the names of menus that you can pull down by clicking them. Each pulled-down menu contains a list of commands from which you can choose.

12. The *Standard* (upper) and *Formatting* (lower) *toolbars* contain buttons you can click to execute the most frequently used commands. To see the name of any button, point to it with the mouse pointer, and a box called a ToolTip is displayed. A description of the button's function is also displayed on the status bar.

13. The *horizontal ruler* changes indents, margins, and tab stops using the mouse. (A vertical ruler is also displayed in page layout view.)

UNDERSTANDING
The Status Bar

The status bar describes highlighted commands or buttons you point to, prompts you for the information it needs you to enter to complete a command, and informs you of the progress of some commands. Here is a brief description of the things you see displayed on this bar.

| Page 1 | Sec 1 | 1/1 | At 1.1" | Ln 2 | Col 1 | REC | MRK | EXT | OVR | WPH | |

- *Page* tells you the page that is displayed on the screen.
- *Sec* tells you the section that is displayed.
- *1/1* indicates the page that is displayed on the screen and the total number of pages in the document.
- *At* indicates the distance from the line with the insertion point to the top of the page.
- *Ln* indicates the number of lines from the line with the insertion point to the top of the text page.
- *Col* indicates the number of characters, including spaces and tabs, between the left margin and the insertion point.
- *REC*, when not dimmed, indicates the macro recorder is active.
- *MRK*, when not dimmed, indicates that revision marking is on.
- *EXT*, when not dimmed, indicates that you have pressed F8 (the Extend Selection key). Press F8 again to turn it off.
- *OVR*, when not dimmed, indicates that overtype is on. Text you type in existing text types over the original text. Press Ins to turn overtype off.
- *WPH*, when not dimmed, indicates that help for WordPerfect users is active.
- When automatic spell checking is on, an icon appears at the right end of the status bar when you enter text. If any words are misspelled, it displays a red X.

PAL ON-LINE ACTIVITIES CHECKLIST

- ☐ **1-2 CONCEPTS.** Word's window is similar to those of other Windows applications. In this concepts section you explore some of its elements and then practice minimizing, restoring, and maximizing it.

- ☐ **1-2 TUTORIAL.** In this tutorial you explore Word's window to familiarize yourself with some of its elements.

- ☐ **1-2 DRILL.** All application windows have buttons you can click to change their size. In this drill you practice using these buttons.

1-3 OPENING AND CLOSING DOCUMENTS

To use Word or any other Windows program you must know how to open and close documents. You open a Word document just as you open documents in all Windows programs. When you first start Word, a new document is automatically opened containing only the flashing insertion point and end-of-document mark. You can't move the insertion point until the document contains some text.

Opening New Documents

Although Word opens a new document automatically when you start it, if you are already working in Word and want to create another new document, you will need to open it. The title bar of each new document that you open reads *Documentx*, where x stands for the number of new documents you have opened in the current session. This automatically assigned name is replaced with the name you give to the document when you save it.

You can open a new document by clicking the **New** button on the Standard toolbar, or by pulling down the **File** menu and clicking the **New** command. When you use the menu command, a tabbed dialog box lists available *templates*. A template is a stored document layout with preset margins, fonts, and other formats. It can also have customized menus, toolbars, or macros. Usually, documents are created using the *Blank Document* template listed on the *General* tab, but you can also base a new document on templates designed to create letters and faxes, memos, and reports. Some templates include a Wizard, a simple answer-the-question type of automated formatting. Both templates and Wizards are topics beyond the scope of this text.

Click the **New** button to open a new document.

<table>
<tr><td>

QUICKSTEPS

Opening a New Document

To open a new document, do one of the following:

▶ Click the **New** button on the Standard toolbar.

▶ Pull down the **File** menu and click the **New** command to display the New dialog box. Click the *General* tab to display it, and then click the icon for the *Blank Document* template. (If you want, you can click other tabs or select another template. You can also click buttons on the toolbar to change the way templates are listed.) Click the **OK** button and the new document appears on the screen.

▶ Right-click Windows' desktop to display a shortcut menu. Point to or click the **New** command to cascade the menu and list things you can create. Click *Microsoft Word Document* to place an icon on the desktop. Type its name and press Enter ↵. To open the document, double-click it. (Documents created this way are saved in the *Desktop* subfolder located in the *Windows* folder.)

</td></tr>
</table>

Tabs list different kinds of templates.

The *Blank Document* template on the *General* tab is the one you use most frequently.

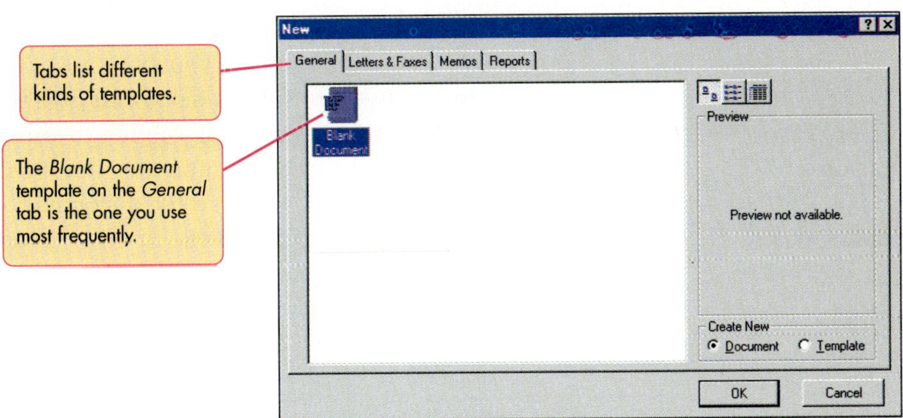

Opening Existing Documents

To open an existing document (also called a *file*), you have to know three things about it: the drive it is on, the folder it is in, and its name. When you use the Open command, the Open dialog box appears so you can use this information to locate the document.

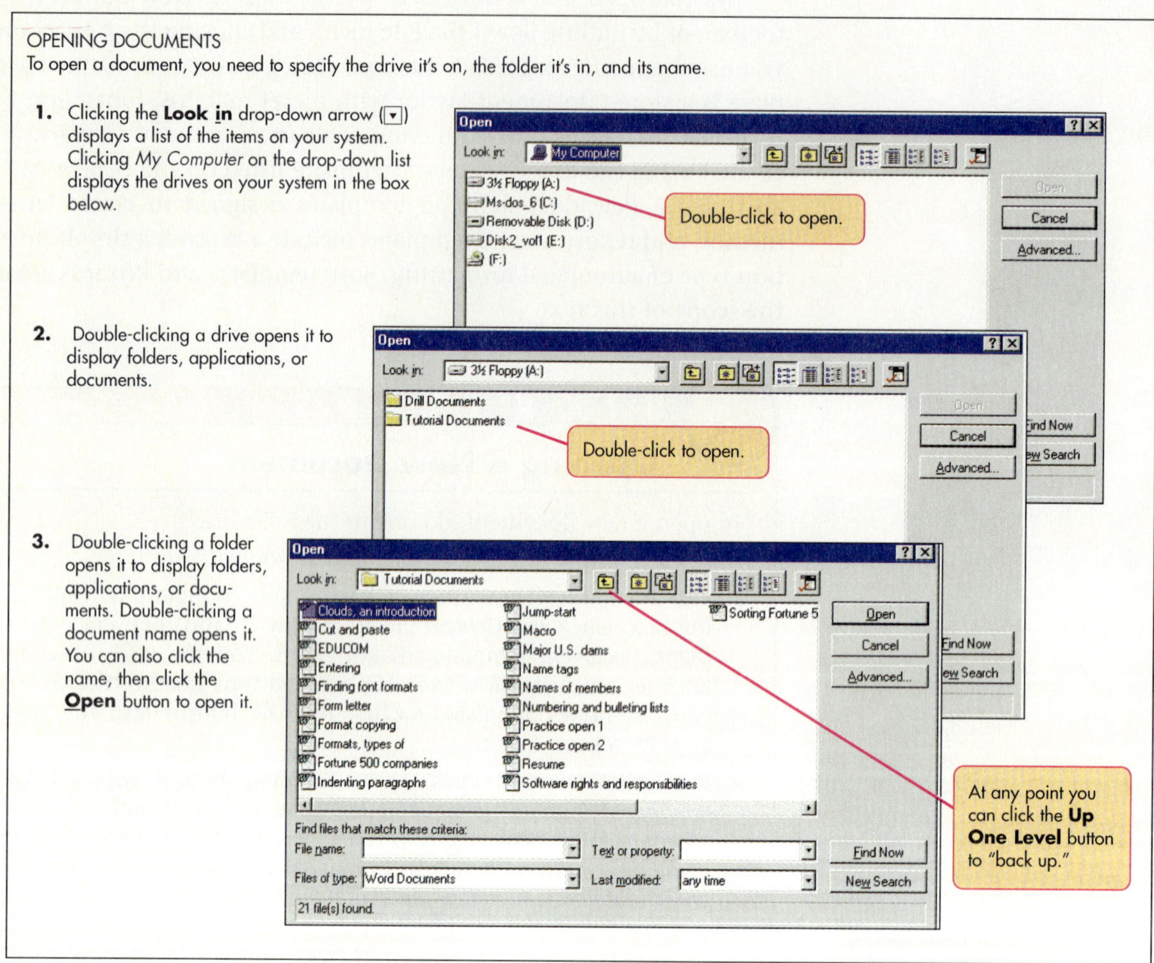

To locate a document, you have to open the folder in which it is stored. Dividing a disk into folders helps you organize your files better. A disk is like an empty drawer in a new filing cabinet: It provides storage space but no organization. To make it easier to find items in a file drawer, you divide it into categories with hanging folders. You can file documents directly into the hanging folders, or you divide the hanging folders into finer categories with manila folders. A folder in a drive is like either a hanging folder or a manila folder within a hanging folder. A document or file within a folder is like a letter, report, or other document in a filing cabinet.

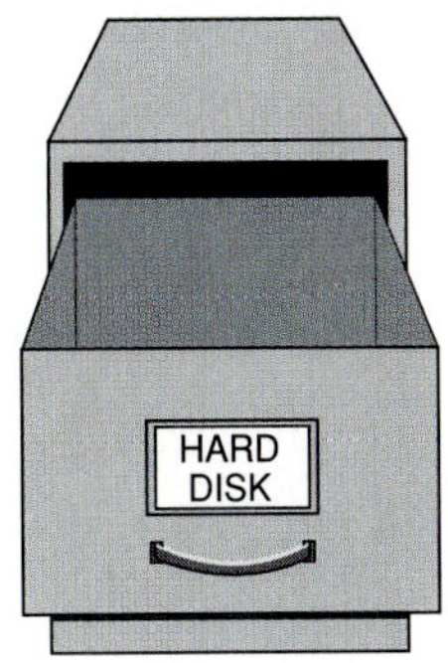

A new hard disk is like an empty file drawer. It has lots of room for files but no organization.

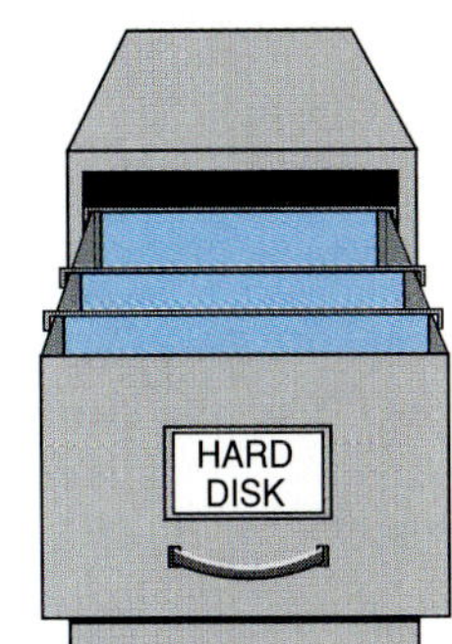

You can divide the hard disk into folders, which is like dividing the file drawer with hanging folders.

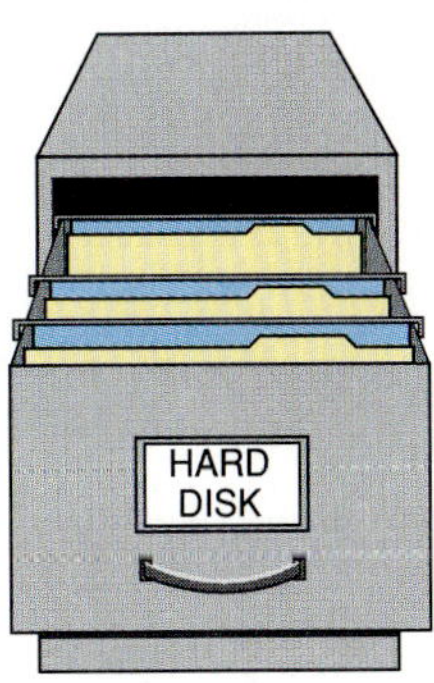

If you want, you can then subdivide the folders into smaller subfolders, which is like dividing the hanging folders with manila folders.

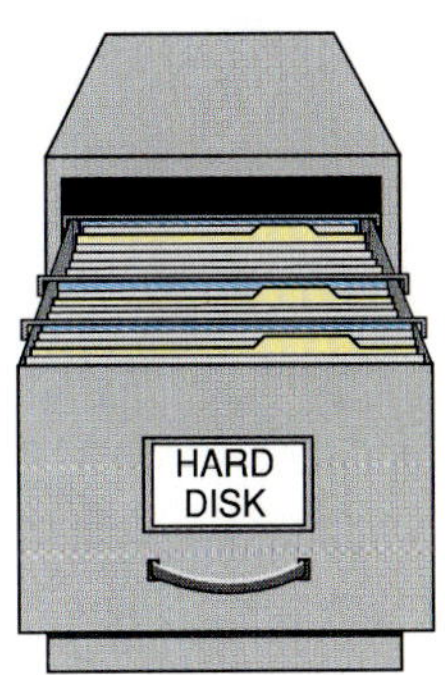

You can save files in any of these folders or subfolders the same way you would file a document in one of the hanging or manila folders.

Folders are organized in a hierarchy called *tree*. The main folder, the one that isn't contained in any other folder, contains other folders, and those may contain still other subfolders. Any of these folders can also contain programs or documents. To move down the tree to see what a folder contains, double-click any folder you want to open. To move back up the tree, click the **Up One Level** button on the toolbar.

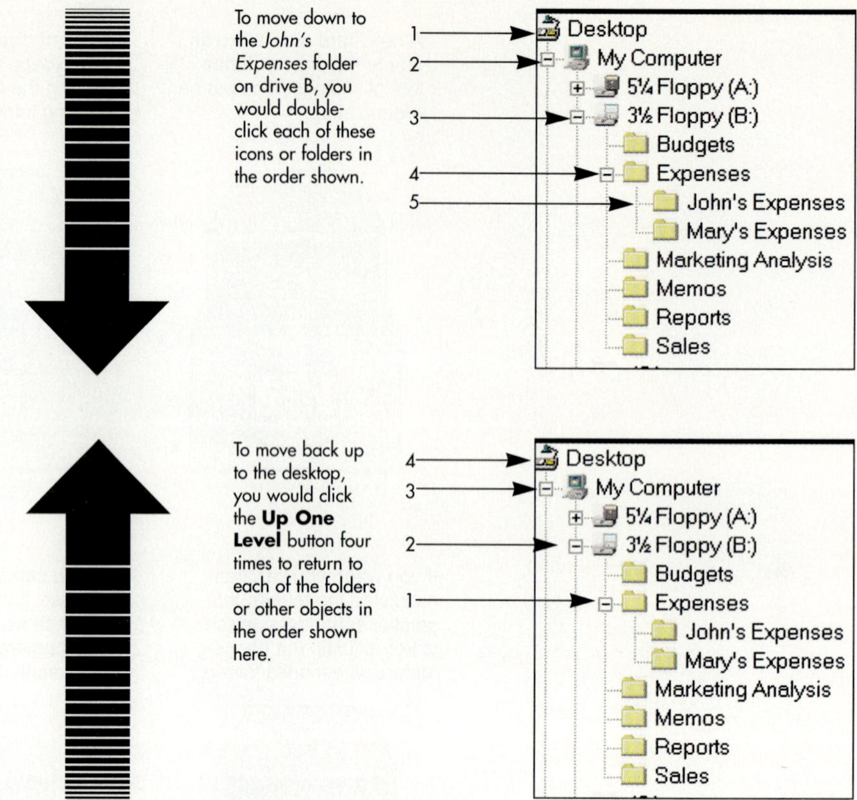

QUICKSTEPS

Opening Existing Documents

1. Click the **Open** button on the toolbar, or pull down the **File** menu and click the **Open** command to display the Open dialog box.

2. To specify the drive the document is on, click the **Look in** drop-down arrow (▼) and select the drive from the list that appears. A list of folders or documents on that drive appears in the box below—how it looks and what is shown depends not only on its contents but also on whether the **List**, **Details**, or **Properties** button on the toolbar is on.

3. The name of the open folder is displayed in the **Look in** box and a list of the folders and documents it contains appears in the box below. To open the folder the document is in:

   ▶ To move down the tree, double-click a folder you want to open.

   ▶ To move up the tree, click the **Up One Level** button on the toolbar.

4. To open a document once you locate it, click its name or icon to select it and then click the **Open** button. You can also double-click the document's name to open it without clicking the **Open** button. To see what's in the selected document before you open it, click the **Preview** button on the toolbar.

When the Open dialog box is displayed, you can click buttons on its *toolbar* to change the way document names are displayed.

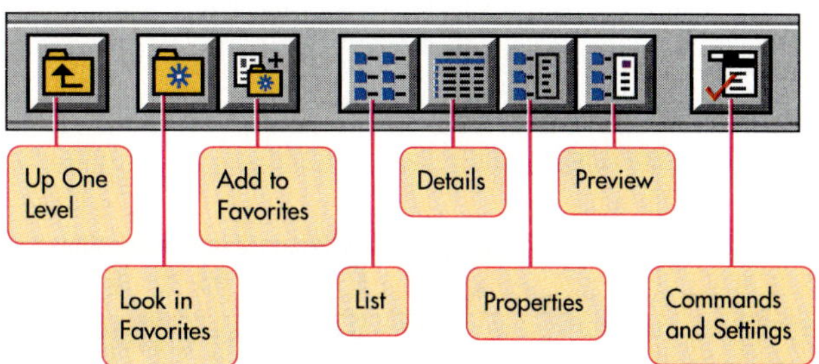

▶ **Up One Level** moves you up the tree.

▶ **Look in Favorites** displays a list of documents that you have designated as favorites with the **Add to Favorites** button (see below).

▶ **Add to Favorites** adds any selected documents to your list of favorite documents when you click it. This is a shortcut you can use to quickly locate documents you work on frequently.

▶ **List** displays just icons and the names of folders or documents.

▶ **Details** displays information about documents including their size, type, and date last modified.

▶ **Properties** displays information about any highlighted document including the name of its creator, the number of times it's been revised, and its size in pages, words, characters, and bytes.

▶ **Preview** displays a small image of the document so you can check that it's the one you want before opening it.

▶ **Commands and Settings** displays a menu you can use to print selected documents, sort the list of documents, or perform other procedures.

When the Open dialog box is displayed, you can also enter the name of a document you want to find in the **File name** text box and click the **Find Now** button to search for it. It will search the drive or folder listed in the **Look in** text box.

Opening a Recently Opened Document

After you've opened and then closed a document, there may be a shortcut to opening it again. The four most recently opened documents are listed at the bottom of Word's **File** menu. (Four is the default number but you can change it.) The fifteen most recently opened documents of any type are listed on Windows' Start menu in the **Documents** folder.

Opening a Recently Opened Document

▶ If Word is already running, pull down Word's **File** menu and click one of the four most recently opened documents listed at the bottom of the menu.

▶ If Word is running or even if it isn't, click the **Start** button on Windows' taskbar to display the Start menu; then point to the **Documents** folder to cascade the menu and display the fifteen most recently opened documents of all kinds. Click the name of the document you want to open. If Word isn't already running, Windows will start it for you.

COMMON WRONG TURNS
Removing a Floppy Disk Too Soon

When you work on Word documents, Windows creates temporary files on the disk. When saving a document to and opening a document from a floppy disk, do not remove the disk from the drive until you have quit Word. If you do, you may see a message telling you that there is a disk error. If this message appears, reinsert the disk and click the **OK** button.

Closing Documents

When you are finished with a document, you close it. This removes it from the computer's memory and removes its window from Word's window.

Closing a Document

To close a document, do any of the following:

▶ Click the document's **Close** button. It's at the far right of the title bar when the database is displayed restored and at the far right of the menu bar when it's displayed maximized. (When a document is open, there are two **Close** buttons. Clicking the upper one closes Word; clicking the lower one closes the open document.)

▶ Pull down the **File** menu and click the **Close** command.

▶ Double-click the Word document icon, or click it to display a shortcut menu, and click the **Close** command. It's at the far left of the document's title bar when the document is displayed restored and at the far left of the menu bar when it's displayed maximized.

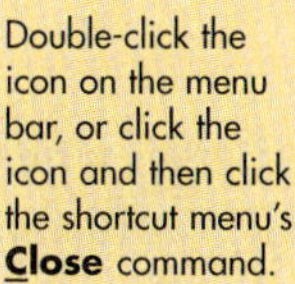

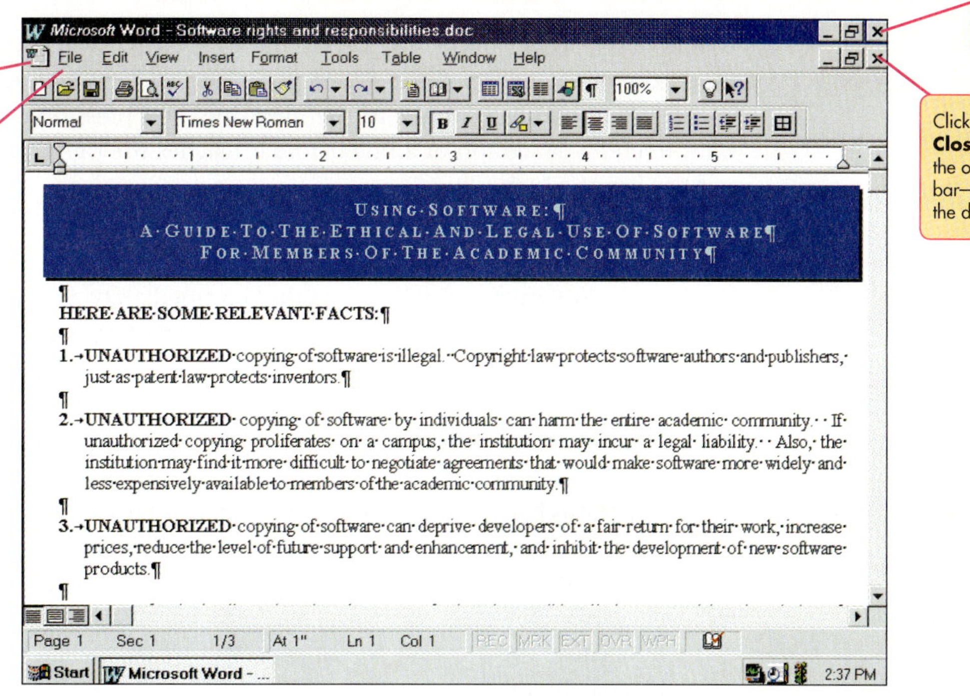

PAL ON-LINE ACTIVITIES CHECKLIST

☐ **1-3 CONCEPTS.** Opening and closing documents is one of the most basic of all skills. In this concepts section you are introduced to these procedures.

☐ **1-3 TUTORIAL.** In this tutorial you open an existing document supplied to you on the *Word Student Resource Disks* designed to be used with this PAL. These disks contain all of the documents on which you will work while completing the on-line and text-based activities in this PAL. If you do not have a copy of these disks, you will need to make one using the *MakeSRD* program on your PAL CD. The document you open in this tutorial is a memo containing only a heading. (You will enter the document's body paragraphs in the next section.)

☐ **1-3 DRILL.** In this drill, you open and close a number of documents. If your system is slow, you need not open and close all of the documents if you feel that you have mastered the procedures. As you complete this drill, and others in this text, you will have to insert the correct disk because the *Tutorial Documents* and *Drill Documents* folders are on one disk, and the other folders are on another.

To enter text, you just type it in. As you do so, the insertion point indicates where the next character will appear. When you reach the end of a line, any word that won't fit automatically wraps to the next line. You press [Enter ↵] only when you want to end a paragraph or a line before it reaches the right margin or when you want to insert a blank line.

Correcting Typos

If you make any mistakes and notice them immediately, you can press [← Bksp] to delete them. You can also click to the left of an error, and press [Del].

Automatic Spell Checking

By default, Word checks your spelling automatically as you type, as you will see in Section 2-3. When automatic spell checking is on, an icon appears at the right end of the status bar when you enter text. If you enter a word that is not in Word's dictionary, the icon displays a red X. The word is also underlined in the document with a wavy red line. Both the line and the X on the icon go away when you correct the word. (However, the word may not be misspelled. For example, your name may cause these events to happen even when spelled correctly because it isn't in the dictionary.)

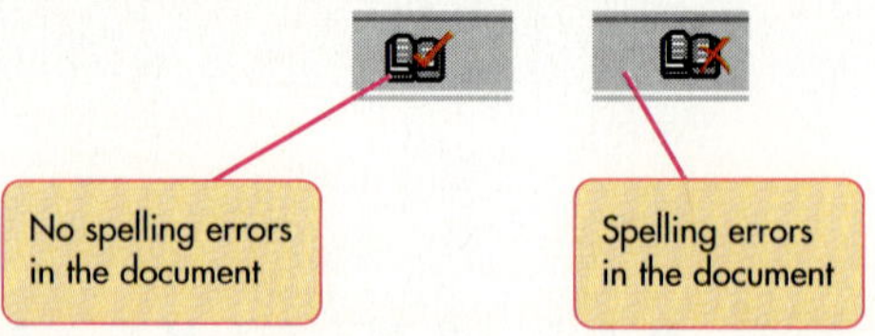

Zooming a Document

Once a document has been entered or opened, you can zoom it or display it in two views, normal view or page layout view. Normal view is the view you normally use to enter and edit text since it is faster. Page layout view is used to check the layout of the document and to see such elements as headers and footers as they will appear when printed.

> ### QUICKSTEPS
> ### Changing Views
>
> ▶ To change the size of the document on the screen, click the **Zoom Control** drop-down arrow ([▼]) on the Standard toolbar to display a list of zooms, and click the zoom you want to use. You can also pull down the **View** menu, click the **Zoom** command, then click the option button to turn on (◉) the zoom you want to use. (**Page Width** is often the best zoom to use when entering and editing text.)
>
> ▶ To change the way a document is displayed, click the **Normal View** or **Page Layout View** buttons to the left of the horizontal scroll bar. You can also pull down the **View** menu and click the **Normal** or **Page Layout** command.

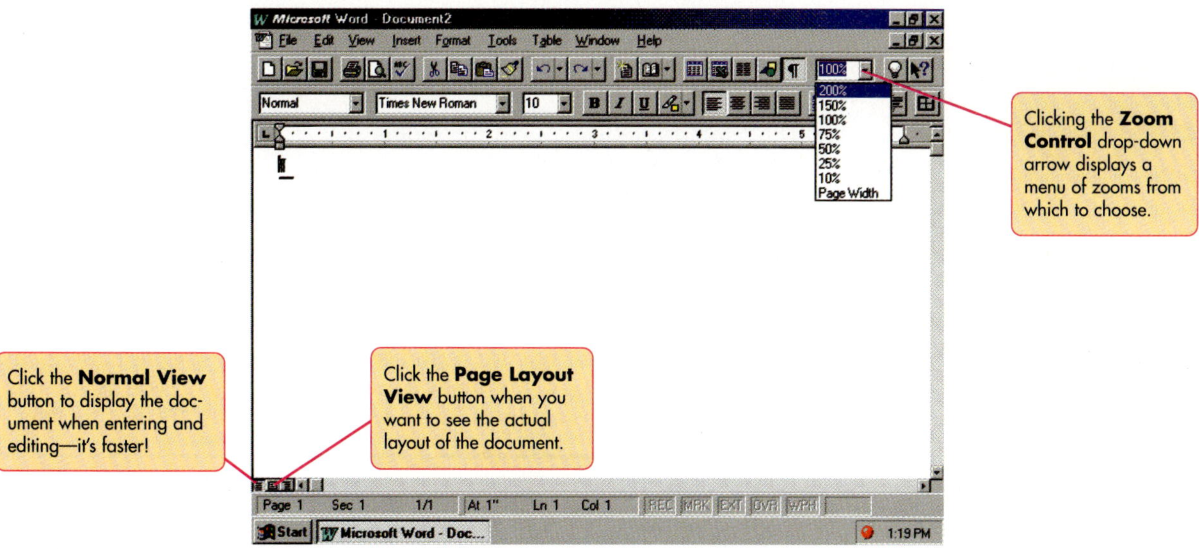

☐ **1-4 CONCEPTS.** The point of learning Word is to use it to create documents. In this concepts section movies demonstrate how text is entered and edited, and you explore various ways to view the document.

☐ **1-4 TUTORIAL.** In this tutorial you open the *Jump-start* document containing only a heading and then enter a few paragraphs to become familiar with entering text. You then practice changing the document's display on the screen.

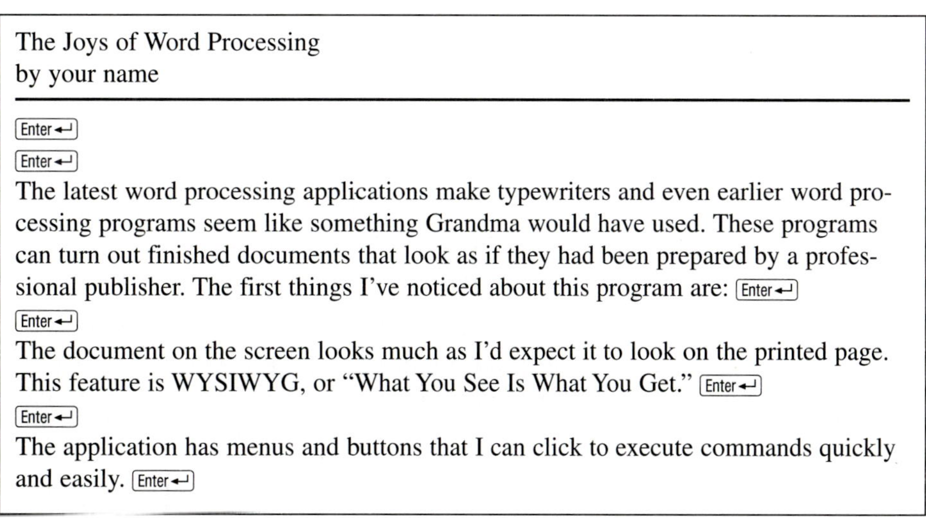

The Jump Start document

Entering Text

▶ The blinking vertical line in the typing area is called the *insertion point*. It indicates where the next character you type will appear.

▶ Press Enter⏎ only where indicated by the Enter⏎ symbol in the illustration of the document. Word automatically wraps text that will not fit on a line—that is, moves it to the next line. Some of your lines will end at places other than the ones shown in the figure; don't worry if they do.

▶ Don't worry about mistakes; you'll see how to correct them later. However, If you make typos you want to correct immediately, press ←Bksp to erase them, and then enter the correct letters. Word may correct some words for you as you type or underline some with red wavy lines. You'll learn more about this feature later.

☐1-4 DRILL. In this drill you enter a short document, view it in different ways, then close it without saving it.

> This may not seem like much, but it is the first paragraph I have typed on my own using this program. It's amazing how easy these programs are to use for the most basic tasks. All you have to do is type and the paragraph is automatically formed. Even printing the document takes just a click of the toolbar's Print button. I could also click the Save button on the same toolbar, but then I would have to know how to direct the document to the disk and folder where I want it stored.

The Entering Text Document

1-5 SAVING DOCUMENTS

You should frequently save the document you are working on. If you turn off the computer, experience a power failure, encounter hardware problems, or make a mistake, you may lose documents that are in the computer's memory. Your documents are not safe from these disasters until you save them onto a disk. You should always save a document:

▶ Before experimenting with unfamiliar commands

▶ Before making major revisions

▶ Before printing it (in case something goes wrong during the process)

▶ Before closing it or exiting Word

On many systems, you save your documents onto a hard disk. On others, especially those you share with other students in a computer lab, you save them onto a floppy disk (usually in drive A or B) so that you can take them with you.

Saving Documents the First Time

Just as when opening documents, you have to decide three things when saving a document the first time: the drive to save it on, the folder to save it in, and its name. When you use a Save command the first time, the Save As dialog box appears so you can specify this information. Once a document has been saved, you can save it again after making any changes just by clicking the **Save** button on the toolbar.

There are certain rules to keep in mind when naming documents:

▶ Filenames can be up to 255 characters long.

▶ Filenames can include spaces and as many periods as you want.

▶ Filenames cannot include the characters \ / : * ? " < > or |. If you use any of these characters, a message box appears and lists them for you so you can change the name.

▶ Each filename should be unique. If you assign a document the same name as a file that is already on the disk in the same folder, the new file can overwrite the previous file and erase it (although you will be warned first).

▶ Filenames retain the capitalization you use to enter them. For example, you could type a filename as *filename*, *Filename*, *FileName*, or *FILENAME*.

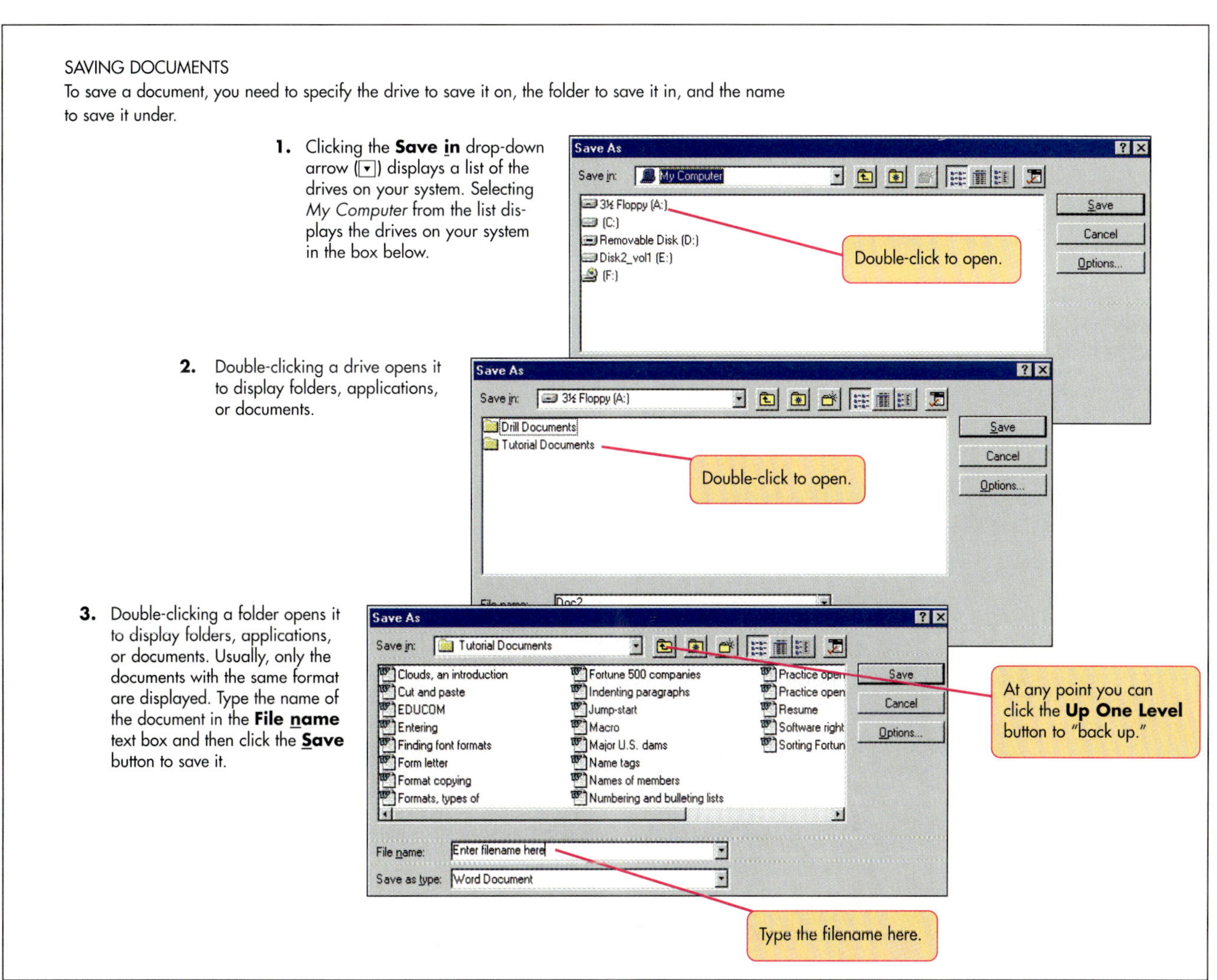

SAVING DOCUMENTS
To save a document, you need to specify the drive to save it on, the folder to save it in, and the name to save it under.

1. Clicking the **Save in** drop-down arrow (▼) displays a list of the drives on your system. Selecting *My Computer* from the list displays the drives on your system in the box below.

2. Double-clicking a drive opens it to display folders, applications, or documents.

3. Double-clicking a folder opens it to display folders, applications, or documents. Usually, only the documents with the same format are displayed. Type the name of the document in the **File name** text box and then click the **Save** button to save it.

Saving Documents for the First Time

1. Click the **Save** button on the Standard toolbar, or pull down the **File** menu and click the **Save** command to display the Save As dialog box.

2. To specify the drive to save the document on, click the **Save in** drop-down arrow and select the drive from the list that appears. A list of folders or documents on that drive appears in the box below—how it looks and what is shown depends not only on its contents but also on whether the **List**, **Details**, or **Properties** button on the toolbar is on.

3. To open the folder the document is to be saved in:

   ▶ To move down the tree, double-click a folder you want to open.

   ▶ To move up the tree, click the **Up One Level** button on the toolbar.

4. The first characters in the document are highlighted in the **File name** text box (up to 255 characters or the first punctuation mark). Type the name you want to use and the first character you type deletes the existing entry.

5. Press Enter ↵ or click the **Save** button.

Click the **Save** button to save the document.

When the Save As dialog box is displayed, you can click buttons on its *toolbar* to change the way documents are displayed.

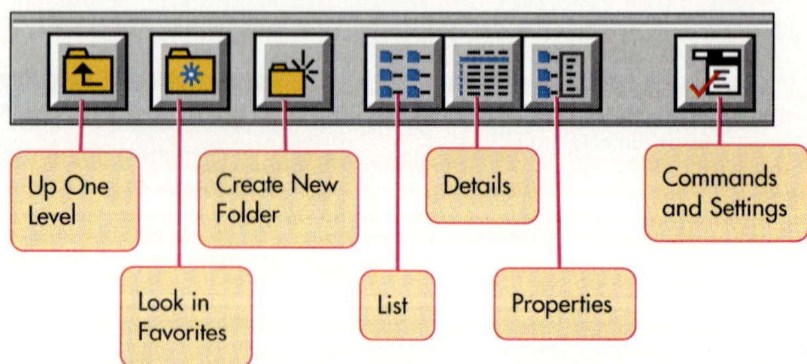

▶ **Up One Level** moves you up the tree.

▶ **Look in Favorites** displays a list of documents that you have added to your list of favorite documents.

▶ **Create New Folder** creates a new folder in which to save documents.

▶ **List** displays just icons and the names of folders or documents.

▶ **Details** displays information about documents including their size, type, and date last modified.

▶ **Properties** displays information about the highlighted document including the name of its creator, the number of times it's been revised, and its size in pages, words, characters, and bytes.

▶ **Commands and Settings** displays a menu you can use to sort the list of documents or perform other procedures.

Saving a Document Under a New Name

There are times when you want to save a document under a new name. You may have made a mistake and don't want to overwrite the version on the disk with the new version until you are certain it's OK to do so. Or you may have opened an existing document that you want to revise into a new and different one. To save an already saved document under a new name, you use the **Save As** command on the **File** menu.

Q U I C K S T E P S

Saving a Document Under a New Name

1. Pull down the **File** menu and click the **Save As** command instead of the **Save** command.
2. Type a new filename into the **File name** text box or edit the one that is there and click the **Save** button. (You can also specify a new drive and folder before clicking **Save**.)

PAL ON-LINE ACTIVITIES CHECKLIST

☐ **1-5 CONCEPTS.** Your work isn't safe until you save it onto a disk. In this concepts section you explore this procedure.

☐ **1-5 TUTORIAL.** In this tutorial you explore the three variations of saving files. First you save a previously saved document by clicking a button. This saves the document under the same name and in the same folder from which you opened it or in which you previously saved it. You then use the Save As command to save the same document under a new name. Finally, you create and then save a new document.

☐ **1-5 DRILL.** In this drill you create three very short poems and save each in a specified folder on your disk. Entering text is as easy as typing it in and pressing ⌷Enter↵⌷ where necessary.

IT ISN'T THE COUGH
It isn't the cough
That carries you off;
It's the coffin
They carry you off in.
--Anonymous

Poem 1

RELATIVITY
There was a young lady named Bright
Who traveled much faster than light.
She started one day
In the relative way,
And returned on the previous night.
--Anonymous

Poem 2

Poem 3

1-6 GETTING AROUND DOCUMENTS WITH THE MOUSE

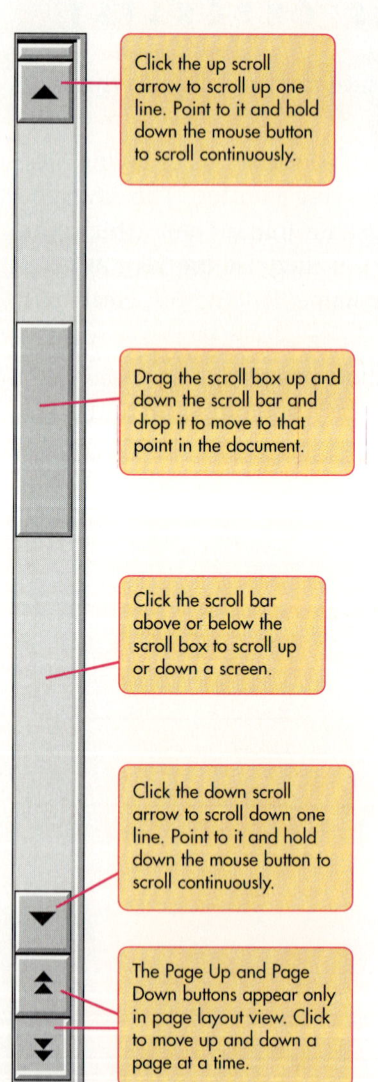

The fastest way to move the insertion point in the document on the screen is to point to where you want to move it and click. However, if the place you want to move it to isn't displayed on the screen, you have to scroll the document. You can do so using the mouse and scroll bars. A *vertical scroll bar* is located on the right edge of the document window, and a *horizontal scroll bar* is located on the bottom edge of the document window.

The vertical scroll bar contains three basic elements: the *up scroll arrow* (▲), the *down scroll arrow* (▼), and the *scroll box* (▢). The horizontal scroll bar contains the same three elements, but its scroll arrows are left and right. Below the vertical scroll bar in page layout view are two buttons you can click to page up and down through the document (see the margin illustration).

You scroll through a document by clicking the scroll arrows or by dragging the scroll box. The scroll box (▢) serves three functions:

▶ When you drag it up or down the vertical scroll bar with the mouse, you move quickly to any point in a document. As you drag it in a multipage document, the current page is indicated in a small box called a ScrollTip to the left of or above the scroll bar you are using.

▶ The scroll box also indicates where you are in a document. If it is at the top of the scroll bar, you are at the top of the document. If it is at the bottom of the scroll bar, you are at the bottom of the document. If it is halfway between the top and bottom of the scroll bar, you are at the middle of the document.

▶ In page layout view, the size of the scroll box varies to reflect the difference between what is visible in the window and the entire content of the document. For example, it is small when only a small portion of the document can be displayed at one time, and large when a large portion can be displayed. Basically, the longer the document, the smaller the scroll box.

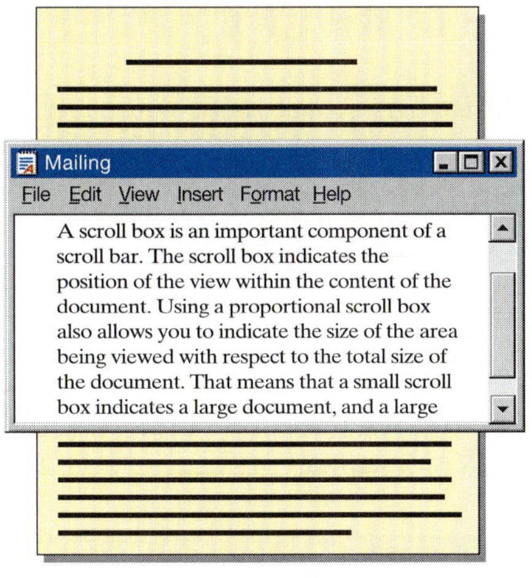

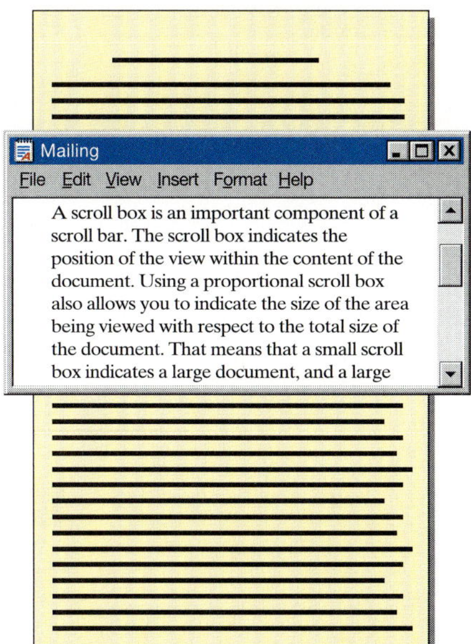

The insertion point always remains displayed on the screen except when you use the scroll bars to scroll the document. This is because scrolling the screen doesn't move the insertion point. To move it, you have to point with the I-beam-shaped mouse pointer ([) to where you want to move it and then click. If you click in an area that contains no text, the insertion point jumps to the nearest place on the line that does or to the left margin.

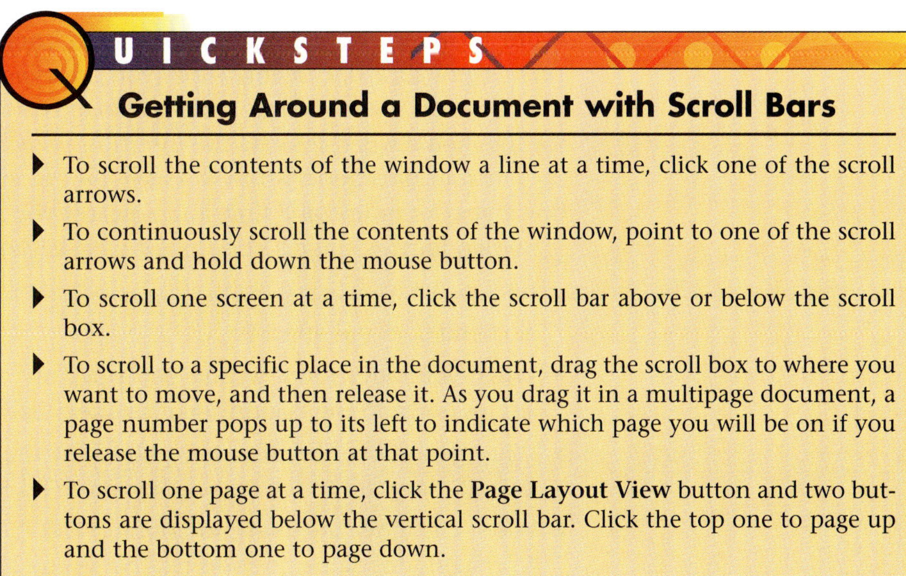

QUICKSTEPS

Getting Around a Document with Scroll Bars

▶ To scroll the contents of the window a line at a time, click one of the scroll arrows.

▶ To continuously scroll the contents of the window, point to one of the scroll arrows and hold down the mouse button.

▶ To scroll one screen at a time, click the scroll bar above or below the scroll box.

▶ To scroll to a specific place in the document, drag the scroll box to where you want to move, and then release it. As you drag it in a multipage document, a page number pops up to its left to indicate which page you will be on if you release the mouse button at that point.

▶ To scroll one page at a time, click the **Page Layout View** button and two buttons are displayed below the vertical scroll bar. Click the top one to page up and the bottom one to page down.

☐ **1-6 CONCEPTS.** The mouse helps you navigate documents very quickly. In this concepts section you explore some of the techniques used.

☐ **1-6 TUTORIAL.** In this tutorial you are introduced to many of the basic techniques for getting around the screen with a mouse. To explore these procedures, you open a long document that is a guide to your rights when using a program such as Word.

☐ **1-6 DRILL.** To navigate documents you have to know how to use the scroll bars and how to move the insertion point by pointing and clicking. In this drill you practice those procedures.

STATUS BAR INFORMATION			
Number	**At**	**Ln**	**Col**
]①	—	—	—
①[	—	—	—
]②	—	—	—
②[	—	—	—
]③	—	—	—
③[	—	—	—

1-7 GETTING AROUND DOCUMENTS WITH THE KEYBOARD

Word provides you with several keyboard commands that move the insertion point through a document. Since you are typing much of the time and your hands are on the keyboard, these commands are frequently faster than reaching for the mouse when moving the insertion point to where you want it.

The four directional arrow keys (←, →, ↑, and ↓) move the insertion point one character or line at a time and repeat if you hold them down.

When moving the insertion point with keyboard commands, you will notice:

▶ When you move the insertion point along a line of text, it moves through the text and does not affect it.

▶ When you move the insertion point past the rightmost character on a line, it jumps down to the beginning of the next line.

▶ When you move the insertion point past the leftmost character on a line of text, it jumps up to the end of the preceding line.

▶ When you move the insertion point up and down through a document, it stays in roughly the same position relative to the left margin unless a line contains little or no text.

▶ If the document is longer than the number of lines displayed on the screen, it can be scrolled into view by moving the insertion point to the top or bottom of the screen and pressing ↓ or ↑. Instead of moving off the screen, the insertion point stays on the top or bottom row, and the text scrolls into view.

▶ You cannot move the insertion point off the screen (except with the scroll bar), and you cannot move it past the end of the document.

Some commands move you slowly over short distances and some move you quickly over long distances. In that respect, these commands are much like the gas pedal in your car. You may want to crawl down the driveway but you'll want to fly on the freeway. For example, pressing the arrow keys moves the insertion point one character or line at a time. When you hold down `Ctrl` while pressing the arrow keys, the insertion point moves in larger jumps. These keys are like accelerators. For example, pressing `Ctrl`+`↓` moves the insertion point to the beginning of the next paragraph. Pressing `Ctrl`+`→` moves it to the beginning of the next word.

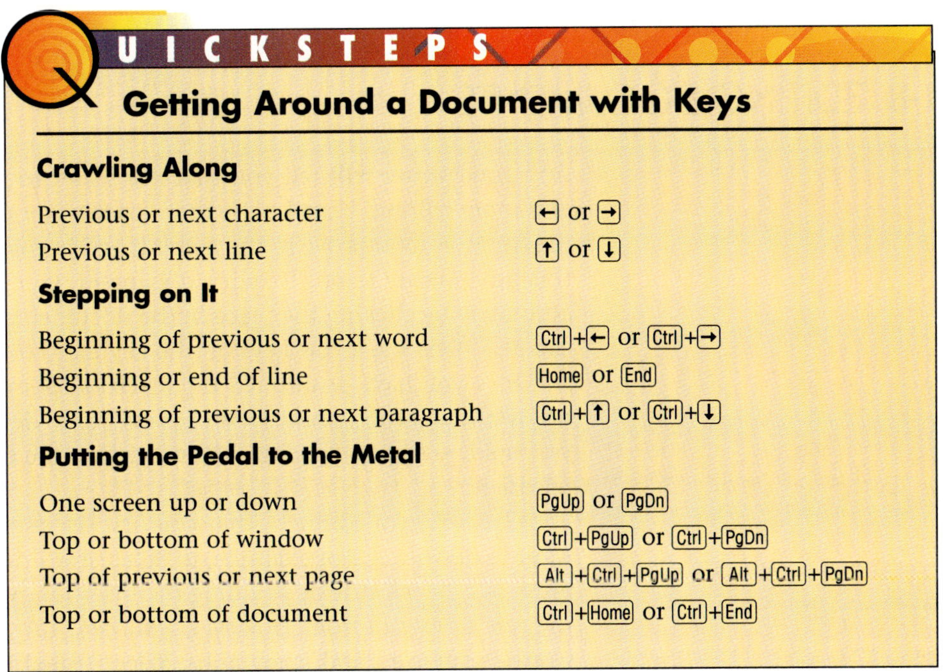

QUICKSTEPS

Getting Around a Document with Keys

Crawling Along

Previous or next character	`←` or `→`
Previous or next line	`↑` or `↓`

Stepping on It

Beginning of previous or next word	`Ctrl`+`←` or `Ctrl`+`→`
Beginning or end of line	`Home` or `End`
Beginning of previous or next paragraph	`Ctrl`+`↑` or `Ctrl`+`↓`

Putting the Pedal to the Metal

One screen up or down	`PgUp` or `PgDn`
Top or bottom of window	`Ctrl`+`PgUp` or `Ctrl`+`PgDn`
Top of previous or next page	`Alt`+`Ctrl`+`PgUp` or `Alt`+`Ctrl`+`PgDn`
Top or bottom of document	`Ctrl`+`Home` or `Ctrl`+`End`

TIP
The Go To Command

To jump to a specific page, press `F5`, or pull down the **Edit** menu and click the **Go To** command to display the Go To dialog box. With **Page** selected on the **Go to What** list, type the number of the page you want to jump to into the **Enter Page Number** text box and click the **Go To** button or press `Enter ↵`. Then click the dialog box's **Close** button.

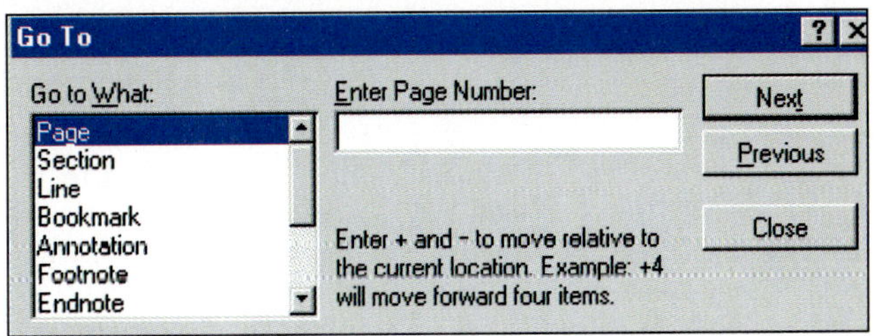

☐ **1-7 CONCEPTS.** When typing, you can move the insertion point with keys on the keyboard. In this concepts section, movies and interactive demonstrations help you explore these procedures.

☐ **1-7 TUTORIAL.** In this tutorial you are introduced to many of the basic techniques for getting around a document on the screen with keyboard commands.

☐ **1-7 DRILL.** When typing, it's often faster to move the insertion point with keyboard commands than it is to reach for the mouse. In this drill you practice these procedures.

1-8 EDITING DOCUMENTS

Any good writer will tell you that the secret to good writing is editing, editing, and more editing. Usually, the more passes you make through a document looking for ways to improve it, the better it will become. Programs such as Word make this process easy to do. To edit a document, you first position the insertion point accurately by clicking the place in the document where you want to move it. You can also press the arrow keys on the keyboard to make final adjustments.

Once you have positioned the insertion point, press ⬅Bksp to delete characters to the insertion point's left or press Del to delete any character to the right. If you hold ⬅Bksp or Del down, it will delete one character after another until you release it.

A basic rule of editing is that you first select text and then tell Word what you want to do with it. For example, to delete a word or phrase, you select it and then press Del. To select text, you drag the insertion point over it while holding down the left mouse button. However, you can also click with the mouse to select words, sentences, and paragraphs. Selected text is highlighted—usually as white text against a black background.

☐ **1-8 CONCEPTS.** Editing documents involves inserting and deleting text, sometimes to correct mistakes, sometimes to make the document read better. In this concepts section movies and interactive demonstrations introduce some basic editing procedures.

☐ **1-8 TUTORIAL.** It's a rare document indeed that needs no editing. In this tutorial you are introduced to some very basic editing commands.

The latest word processing applications such as Word for Windows make typewriters and even earlier word processing programs seem old fashioned. These programs can turn out finished documents that look as if they had been prepared by a professional printer. The first things I've noticed about this program are:

The Finished Document

☐ **1-8 DRILL.** In this drill you practice editing a document by inserting and deleting text.

This may ~~not~~ seem like ~~very~~ much, but it is the first paragraph I have typed ~~on my own~~ using this ~~amazing~~ program. It's amazing how easy these programs are to use ~~for the most basic tasks~~. All you have to do is type ~~in your text~~ and the paragraph is automatically formed. Even printing the document takes just a click ~~of the toolbar's Print button~~. I could also click the Save button on the same toolbar, but then I would then have to know how to direct the document to the ~~disk and~~ folder where I want it stored.

The Editing Text Document

1-9 EXPLORING THE TOOLBAR AND BASIC PRINTING

The Standard and Formatting toolbars just below the menu bar contain buttons, any one of which you can click to execute a command. You can also display other toolbars—or even create your own. All of these button commands can also be executed using the menus, but the toolbar buttons are faster—one click and the command is executed.

Understanding Toolbars

The Standard toolbar (the top one) includes buttons that open new or existing documents, save documents, or print them.

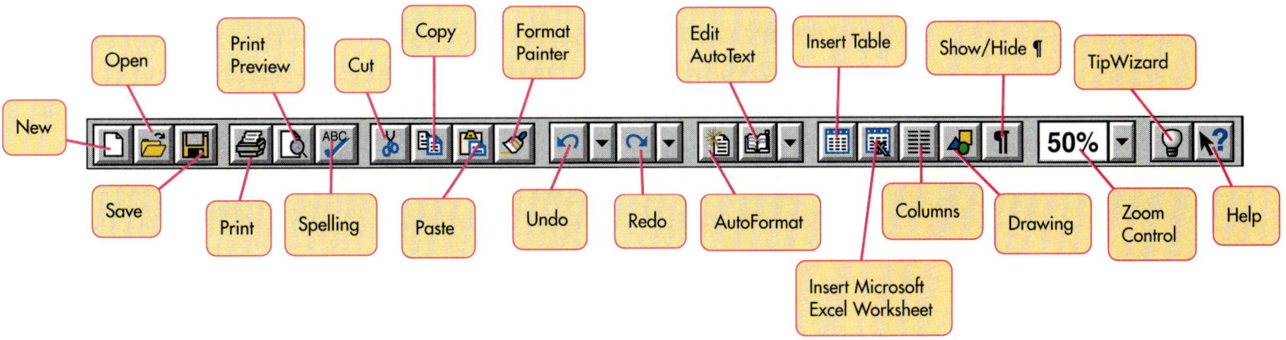

The Formatting toolbar (the lower one) contains buttons and drop-down arrows (▾) you use to format your text. The text boxes and buttons on the Formatting toolbar indicate the format settings in effect at the insertion point. For example, in a new document you may see that the **Style** is *Normal*, the **Font** is *Times New Roman*, and the **Font Size** is *10*. The alignment button that appears depressed indicates that text is set to **Align Left**.

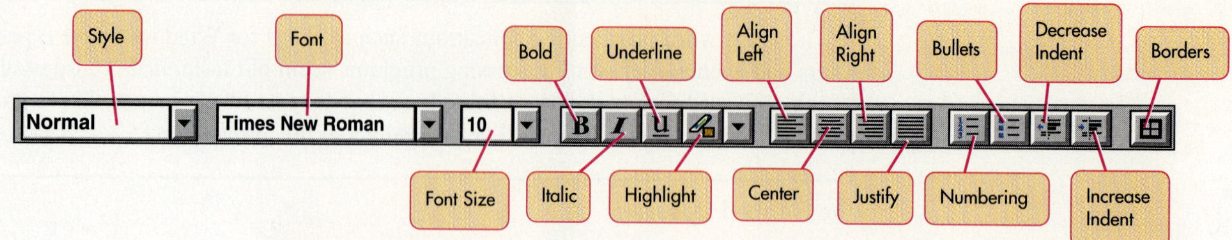

QUICKSTEPS

Displaying and Hiding Toolbars

1. Right-click anywhere on the toolbar to display a shortcut menu, or pull down the **View** menu and click the **Toolbars** command to display the Toolbars dialog box.

2. Click any toolbar names or check boxes to turn them off or on. (Normally, the *Standard* and *Formatting* toolbars are on and all others are off.) If you used the **View**, **Toolbars** command, click the **OK** button.

Printing from the Toolbar

When you want to share a document with others or file a copy for future reference, you usually make a printout. You can do so by just clicking the **Print** button on the Standard toolbar. Before you do so, you can preview how the document will look when printed by clicking the **Print Preview** button on the toolbar. If you find that you need to make adjustments, you can do so without wasting a sheet of paper. (The Print Preview command is discussed in detail in Section 2-4.)

PAL ON-LINE ACTIVITIES CHECKLIST

☐ **1-9 CONCEPTS.** The buttons on Word's toolbar make executing commands fast and easy. Here you are introduced to some of these buttons including the one that prints your documents.

☐ **1-9 TUTORIAL.** The buttons on the toolbar make executing commands fast and easy. In this tutorial you practice executing commands by just clicking buttons. Before beginning, make sure your printer is on, is connected, and has paper in it.

☐ **1-9 DRILL.** In this drill you point to each of the buttons on Word's Standard toolbar so its name is displayed on the mouse pointer and its description is displayed on the status bar.

When you are using Word, you can have tips automatically displayed as you go about your usual tasks, or you can ask for detailed help whenever you want information on a specific procedure.

The TipWizard

Word's *TipWizard* watches how you perform a procedure, and if there is a faster or more efficient way to do it, the **TipWizard** button on the toolbar lights up by changing from white to yellow. If the TipWizard box just below the toolbar isn't displayed, you can turn it on or off by clicking the **TipWizard** button on the toolbar. When displayed, you can do the following:

▶ Click the spinner buttons (⬍) at the right end of the TipWizard box to scroll through all tips offered so far in a session.

▶ To hide the TipWizard box, just click the **TipWizard** button on the Standard toolbar again.

▶ After the TipWizard has made a suggestion once, it won't make it again unless you reset it. To reset it, hold down Ctrl when you click the **TipWizard** button on the toolbar.

▶ The **Change** button appears when TipWizard senses a change it can make automatically. Read the accompanying text in the TipWizard box and then click the button to accept or reject the change.

▶ Click the **Show Me** button for more information about a tip.

ScreenTips

When you click the **Help** button on the Standard toolbar, it adds a question mark to the mouse pointer. You can then click buttons or areas of the screen to display a pop-up description called a ScreenTip. To close the ScreenTip, click it. Also, many Help windows and dialog boxes have a question mark button on their title bar. To use it to learn about parts of the Help window or dialog box, click the question mark button, then click the item in question to display a ScreenTip. To close the ScreenTip, click it. If there is no question mark button, look for a **Help** button or try pressing F1.

The Help System

Word has extensive *on-line Help* available from almost anywhere in the program. When you call up Help, you'll find that it is organized into topics, much like sections in a book. To find Help on a specific topic, you click one of the four tabs in the Help Topics window: *Contents, Index, Find,* and *Answer Wizard.* Each tab uses a different method of locating Help.

Help—The Contents Tab

The *Contents* tab lists topics group by subject much as the table of contents in a book.

1. Click to display the *Contents* tab.

2. Double-click a book icon to open it.

3. Double-click a topic or click it and then click the **Display** button to display Help.

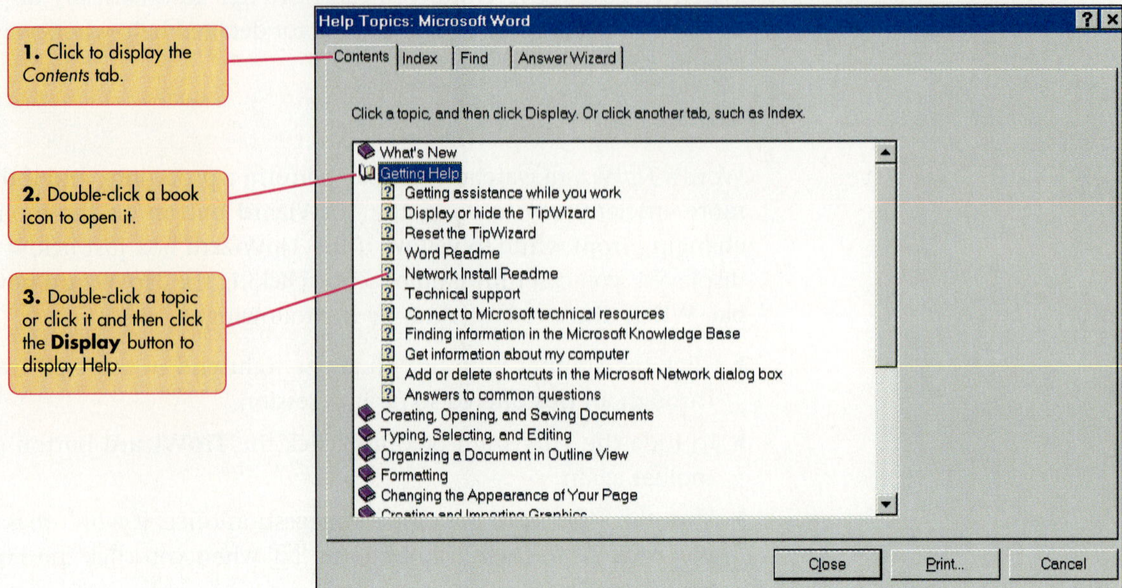

Help—The Index Tab

The *Index* tab lets you look up topics much as you would in the index of a book.

1. Click to display the *Index* tab.

2. Type the first letters of the topic you are looking for and the list below scrolls to topics that begin with those letters.

3. Double-click a topic to display it, or click it and then click the **Display** button.

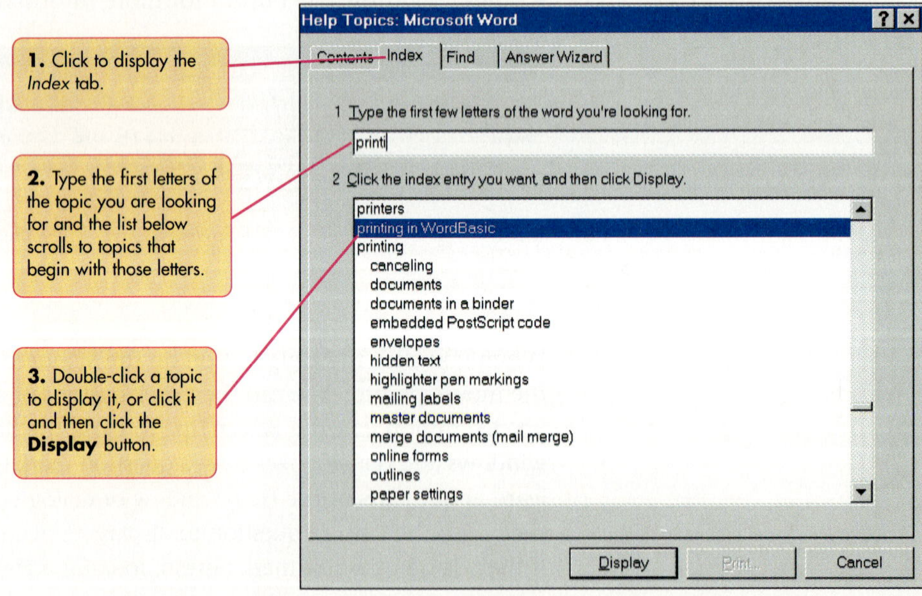

Help—The Find Tab

The *Find* tab lets you search for words or phrases that might appear in a Help topic's title.

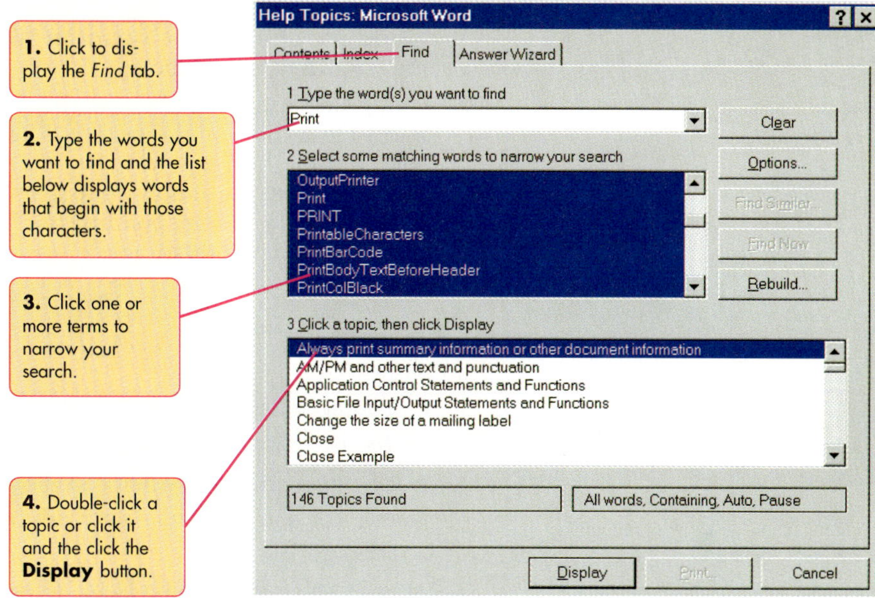

Help—The Answer Wizard Tab

The *Answer Wizard* lets you ask questions in your own words. It then not only provides Help, but it also guides you through many procedures step by step.

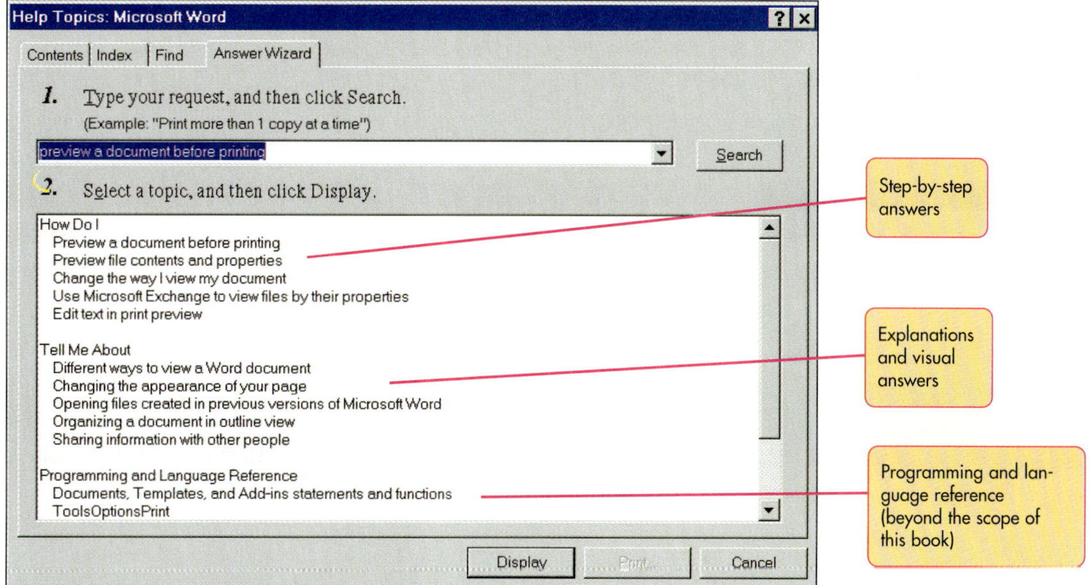

Displaying Help

1. Double-click the **Help** button on the Standard toolbar, or pull down the **Help** menu and click the **Microsoft Word Help Topics** command to display the Help Topics dialog box.

2. Locate Help using the tabs *Contents*, *Index*, *Find*, or *Answer Wizard* as shown in the illustrations in the section "The Help System." You may see *hypertext links* within the Help windows that take you directly to other places. Hypertext links are simply "hot spots" you click to jump to another location. (You know you are pointing to a hypertext link when the mouse pointer turns into a pointing finger.)

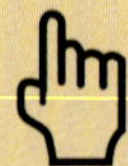

   ▶ *Shortcut buttons* take you directly to the dialog box where you make the changes related to the Help topic.

   ▶ *Pop-ups* are displayed when you click red boxes or text with green underlines. Click in a pop-up or any area but a button or menu command to close it.

3. After locating and reading Help, do one of the following:

   ▶ Pull down the **Options** menu and click the **Print Topic** command.

   ▶ Click the **Help Topics** button to return to the Help Topics dialog box.

   ▶ Click the Help window's **Minimize** button to display it as a button on the taskbar.

   ▶ Click the Help window's **Close** button to close it.

   ▶ Click the shortcut button to perform the procedure.

PAL ON-LINE ACTIVITIES CHECKLIST

☐ **1-10 CONCEPTS.** Help is always just a few keystrokes away. In this concepts section you explore the ways it's organized.

☐ **1-10 TUTORIAL.** In this tutorial you practice using Word's on-line Help to locate information on some of the topics you have explored in this PicTorial.

☐ **1-10 DRILL.** The best thing about Word's on-line Help is that it's always available, even long after you've lost the manual. In this drill you use Help to identify items on the screen and get help on procedures.

What if you want to copy, move, delete, rename, or explore documents or folders? You can do so from within Word without opening My Computer or Windows Explorer. To do so, you right-click in the Open or Save As dialog boxes, and a shortcut menu appears. Which menu appears depends on whether you right-click a document, a folder, or elsewhere in the box. The commands listed on the menus are described below, although not all of these commands appear on the same menu.

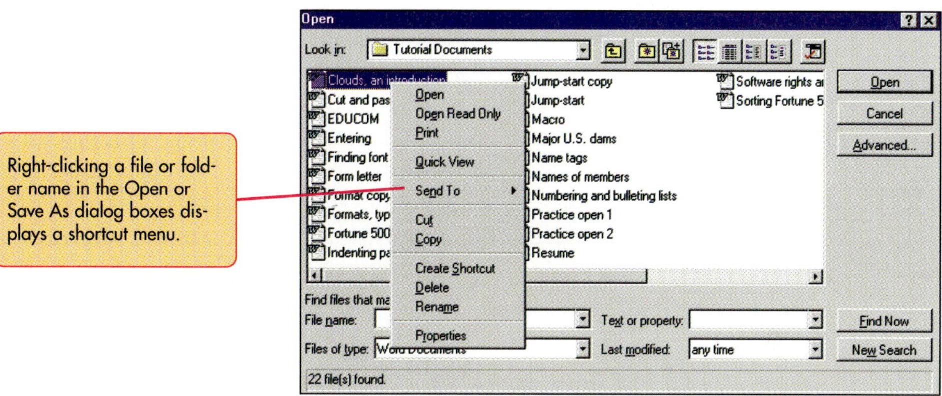

▶ **Open** opens the selected object in the dialog box.

▶ **Open Read Only** opens the selected document so you can read it but not change it.

▶ **Print** prints the selected document.

▶ **Save** saves the document using the selected filename.

▶ **Quick View** displays the contents of the selected document.

▶ **Explore** opens the selected folder and displays it in Windows Explorer.

▶ **Send To** sends a copy of the selected document or folder to a floppy disk, or to a fax or e-mail recipient.

▶ **Cut** moves the selected folder or document to the Clipboard.

▶ **Copy** copies the selected folder or document to the Clipboard.

▶ **Paste** pastes the cut or copied document or folder into the current folder.

▶ **Create Shortcut** creates a shortcut to the selected folder or document in the same location. You can then drag or move this shortcut to another folder or to the desktop.

▶ **Delete** deletes the selected folder or document to the Recycle Bin.

▶ **Rename** highlights the name of the selected folder or document so you can type a new name.

▶ **Properties** displays the properties of the selected folder or document.

Managing Documents

1. To manage your documents, do one of the following:

   ▶ Click the **Open** button on the toolbar, or pull down the **File** menu and click the **Open** command to display the Open dialog box.

   ▶ If you are saving the document for the first time, click the **Save** button on the toolbar, or pull down the **File** menu and click the **Save** command to display the Save As dialog box.

   ▶ If you have already saved the document once, pull down the **File** menu and click the **Save As** command to display the Save As dialog box.

2. Locate the folder or document you want to manage, and right-click it to display a shortcut menu. If you right-click in the box, but not on a specific folder or document, the shortcut menu choices apply to the drive or folder listed in the **Look in** text box.

3. Click any of the menu commands described above.

PAL ON-LINE ACTIVITIES CHECKLIST

☐ **1-11 CONCEPTS**. You don't have to leave Word to copy, move, or delete documents. You can do so when opening or saving documents. In this concepts section you are introduced to these procedures.

☐ **1-11 TUTORIAL**. In this tutorial you use the Open dialog box to manage a few documents. Although you normally use this dialog box to open documents, you can also use it to move, copy, rename, or delete files.

☐ **1-11 DRILL**. In this drill you practice managing documents when the Open dialog box is displayed.

LAB ACTIVITIES

1-1 Exploring the Formatting Toolbar

Point to each of the buttons on Word's Formatting toolbar so its name is displayed on the mouse pointer and its description is displayed on the status bar. Write down the name of each button on the list below that is labeled with a letter on the illustration.

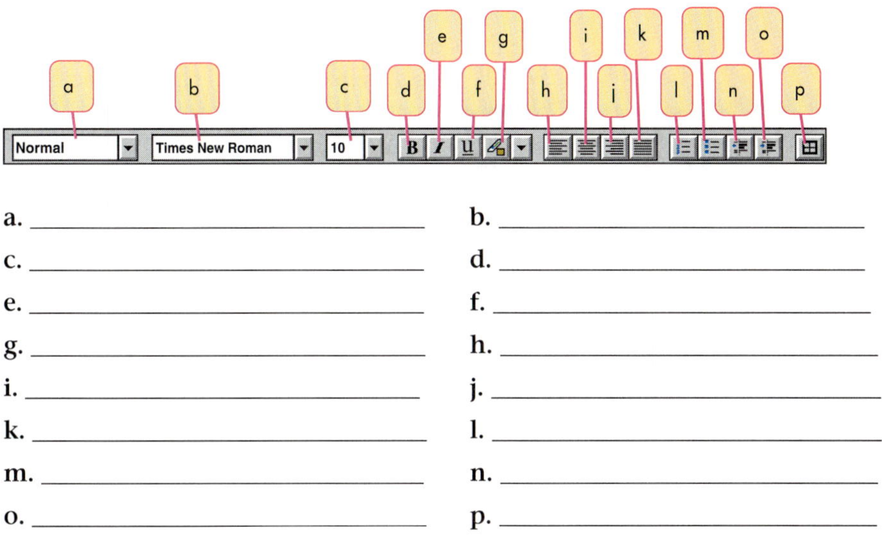

a. _______________________________ b. _______________________________

c. _______________________________ d. _______________________________

e. _______________________________ f. _______________________________

g. _______________________________ h. _______________________________

i. _______________________________ j. _______________________________

k. _______________________________ l. _______________________________

m. _______________________________ n. _______________________________

o. _______________________________ p. _______________________________

1-2 Creating and Saving Documents

In this exercise you practice many of the procedures you learned in this PicTorial.

1. Open a new document.

2. Type the paragraphs shown in the figure "The Darkroom Document." Correct any misspellings that appear underlined in red.

The 1880s was a time of rapid transition to the modern period. Prior to this period, the really slow paper emulsions required very bright light and the paper was so very slow that contact printing was the only feasible way to make prints. This meant that new prints were the same size as the negative. If one wanted large prints, one needed large negatives to take them. The simplification of making enlargements enabled the photographer to use smaller negatives and cameras; with the new faster paper emulsions large prints could be made.

The introduction of dry plates contributed to making the photographer more mobile as well. With these technological changes photographers were free from burdensome equipment. They were now able to travel light and return periodically to a darkroom to develop negatives and make enlargements.

What was this new darkroom of the 1880s like? The photographer's needs were essentially the same as today's and Victorian ingenuity developed many gadgets to make work easier and more exact. Many of these have survived the passage of time and the fickleness of photographers to appear in only slightly revised form today.

The Darkroom Document

3. Using the illustration "The Edited Darkroom Document" as a guide, insert the text shown underlined and delete the text shown struck through.

The 1880s was a time of ~~rapid~~ transition to the modern period <u>in photography as new, faster emulsions were introduced, simplifying the making of enlargements.</u> Prior to this period, the ~~really~~ slow paper emulsions required very bright light and the paper was so ~~very~~ slow that contact printing was the only feasible way <u>for amateurs</u> to make prints. This meant that ~~new~~ prints were the same size as the negative. If one wanted large prints, one needed large negatives <u>and a large camera</u> to take them. The simplification of making enlargements enabled the photographer to use smaller negatives and cameras; with <u>access to a darkroom and</u> the new faster paper emulsions large prints could be made.

The introduction of dry plates contributed to making the photographer more mobile as well. With these technological changes photographers were free from burdensome equipment<u> on their travels</u>. They were now able to travel light and return periodically to a darkroom to develop negatives and make enlargements.

What was this new darkroom of the 1880s like? <u>It was surprisingly like the darkroom of the 1990s.</u> The photographer's needs were essentially the same as today's and Victorian ingenuity developed many gadgets to make work easier and more exact. Many of these have survived the passage of time and the fickleness of photographers to appear in only slightly revised form today.

The Edited Darkroom Document

4. Save the document as *The darkroom document* in the *Project Documents* folder on the *Word Student Resource Disk*.

5. Click the **Print** button on the Standard toolbar to make a printout of the document, then close the document.

6. Close the document, then use the Open dialog box to cut the document from the *Project Documents* folder and paste it into the *Exercise Documents* folder.

7. Rename the document *Moved and renamed darkroom document*. (Click it once to select it, then again to move the insertion point into the name for editing.)

8. Close the Open dialog box, then close Word.

PicTorial TWO

MASTERING THE ESSENTIALS

After completing this PicTorial, you will be able to:

▸ **Enter and edit text**
▸ **Spell-check documents**
▸ **Preview and print documents**
▸ **Select text and copy and move it**
▸ **Find and replace text**
▸ **Look up synonyms and antonyms in the thesaurus**

T HERE are only a few procedures that you absolutely must know to begin getting value from a program such as Word, and they are covered in this PicTorial. These procedures include entering and editing text, printing documents, and copying and moving larger sections of text. This PicTorial also shows how to use Word's built-in spelling checker and the-saurus, which are so handy that you will not want to work without them.

If you have just started Word or opened a new document, the insertion point is at the top of the document waiting for you to enter text. As you type a character, the character appears where the insertion point is, and the insertion point then moves one space to the right. To enter text into the middle of existing text, move the insertion point to where you want to enter it and then type it in.

When you are typing paragraphs, you do not have to press [Enter ←] at the end of each line. Word has a feature, called *word wrap*, that automatically does this for you. When the end of a line is reached, Word calculates whether the word being entered fits on the line. If it will not fit, Word automatically begins a new line of text by moving the entire word to the next line.

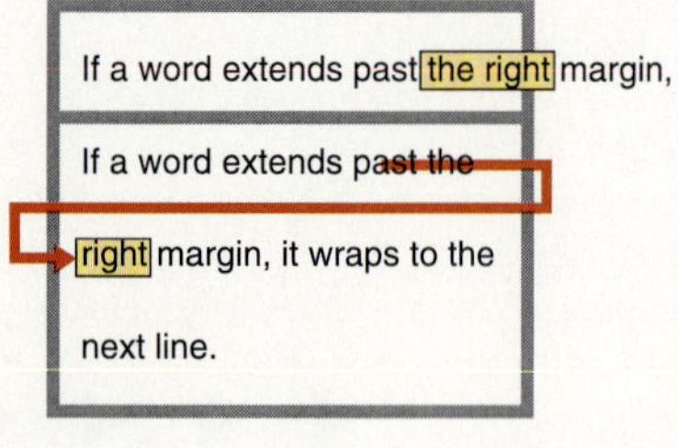

Hard and Soft Returns

Returns (sometimes called carriage returns) are codes in the document that indicate where lines end. When you print the document, these codes are not printed, but they tell the printer when to move down one line and back to the left margin. Word (like all word processing programs) has two kinds of returns: soft and hard.

Word automatically enters *soft returns* at the end of a line as you enter text whenever it reaches the right margin and wraps a word to the next line. Soft returns automatically adjust their position if you revise the text. For example, when you insert or delete text or when you change the margins, existing soft returns are automatically rearranged so that they are always positioned at the end of each line.

Unlike soft returns, *hard returns*, also called paragraph marks (¶), remain fixed in place where you enter them by pressing [Enter ←]. You enter a hard return whenever you want to end a line before you reach the right margin—for example:

▶ To end a paragraph and start a new one.

▶ To enter an inside address, a salutation, or a heading.

▶ To insert a blank line, as you would following an inside address, the date, and the closing of a letter. Each time you press [Enter ←], you insert another blank line.

Entering Letters, Numbers, and Symbols

You can enter letters, numbers, and shifted characters such as % and &.

To enter uppercase letters, either hold down [⇧ Shift] while typing a letter or press [CapsLock] to enter all uppercase letters. Press [CapsLock] again to return to lowercase. If you press [⇧ Shift] to enter text when [CapsLock] is engaged, you enter lowercase letters. Most keyboards have lights that indicate when [CapsLock] is engaged.

To enter shifted characters like !, @, and # that appear on the top half of some keys, hold down [⇧ Shift] while you press the keys.

To enter numbers, either use the number keys on the top row of the keyboard or use the numeric keypad. The keys on the numeric keypad not only enter numbers; they also move the insertion point. When [NumLock] is engaged, pressing the keys enters numbers. When [NumLock] is not engaged, pressing the keys moves the insertion point. Most keyboards have lights that indicate when [NumLock] is engaged.

If you are an experienced typist and are used to typing a lowercase letter ell (l) for the number one (1), or an uppercase letter oh (O) for zero (0), do not do this on your computer. The computer treats numbers and letters differently, and although you usually won't have problems, you could run into difficulties by disregarding this distinction.

COMMON WRONG TURNS
Using Spaces to Align Text

With a program such as Word, you should never use spaces to align text as you might on a typewriter. Word will expand and compress spaces at times so your text may look aligned on the screen but then print out of alignment. When using Word, use tab stops or paragraph indents to align your text, as you will see in PicTorial 3.

TIP
The Changing Rules on Spaces Following Periods and Colons

When documents were typed on typewriters, it was common practice to enter two spaces following periods and colons. However, in publishing, it has always been standard practice to use only one space. As the power of word processors has begun to rival that of desktop publishing programs, it is more common to follow publishing practices, so one space is becoming increasingly acceptable.

Entering Symbols and Special Characters

There are times when you want to enter characters that are not on the keyboard. Word makes this easy to do. Each font on your system (there are usually quite a few) has a set of symbols with it. To select one of these fonts, you display a grid showing all of the characters in the font, and choose the one you want to insert. Other special characters, such as ©, ®, and ™, can be used with any font. To insert one of these commonly used symbols, you just select it from a list.

QUICKSTEPS
Entering Symbols and Special Characters

1. Position the insertion point where you want the symbol, pull down the **Insert** menu and click the **Symbol** command to display the Symbol dialog box.
2. Do one of the following:
   ▶ On the **Symbols** tab, click any character to select it and enlarge it and then click the **Insert** button to insert it into the document. To change the displayed characters, click the **Font** drop-down arrow and select another font.
   ▶ On the **Special Characters** tab, click any character to select it and then click the **Insert** button to insert it into the document.
3. Click the **Close** button to close the dialog box.

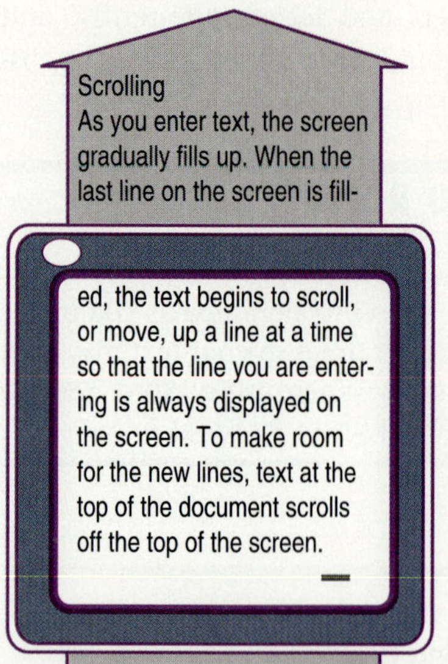

Scrolling

As you enter text, the screen gradually fills up. When the last line on the screen is filled, the text begins to scroll, or move, up a line at a time so that the line you are entering is always displayed on the screen. To make room for the new lines, text at the top of the document scrolls off the top of the screen. But it is not gone for good; you can scroll back to it whenever you want using the scroll bar or keyboard commands.

Page Breaks

When you enter enough lines of text so that they will fill a page when you print the document, Word automatically inserts a page break. This is called a *soft page break*. If you insert or delete text above this soft page break, it adjusts its position automatically. The soft page break is indicated by a thin dotted line across the screen in normal view and a separation between pages in page layout view. You cannot delete a soft page break. The only way to change its position is to add or delete text above it.

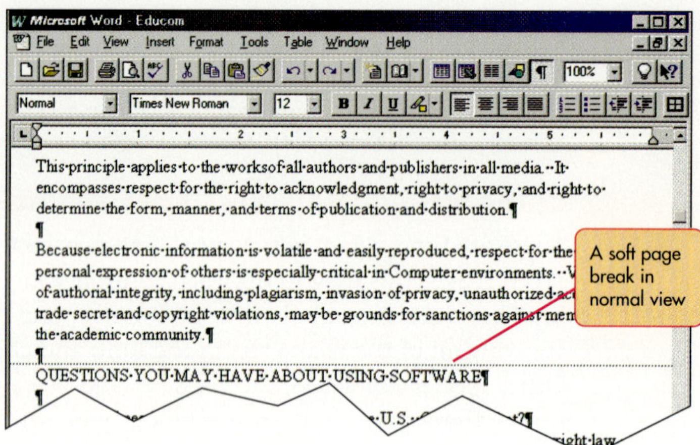

Correcting Mistakes

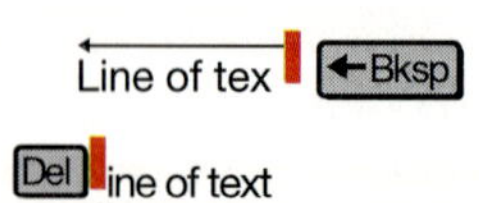

If you make a mistake when typing, press ←Bksp to delete characters to the insertion point's left; then type the characters correctly. You can also move the insertion point through the text and press Del to delete any character to the right of the insertion point, as shown in the margin illustration. If you hold ←Bksp or Del down, it will delete one character after another until you release it.

If a word you type isn't in the dictionary, Word underlines it with a wavy red line. You can edit the word, or right-click it to display a shortcut menu listing suggested replacements.

Undoing Mistakes

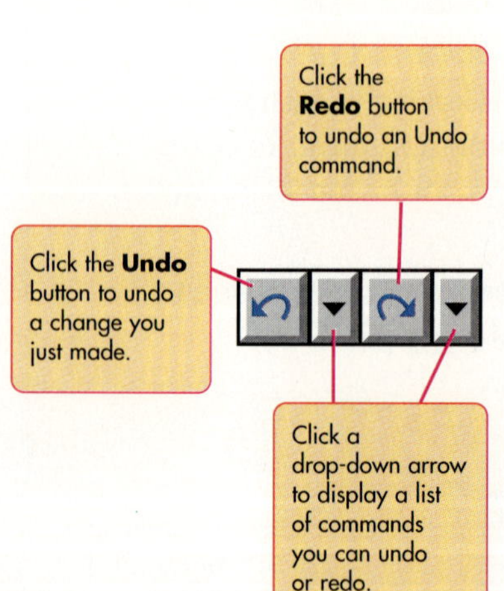

Word has a very powerful command that allows you to undo mistakes. This way, if you delete text by mistake, or make some other error, you can often undo it. In fact, you can undo an entire series of commands with just a few clicks of the Undo button on the toolbar.

▶ To undo the last command, click the **Undo** button on the toolbar.

▶ To undo the last command and any number of commands before it, click the drop-down arrow (▼) next to the **Undo** button to display a list of commands you can undo. Click the last command on the list to be undone.

You can also pull down the **Edit** menu and click the **Undo** command. The word **Undo** on the menu is followed by the name of the command that will be undone. If no command can be undone, the command will read **Can't Undo**.

If you make a mistake in undoing a command, click the **Redo** button to undo it. The **Redo** button works just like the **Undo** button.

☐ **2-1 CONCEPTS.** In this concepts section you view two movies, one that explores word wrap and one that demonstrates the ⌜Enter ↵⌟ key.

☐ **2-1 TUTORIAL.** Entering text is what word processing is all about. You can't do anything else until you have mastered this basic skill. In this tutorial you open a document with a pre-existing letterhead and heading and enter your own body text.

COMPUTER **C**URRICULUM **C**ENTER

MEMORANDUM

123 NORTH MONROE STREET   PHONE: 456 385-2578
CLEVELAND, OHIO 65743   FAX: 456 385-3456

TO: Janie Czarnecki, Word Instructor

FROM: your name, Educational Director

SUBJECT: Interesting documents needed

DATE: November 11, 1997

⌜Enter ↵⌟
⌜Tab⇆⌟ We need to come up with a document to use in the introductory Word class in the section on entering text. The document should be short because some students don't type well. It should also be interesting or useful. Too many documents used in textbooks are DULL! I'd like to suggest the paragraphs describing OLE, one of the newest features of application programs. ⌜Enter ↵⌟
⌜Enter ↵⌟
⌜Tab⇆⌟ "One of the recent trends in computing has been to make data, rather than applications, the focus of software design. Advances in design make it possible to include data in a document that has been created by other applications. For example, you can create a table in Access and then place it in an Excel worksheet. You can also use other types of applications to create and paste in line drawings, photographs, sounds, and even video. ⌜Enter ↵⌟
⌜Tab⇆⌟ Windows gives you more than one way to get data from one application into another. One of the easiest ways to insert data from one application into another is to cut and paste it. To do so, you just copy some data from one application to the Windows Clipboard and then paste it into another application's document. You can even drag data from one application and drop it into another. It's as if you cut a picture out of a magazine and pasted it into a scrapbook. ⌜Enter ↵⌟

> [Tab⇆] As useful as copying data is, it has some drawbacks, the biggest one being that the copied data has no links to the application that created it. If you needed to update the data you pasted into a document, you couldn't do it from the document you copied it to. You'd have to open the application that created it, change the data, cut and paste it again, and then delete the old version. [Enter↵]
> [Tab⇆] To overcome the shortcomings of copying data, most new Windows applications support a process called object linking and embedding, or OLE. OLE allows you to insert data from one application into another just as if it were copied. However, when it is linked or embedded, you can edit it within the document you copied it to." [Enter↵]

The Entering document

☐2-1 DRILL. To enter text, you just type it in, pressing [Enter↵] whenever you want to end a paragraph or insert a blank line. In this drill, you practice these procedures by typing a short document describing geysers.

> What Is a Geyser? [Enter↵]
> [Enter↵]
> A geyser is a special kind of hot spring that from time to time spurts water above ground. It differs from most hot springs in having periodic eruptions separated by intervals without flow of water. The temperature of the erupting water is generally near the boiling point for pure water. Some geysers erupt less than a foot, and a few erupt more than 150 feet. Some small geysers erupt every minute or so, but others are inactive for months or even years between eruptions. Contrary to popular opinion, most geysers are very irregular in their behavior, and each is different in some respect from all others. Among the major geysers, only a few, such as Old Faithful in Yellowstone National Park, are predictable enough for the impatient tourist. But even for Old Faithful the interval between eruptions varies from about 30 to 90 minutes, with an average of about 65 minutes. [Enter↵]
> [Enter↵]
> Donald E. White [Enter↵]
> U.S. Department of the Interior [Enter↵]

The Geyser document

2-2 EDITING TEXT

To edit text, you move the insertion point through the document and insert characters by typing them in or delete them by pressing [←Bksp] or [Del]. You can also switch between insert and overtype modes, make new paragraphs from existing ones, and join existing paragraphs into one paragraph.

Switching Between Insert and Overtype Modes

Word's default setting is the insert mode, so if you enter characters into existing text, the text moves over to make room for them. However, you can switch to overtype mode so that characters you enter type over and replace any existing characters in their way. The current status is listed on the status bar. When *OVR* is dimmed, you are in insert mode. When it's not dimmed, you are in overtype mode.

Switching Between Insert and Overtype Modes

Do either of the following:

▶ Press [Ins].

▶ Double-click *OVR* on the status bar.

Displaying Nonprinting Characters

Nonprinting Characters	
Character name	**Character**
Tab characters	→
Spaces	•
Paragraph marks	¶

When you press [Enter ↵], [Tab ⇥], and [Spacebar], you enter nonprinting characters into the document. When these characters are displayed, it's easy to see if you have inserted spaces, tabs, or returns. It also makes it easy to delete these hidden characters. Some of the nonprinting characters that you can display are listed and described in the table "Nonprinting Characters."

Displaying Nonprinting Characters

Fastest

▶ Click the **Show/Hide ¶** button on the Standard toolbar to display or hide nonprinting characters.

Menus

1. Pull down the **Tools** menu and click the **Options** command to display the Options dialog box.

2. On the **View** tab, click any of the check boxes in the *Nonprinting Characters* section to turn them on, and then click the **OK** command button.

Paragraph mark in a document.

TIP
Inserting Text

When you position the insertion point to insert text between two existing words, you can position it on either side of the space that separates the words. If you position it on the left side of the space, you press [Spacebar] before typing the new word. If you position it on the right side of the space, you press [Spacebar] after typing the new word. If you click the Show/Hide ¶ button on the Standard toolbar to display nonprinting characters, it is easy to see which side of the space you are on.

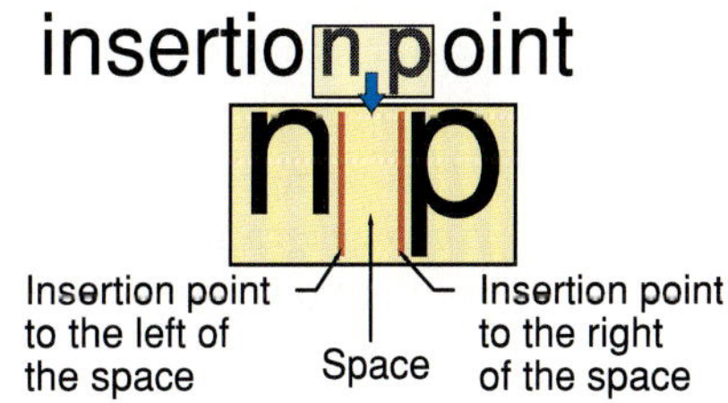

Making One Paragraph into Two

You can enter paragraph marks as you type a document, or you can enter them into existing text. You enter paragraph marks in existing text whenever you want to break an existing paragraph into two paragraphs. To do so, move the insertion point just to the left of the character that you want to be the first character in the new paragraph and press [Enter←]. This moves the insertion point, and all text to its right, down one line and back to the left margin. If you press [Enter←] a second time, a blank line is inserted above the new paragraph.

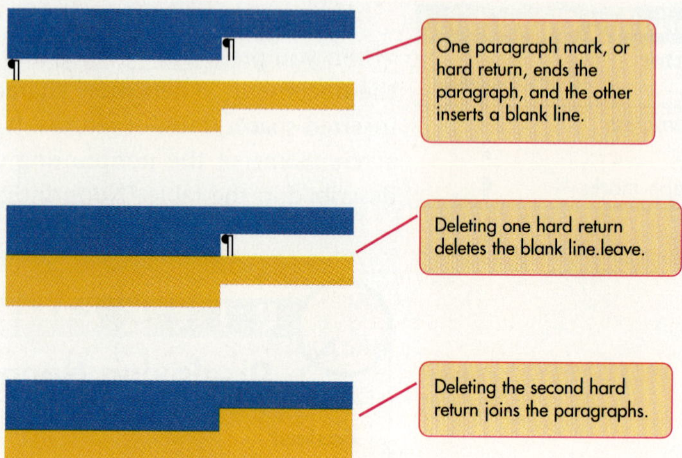

Joining Two Paragraphs into One

To join two paragraphs into one, you can use [←Bksp] or [Del] to delete the paragraph marks (hard returns) that separate them. (Click the **Show/Hide ¶** command on the toolbar to turn it on so you can see them). When you join paragraphs like this, strange things can happen because Word stores all paragraph formats, like alignment, indents, and spacing, in the paragraph mark symbol. When you delete the paragraph mark at the end of a paragraph, the paragraph that follows takes its formatting from the paragraph above it. The paragraph mark at the end of that first paragraph determines the format of the combined paragraphs.

Before Paragraphs Are Joined:

This paragraph is aligned with the left margin and separated from the paragraph below by a paragraph mark.¶

The paragraph below is aligned with the right margin. ¶

After Paragraphs Are Joined:

This paragraph is aligned with the left margin and separated from the paragraph below by a paragraph mark. The paragraph below is aligned with the right margin. ¶

☐ **2-2 CONCEPTS.** In this concepts section you view a series of movies that demonstrate inserting text, overtyping text, displaying nonprinting characters, and breaking and joining paragraphs.

☐ **2-2 TUTORIAL.** In this tutorial you open the document you created in a previous tutorial and revise it by inserting and deleting text.

We need to come up with a useful document to use in the introductory Word class in the section on entering text. The document should be as short as possible because some students don't type well. It should also be interesting or useful. Too many textbooks use documents that used in textbooks are DULL! I'd like to suggest the following paragraphs describing OLE, one of the newest features of applications programs.

The Edited Entering document

☐ **2-2 DRILL.** Any successful newspaper, magazine, or book writer can tell you that writing is revising. No one sits down and jots down deathless prose. Writers write and then they revise, revise, revise. It's word processing's ability to make the mechanics of revision painless that makes writers love it. Only a few years ago each major draft had to be typed all over again. Now writers just insert and delete on the fly. In this drill you practice some of the basic editing procedures.

2-3 CHECKING SPELLING

Word's built-in spelling checker will correct the spelling of words in your documents—a valuable aid upon which you should not rely too much. If you do so, you are sure to be embarrassed at some point. It checks only for spelling, not usage. For example, spelling checkers would find no problems in the sentences *Eye wood like two except you're invitation, butt can not. unfortunately, their are another things I half too due* or *Too bee oar knot two bee.* These sentences, concocted from words that sound like the ones that are intended, will not be flagged by Word's automatic spell checking or its **Spelling** command because each word in them is an actual word, correctly spelled, that is in Word's dictionary. Also, Word's default settings are to ignore words in all uppercase (ATTENTION) or that contain numbers (3-D) so these might be missed. Because of these limitations, you must proofread documents carefully for content and context.

Automatic Spell Checking

When Word's automatic spelling checker is on, Word will detect possibly misspelled words as you type them. It indicates that a word isn't in the dictionary in two ways:

▸ It underlines the word with a wavy red line as soon as you press [Spacebar] or click elsewhere in the document.

▸ It puts a red X in the open dictionary icon that is displayed at the right end of the status bar.

This icon on the status bar indicates that automatic spell checking is on. The red X indicates the document contains is in a word that isn't in Word's dictionary

When a word appears with this red line, check it to see if it is spelled incorrectly. Not all words are. For example, your name may be spelled correctly but if it isn't in the dictionary, Word won't know that so it will underline it. If a word is spelled incorrectly, there are a number of ways to correct it:

▶ Edit the word just as you would edit any other word.

▶ Right-click the word to display a list of suggested replacement words and select one.

▶ Spell-check the entire document as described in the next section.

▶ Double-click the icon with a red *X* in it on the status bar and the highlight jumps to the next underlined word in the document and displays a shortcut menu of suggested replacement words.

QUICKSTEPS

Turning Automatic Spell Checking On and Off

1. Pull down the **Tools** menu and click the **Options** command to display the Options dialog box.

2. On the **Spelling** tab, click the **Automatic Spell Checking** check box to turn it on or off.

3. Click the **OK** button to close the dialog box.

The Spell Checking Command

When you use the **Spelling** command with automatic spell checking on, Word only checks those words that have been underlined with wavy red lines. At the end of spell checking no wavy red lines will remain in the document. If automatic spell checking is off, Word checks each word in the document against its dictionary. If Word can't find the word in its dictionary, it highlights the word, and you are given the option of ignoring, changing, editing, or adding it to the dictionary if it is spelled correctly. Adding a word to the dictionary keeps it from being flagged in other documents.

Click the **Spelling** button to check the document's spelling.

QUICKSTEPS

Checking Spelling

1. The insertion point can be anyplace in the document but if you want to check the spelling of a single word or a section of text, select it before using the **Spelling** command. (Selecting text is discussed in Section 2-5.)

2. Click the **Spelling** button on the toolbar or pull down the **Tools** menu and click the **Spelling** command.

3. If a "misspelled" word is highlighted in the document,. use any of the commands described in the box "Understanding the Spelling Dialog Box."

4. When spell-checking is complete, a dialog box tells you so. Click the **OK** command button to close the dialog box.

When you spell check a document, the Spelling dialog box appears whenever Word locates a word that isn't in its dictionary.

▶ To replace the word in the document with the word in the **Change To** text box, click the **Change** command button. To replace it and all subsequent occurrences of the same word, click the **Change All** button.

▶ To replace the word in the document with a word on the **Suggestions** list, click the replacement word to select it and then click the **Change** or **Change All** command button.

▶ To edit a word displayed in the **Change To** text box, press ➡ to remove the highlight from the word or click in the text box to move the insertion point there. After editing the word, click the **Change** or **Change All** command button.

▶ To leave the word in the document unchanged, click either the **Ignore** or **Ignore All** command button.

▶ To add the word in the document to the dictionary, click the **Add** command button.

▶ To delete one of a pair of repeated words, click the **Delete** command button when it appears.

▶ To correct the word and also add the misspelling and corrected word to the AutoCorrect list so Word corrects it automatically should you type it wrong again, click the **AutoCorrect** button.

▶ To undo the last correction if you change your mind, click the **Undo Last** command button.

PAL ON-LINE ACTIVITIES CHECKLIST

☐ **2-3 CONCEPTS.** In this concepts section you view movies that demonstrate how words that are not in the dictionary are underlined when you type them in and how the lines disappear on those you correct.

☐ **2-3 TUTORIAL.** No one is perfect—that's one reason why spelling checkers are so popular. In this tutorial you use Word's spelling checker to check a document that contains built-in mistakes. Not all words highlighted during a spelling check are spelled wrong. Some are spelled correctly but just aren't in Word's dictionary. The Tip box "EDUCOM Document 'Misspelled' Words" on page 48 contains a table listing words that may be highlighted during your spelling check of the *EDUCOM* document, with comments about each.

☐ **2-3 DRILL.** Checking the spelling in your documents should be a routine procedure. In this drill you spell-check a document that has a number of built-in spelling errors.

EDUCOM Document "Misspelled" Words

Not all words highlighted during a spell check are spelled wrong. Some are spelled correctly but just aren't in Word's dictionary. Here is a list of the words that may be highlighted during your spell check of the *EDUCOM* document, with comments about each.

Word highlighted	Comment
acedemic	academic
unauthorised	unauthorized
wideli	widely
EDUCOM	*Spelled correctly and may not be flagged*
worksof	works of
U.S.	*Spelled correctly but Word suggests version without periods*
distribute distribute	distribute
licenseagreement	license agreement
legel	legal
Shareware	*Spelled correctly*
ADAPSO	*Spelled correctly and may not be flagged*
P.O.	*Spelled correctly but Word suggests version without periods*

2-4 PREVIEWING AND PRINTING DOCUMENTS

Most document are eventually printed so a record can be filed or distributed to others. Word lets you print a document with the click of a button or preview it before you print it to be sure it will print correctly.

Previewing a Document

Print Preview lets you catch layout mistakes before wasting time and paper printing the document. In this view, you can also adjust margins, edit text, and even drag text or graphics between pages, as you will see later.

QUICKSTEPS

Previewing Printouts

1. Click the **Print Preview** button on the Standard toolbar, or pull down the **File** menu and click the **Print Preview** command.
2. Click any of the buttons described in the box "Understanding the Print Preview Toolbar." Use the scroll bar to scroll through a document that has more pages than are currently displayed.
3. Click the **Close** command to return to your previous view of the document.

When you click the **Print Preview** button on the Standard toolbar, or pull down the **F**ile menu and click the **Print Pre**v**iew** command, the Print Preview toolbar is displayed.

Print prints the document.

Magnifier switches the mouse pointer between a magnifier and an I-beam (I). When displayed as a magnifier, click anywhere in the document to enlarge it and again to shrink it. When displayed as an I-beam, you can select text as described in Section 2-5 and drag and drop it as described in Section 2-7.

One Page displays one page at a time.

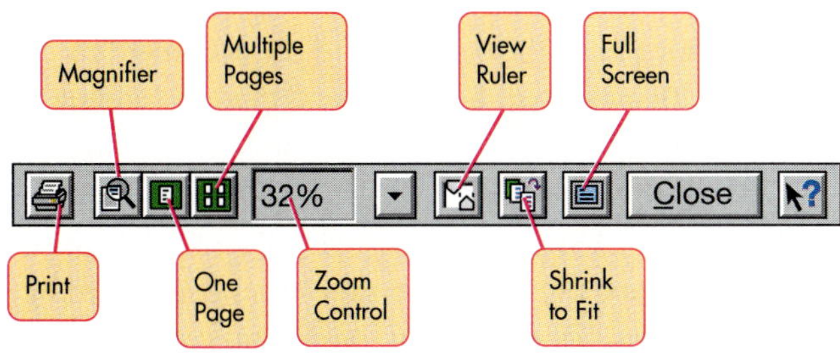

Multiple Pages displays a grid you use to select the number of pages to be displayed. Click the lower right corner of the rectangular grid of pages you would like displayed or point to the upper-left corner of the grid, hold down the mouse and drag the highlight over the grid. It will expand as you drag against a border. When you have highlighted the number of pages you want to display, release the mouse button.

Zoom Control drop-down arrow (▼) displays a list of zooms from which you can choose.

View Ruler turns the horizontal and vertical rulers on and off.

Shrink to Fit reduces the number of pages when there is only a limited amount of text on the document's last page. It does this by making the document's type smaller each time you click it. These changes in type size are permanent, so use this with care (or pull down the **E**dit menu and click the **U**ndo command to reverse them.)

Full Screen hides all screen elements except the Print Preview toolbar when you click it the first time, and reveals them when you click it again.

Close returns you to your previous view of the document.

Printing Documents

When you print the document displayed on the screen, you can print the entire document, specific pages, or a selected block. As pages are printed, the status of the print job is indicated at the right end of the status bar.

QUICKSTEPS

Printing Documents

▶ To print the entire document using the current print settings, click the **Print** button on the Standard toolbar or on the Print Preview toolbar. This prints the document using the current default settings for printing.

▶ To print specific pages, or choose other options, pull down the **F**ile menu and click the **Print** command, to display the Print dialog box that allows you to specify options. Change any of the settings described in the box "Understanding the Print Dialog Box" and then click the **OK** command button.

When you pull down the **File** menu and click the **Print** command, the Print dialog box appears. (It does not appear when you click the **Print** button on the toolbar.) This box allows you to control all aspects of the printout.

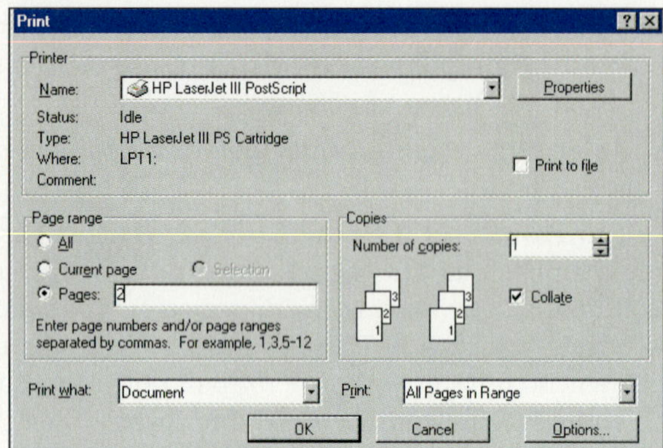

Printer Section

Name text box lists the currently selected printer. To select another printer, click the drop-down arrow (▼) and select one from the list.

Properties command button displays a tabbed dialog box you use to change the default paper sizes, page orientation (portrait, which is like a normal letter, or landscape, which is lengthwise on the page), and number of copies. It also has advanced settings including graphics and device options. After making changes, you can always click the **Restore Defaults** button to cancel them. Click the **OK** command button to return to the Print dialog box.

Print to file check box, when on (☑), sends the printout to a file on the disk rather than the printer.

Page Range Section

▶ **All** (the default setting) prints all pages in the document.

▶ **Current Page** prints the page on which the insertion point is positioned.

▶ **Selection** prints just the text that you have selected in the document.

▶ **Pages** prints ranges of pages using these procedures (do not enter spaces in the page specifications, for they may create problems):

  ▶ To print a single page, enter the page number. For example, to print page 7, type **7**.

  ▶ To print several consecutive pages, enter the starting and ending pages separated by a hyphen. For example, to print pages 2 through 5, type **2-5**.

  ▶ To print several nonconsecutive pages or ranges of pages, separate them with commas. For example, to print pages 1, 5, and 10, type **1,5,10** and to print page 1 and then pages 6 through 8, type **1,6-8**.

  ▶ To print from the beginning of the document to a specific page, type a hyphen and then the ending page number. For example, to print from the beginning of the document to page 10, type **-10**.

  ▶ To print from a specific page to the end of the document, type the beginning page number followed by a hyphen. For example, to print from page 10 to the end of the document, type **10-**.

Copies Section

Copies specifies the number of copies to be printed.

Collate check box, when on (☑), collates multiple copies. When off, all of the first page are printed, then all of the second, and so on.

Other Commands

Print What normally specifies the document, but you can change it to print such things as summary information about the document, annotations, or key assignments.

Print specifies whether you print all pages in the specified range or just odd or even pages.

Options command button displays a dialog box where you can change print options. Click the **OK** command button to return to the Print dialog box.

Managing Print Jobs

When you print a document, you may want to check its status, pause it, or even cancel it. You can do so using the printer icon in the notification area on Windows' taskbar. This printer icon is only displayed when print jobs are being processed.

Managing Print Jobs

1. Do one of the following:

▶ Double-click the printer icon in the notification area on Windows' taskbar.

▶ Right-click the printer icon in the notification area on Windows' taskbar and then click the shortcut menu's **Open Active Printers** command.

▶ Double-click the *My Computer* icon on the Windows desktop, then double-click the *Printers* folder to display icons for the printers on your system. Double-click the printer you want to manage.

2. Use any of the commands described in the box "Understanding the Printer's Dialog Box."

UNDERSTANDING
The Printer's Dialog Box

When you display the dialog box for the printer you are using, its name appears on the title bar. You can use any of the dialog box's commands to manage your print jobs.

Printer Menu

P̲ause Printing pauses all print jobs on the current printer. You have to click the command a second time to resume printing.

P̲urge Print Jobs cancels all jobs waiting to be printed.

Set as De̲fault makes the current printer the default printer for your system.

P̲roperties displays a dialog box where you can change the properties of your printer. For example, you can change the printing mode from portrait (normal) to land-scape (text printed lengthwise on the page) or back again.

C̲lose closes the dialog box.

Document Menu

P̲ause Printing pauses the printing of the document highlighted on the list. You have to click the command a second time to resume printing.

C̲ancel Printing cancels the printing of the document highlighted on the list.

View Menu

S̲tatus Bar turns the dialog box's status bar on or off.

☐ **2-4 CONCEPTS.** In this concepts section you interactively explore previewing documents before you print them.

☐ **2-4 TUTORIAL.** In this tutorial you use the Print Preview command to check a document's layout before printing. You then print only selected pages instead of the entire document.

☐ **2-4 DRILL.** When working on documents, it's smart to use the Print Preview command to check them before making printouts. This not only saves time, but also saves paper. In this drill you practice previewing and printing.

> Selected text is highlighted
> Unselected text isn't.

Word, like most other Windows applications, makes it easy for you to copy, move, delete, or format data in a document. To do so, you first select the text you want to work with and then choose the action to be performed on it. Selected text is displayed in reverse video—white text against a black background.

There are four ways to select text: clicking, dragging with the mouse, using the keyboard, and using the **Edit** menu.

TIP
Replacing Text

The fastest way to replace text in a document is to select it and then type in the new text. The first character that you type deletes all of the selected text.

Clicking the Mouse

The fastest way to select text is often by clicking it. Where you point and how many times you click determine what is selected. These options are described in the table "Selecting Text by Clicking the Mouse." When clicking you should be aware of the invisible area, called the *selection area* (sometimes called the *selection bar*), between the text and the left edge of the screen. When the mouse pointer is positioned in this narrow area, the mouse pointer turns into a right-pointing arrow. Clicking the mouse then selects text to the right of the pointer.

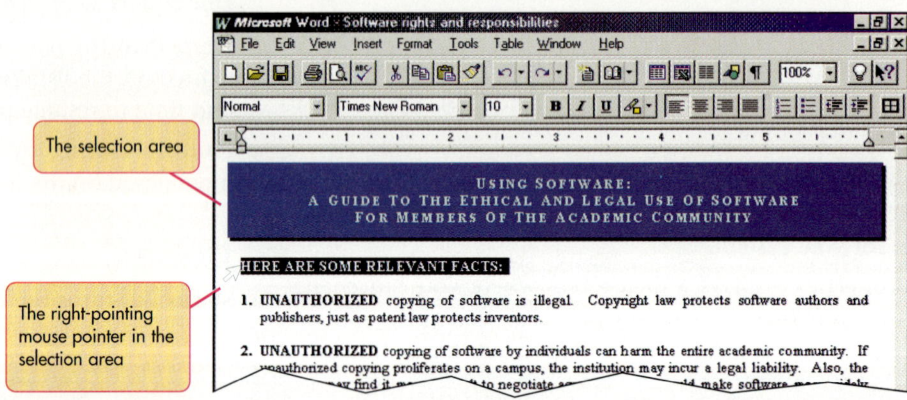

SELECTING TEXT BY CLICKING THE MOUSE

To	Do This
Select a word	▶ Double-click the word.
Select a sentence	▶ Hold down [Ctrl] and click anywhere in the sentence.
Select a line of text	▶ Click in the selection area next to it.
Select a paragraph	▶ Double-click in the selection area next to it.
	▶ Triple-click anywhere in the paragraph.
Select any amount of text	▶ Click at the beginning of the text you want to select and [⇧ Shift]-click at the end.
Select an entire document	▶ Triple-click anywhere in the selection area or hold down [Ctrl] and click once in the selection area.
Unselect selected text	▶ Click anywhere to remove the highlight from selected text.

Dragging the Mouse

You can drag the mouse pointer while holding down the left button to expand the highlight over selected text. When doing so, if you drag it against the upper or lower frame of the window, the document will scroll. When the text that you want to select is highlighted, release the left button and it remains highlighted.

▶ Once you have selected a word by double-clicking it or by dragging the mouse, if you continue to drag the highlight it will select only whole words. You can't select partial words with this procedure.

▶ If you select a sentence or paragraph by clicking and then drag the highlight without releasing the mouse button, you will select adjacent sentences or paragraphs. You can't select partial sentences or paragraphs with this procedure.

To fine-tune your selection, you can use the keyboard, as explained in the next section.

COMMON WRONG TURNS
Dragging Text

Word has a feature called *drag and drop* that allows you to drag text to a new position in the document (it is described in Section 2-7). If you do this by mistake, immediately click the **Undo** button on the Standard toolbar.

You can tell when you are about to drag text because the mouse pointer takes on the shape of a diagonal arrow with a small box attached to it.

Using the Keyboard

You can use the arrow keys to expand the highlight to select text. One way is to hold down ⇧ Shift while you then press the arrow keys (or other keys that move the insertion point). Another way is to press F8 or double-click *EXT* on the status bar (*EXT* will no longer be dimmed). When you then press the arrow keys (or other keys that move the insertion point), or click elsewhere in the document, all text is selected between the original position and where you move the highlight or click. Press F8 again or double-click *EXT* on the status bar again to turn Extend Selection off if you want to press the arrow keys or click without expanding the highlight further.

Using the Edit Menu

To select all of the text in a document, pull down the **Edit** menu and click the **Select All** command.

☐ **2-5 CONCEPTS.** In this concepts section you view movies on selecting text by clicking it, clicking in the selection area, and dragging with the mouse.

☐ **2-5 TUTORIAL.** In this tutorial you practice selecting text by clicking and dragging. To make it more interesting, you click buttons on the toolbar to format your selections.

☐ **2-5 DRILL.** Normally with Word, you select text and then use commands to act on it. Since selecting text is such a fundamental skill, you should master it as soon as possible. In this drill you practice the procedures you use to select various text elements such as words, line, paragraphs, and documents. When completing this drill, refer to the table "Selecting Text by Clicking the Mouse" in Section 2-5 for help.

2-6 COPYING AND MOVING TEXT WITH THE CLIPBOARD

Word, like most other Windows applications, makes it easy for you to copy or move text in a document. To begin, you first select the text you want to copy or move. You then copy or cut the selected text to Windows' Clipboard, where it remains until you copy or cut other text or exit Windows.

▸ When you cut text, it is removed from the original position when pasted elsewhere in the document.

▸ When you copy text, it remains in its original position even when pasted elsewhere in the document.

While the text is stored on the Clipboard, you can paste it anywhere in the document you copied or cut it from. You can also paste it into another document, or even into another application's document.

Q U I C K S T E P S

Copying or Moving Text

1. Select the text you want to copy or move.
2. Do one of the following to copy or cut the selected text:
   ▸ Click the **Cut** or **Copy** button on the toolbar.
   ▸ Pull down the **Edit** menu and click the **Cut** or **Copy** command.
   ▸ Right-click the selected text, then click the shortcut menu's **Cut** or **Copy** command.
3. Do one of the following to paste the cut or copied text:
   ▸ Move the insertion point to where you want the text inserted, then click the **Paste** button on the toolbar.
   ▸ Move the insertion point to where you want the text inserted, then pull down the **Edit** menu and click the **Paste** command.
   ▸ Right-click where you want the text to be pasted, then click the shortcut menu's **Paste** command.

Cutting and Pasting

Copying leaves the original text intact and makes a copy of it on the Clipboard. Cutting removes the original text from the application's file and transfers it to the Clipboard. A copy of the text remains on the Clipboard until you cut or copy other text so you can paste it in a number of places if you wish.

Original document with text selected

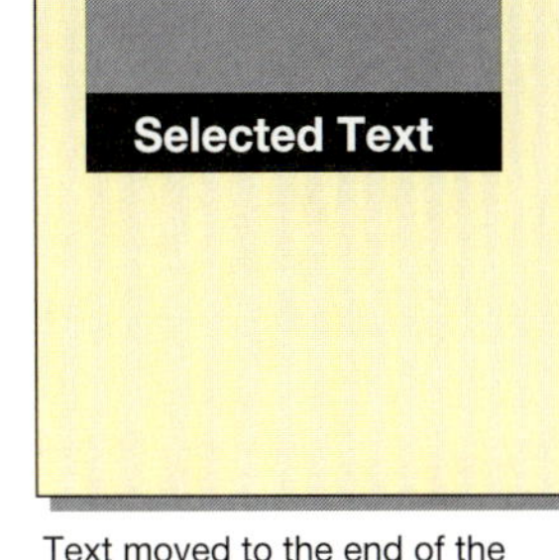

Text moved to the end of the document. Paragraphs below its original position move up.

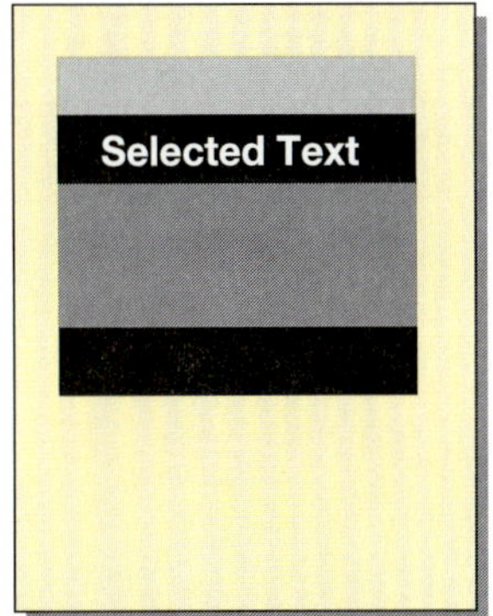

Text copied to the end of the document. The original text remains unchanged.

TIP
Smart Cut and Paste

When you select text and cut, paste, or delete it, Word will automatically adjust spaces to make the text fit the surroundings. For example, if you delete a word at the end of the sentence, Word automatically deletes the space that was in front of the word so there is no space between the new last word and the period. It will also automatically make similar adjustments when you delete text near parentheses or hyphens.

TIP
Fast Cutting, Copying, and Pasting

To copy or cut text as fast as possible, select the text and then press ⇧ Shift + Del to cut it; or press Ctrl + Ins to copy it. Then move the insertion point to where you want it inserted and press ⇧ Shift + Ins.

☐ **2-6 CONCEPTS.** In this concepts section you interactively explore cutting and pasting text using the Clipboard.

☐ **2-6 TUTORIAL.** In this tutorial you are introduced to copying and moving paragraphs and phrases using the Clipboard.

☐ **2-6 DRILL.** Windows' Clipboard is designed to store text and other data that you copy or cut while working on a document. As long as the data remains on the Clipboard, you can paste it elsewhere in the document. In this drill you practice using the Clipboard to copy and move text in a document.

2-7 COPYING AND MOVING TEXT BY DRAGGING AND DROPPING IT

Instead of using the Clipboard to move text, you can drag it from one place to another with the mouse and then release it. This is called *dragging and dropping* and is a quick way to copy and move text.

QUICKSTEPS

Copying and Moving Text by Dragging and Dropping It

1. Select the text to be copied or moved.
2. Point to the selected text and hold down the left button. The mouse pointer changes from an I-beam to a diagonal arrow with a small box attached to it. This indicates you can now drag and drop the selected text. The dotted vertical bar indicates exactly where the text will be pasted when you release the mouse button.
3. Move or copy the selection:
   ▸ To move the selection, drag the pointer to where you want the text moved and release the left button.
   ▸ To copy the selection, hold down Ctrl while you drag it. (A small plus sign is added to the mouse pointer to indicate you are copying text rather than moving it.) To drop the copied text, release first the mouse button and then release Ctrl. (If you reverse the order of release, the selected text will be moved.)

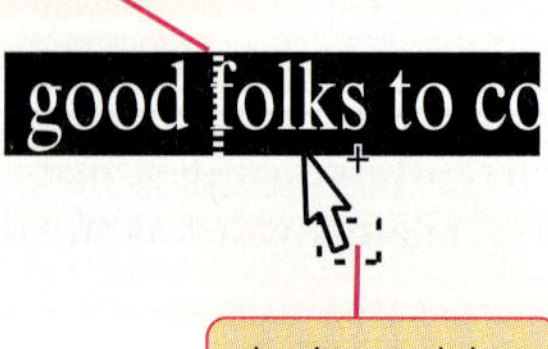

COMMON WRONG TURNS
Can't Drag and Drop

If you can't drag and drop text, someone has turned off a setting. Pull down the **Tools** menu and click the **Options** command to display the Options dialog box. On the **Edit** tab, click the **Drag-and-Drop Text Editing** check box to turn it on, then click the **OK** command button.

☐ **2-7 CONCEPTS**. In this concepts section you view movies on copying and moving text by dragging and dropping it.

☐ **2-7 TUTORIAL**. In this tutorial you are introduced to copying and moving paragraphs using the dragging and dropping.

☐ **2-7 DRILL**. In this drill you practice moving text by dragging and dropping numbered paragraphs so they appear in numerical order.

2-8 FINDING TEXT

Word can help you find text in a document. This is especially useful in long documents. For example, you may want to find an article's title so you can put quotation marks around it or find a word you want to change. (In other cases, you may want to find a format you want to change, as described in Section 4-3.)

QUICKSTEPS

Finding Text

1. Pull down the **Edit** menu and click the **Find** command to display the Find dialog box. Use any of the options described in the Box "Understanding the Find Dialog Box."

2. Enter the text you want to find in the **Find What** box, and then click the **Find Next** command button to begin the find operation. If a match is found in the document, it is highlighted. You may have to drag the Find dialog box out of the way so you can see it. You can click in the text area to edit the document without closing the dialog box.

3. You can then continue to click the **Find Next** command button to find more occurrences, or you can click the **Cancel** command button to remove the dialog box.

TIP
Searching Part of a Document

If you select part of a document before using the **Find** command, only the selected part will be searched.

TIP
Repeating the Previous Find Command

After you have used the Find command and then closed the dialog box, you can repeat the same Find command by just pressing ⇧Shift + F4 .

UNDERSTANDING
The Find Dialog Box

When you use the **Find** command, the Find dialog box appears. (At any point you can click in the document to move the insertion point there to edit text and then click the dialog box to make it active again.) Here is a brief description of the box's commands.

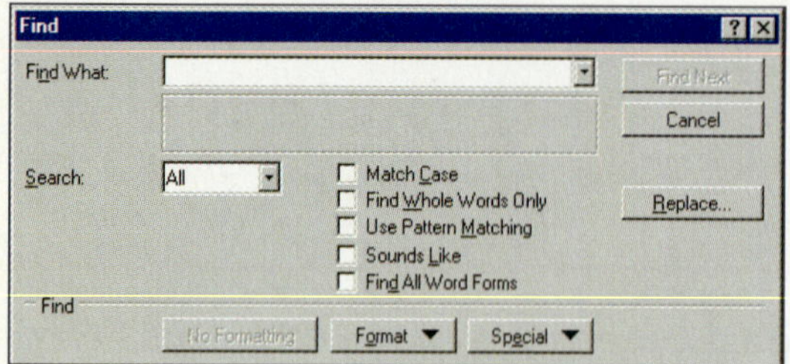

Find What text box is where you enter the text you want to find. Click the drop-down arrow (▼) next to the text box to display previous terms you've searched for and click one to use it again.

Search drop-down arrow (▼) lets you select the direction of search. Your choices are *All* (starting at the insertion point), *Down*, or *Up*.

Match Case check box, when on (☑), will find only text that matches yours in capitalization. For example, when on a search for *mouse* will not find *Mouse.*

Find Whole Words Only check box, when on (☑), will find only matching text that forms whole words. For example, when on a search for *Wind* or *Window* will not find *Windows.*

Use Pattern Matching check box, when on (☑), allows you to use wildcards where ? stands for any single character and * stands for any group of characters. Click the dialog box's **Help** button and then click this option for a more complete description.

Sounds Like check box, when on (☑), finds words that sound like the one you enter. For example, searching for *color* will find *colour.*

Find All Word Forms allows you to find all forms of a word. For example, you can find run, running, and ran.

Find Next command button finds the next match.

Cancel command button close the Find dialog box at any point in the procedure.

No Formatting command button is dimmed unless you have previously searched for formats (see Section 4-3).

Format command button allows you to search for formatted text. (We'll discuss formatting in the next PicTorial.)

Special command button displays a list of nonprinting characters (paragraph marks, tab characters, and so on) you can search for. It also allows you to enter wildcards in the word or phrase you are searching for.

Replace changes the Find dialog box into the Replace dialog box so you can replace one word or phrase with another. Replace is discussed in Section 2-9.

PAL ON-LINE ACTIVITIES CHECKLIST

☐ **2-8 CONCEPTS.** In this concepts section you interactively explore finding text in a document.

☐ **2-8 TUTORIAL.** In this tutorial you are introduced to finding words in a document. You'll explore options such as finding exact matches for case and whole words.

☐ **2-8 DRILL.** Times have changed, and we should be glad they have. The document you use in this drill has been copied from an actual list of rules passed out to freshmen "girls" at a liberal arts college in the 1920's.

Replacing text is much like finding it but goes a step further—one word or phrase is replaced with another. All of the commands and options you can use are the same as when finding text. One difference is the **Match Case** check box. When this setting is off, the case of words is preserved. For example, if you replace *Old* with *new*, *Old* in the document becomes *New*. When **Match Case** is on, *Old* becomes *new*.

QUICKSTEPS

Replacing Text

1. Pull down the **Edit** menu and click the **Replace** command to display the Replace dialog box. Use any of the options described in the Box "Understanding The Find Dialog Box" in Section 2-8.
2. Enter the text you want to find in the **Find What** text box, and the text you want to use instead in the **Replace With** text box.
3. Click the **Find Next** command button to begin the operation. If a match is found in the document, it is highlighted. (You may have to drag the Replace dialog box out of the way so you can see it.)

   ▶ Click the **Find Next** command button to leave the word unchanged and look for the next occurrence.

   ▶ Click the **Replace** command button to replace the word and look for the next occurrence.

   ▶ Click the **Replace All** command button to replace the word and all further occurrences of it. (This command is not recommended for use when you have turned on **Find All Word Forms**.)

   ▶ Click the **Cancel** command button to end the procedure and close the dialog box.

   ▶ Click in the text area to edit the document without closing the dialog box, then click the **Find Next** command button to continue.

TIP
Replacing with Clipboard Contents

You can replace text with anything you have copied to the Clipboard. For example, if you want to find a special symbol, or other item, copy it to the Clipboard. Then pull down the **Edit** menu and click the **Replace** command to display the Replace dialog box. With the insertion point in the **Replace With** text box click the **Special** command button, then select **Clipboard contents**.

COMMON WRONG TURNS
Replace All Gives Unexpected Results

Clicking the **Replace All** command button in the Replace dialog box automatically replaces all text in the selected section of the document without prompting you. This can lead to problems. Immediately click the **Undo** button on the toolbar if you click this command in error.

☐ **2-9 CONCEPTS.** In this concepts section you interactively explore replacing text in a document.

☐ **2-9 TUTORIAL.** In this tutorial you are introduced to replacing words in a document, an operation that takes finding text one step further.

☐ **2-9 DRILL.** Given the age of most freshman today, it would not be appropriate to refer to them as boys and girls. In this drill you first replace all occurrences of the word *girl* with *woman* and *boys* with *men*. You then open a new document and change all director names from being listed as *first name last name* to *last name, first name*.

BUGS REPLACEMENTS	
Search For	**Replace With**
Tex Avery	Avery, Tex
Chuck Jones	Jones, Chuck
Ken Harris	Harris, Ken
Abe Levitow	Levitow, Abe
Friz Freleng	Freleng, Friz
Bob Clampett	Clampett, Bob
Frank Tashlin	Tashlin, Frank
Robert McKimson	McKimson, Robert
Phil Monroe	Monroe, Phil
Gerry Chiniquy	Chiniquy, Gerry

2-10 LOOKING UP SYNONYMS AND ANTONYMS IN THE THESAURUS

Word includes a thesaurus for looking up synonyms (words with the same meaning) and antonyms (words with opposite meanings). For example, when you look up the word *wicked*, the thesaurus may display the synonyms *evil*, *corrupt*, *depraved*, *atrocious*, *henious*, *immoral*, *nefarious*, *amoral*, and *abandoned*. You can choose one of the suggested words to replace the word in the document, look up another word, or quit the thesaurus and return to the document.

QUICKSTEPS

Looking Up Synonyms and Antonyms in the Thesaurus

1. Position the insertion point anywhere in a word you want to look up.
2. Pull down the **Tools** menu and click the **Thesaurus** command to display the Thesaurus dialog box.
3. Click a word in the **Replace with Synonym** list to select it, and then click the **Replace** command button, or use any of the commands described in the box "Understanding the Thesaurus Dialog Box."

When you look up a word in the thesaurus, Word displays the Thesaurus dialog box with the following options and commands.

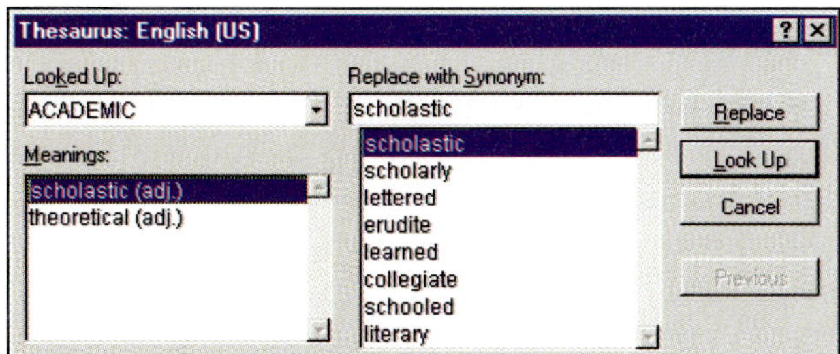

Looked Up text box displays the word being looked up. Click the drop-down arrow (▾) to display words previously looked up in the session/document. To change the word in this box, click the drop-down arrow (▾) to select another, or double-click any word on the list below the **Replace with Synonym** text box.

If the selected word is not found in the thesaurus, the text box's name changes to **Not Found** and the list below changes its name to **Alphabetical List** and lists similarly spelled words from which to choose.

Meanings list allows you to select the meaning that best matches the context of the word you are looking up—for example, antonyms. If the selected word is not found in the thesaurus, the list's name changes to **Alphabetical List** and lists similarly spelled words or phrases from which to choose.

Replace with Synonym or **Replace with Antonym** text boxes list all synonyms, antonyms, or related words for the word listed in the **Meanings** list. To change the word in the text box, click any other word on the list below it. If the insertion point is not in a word, or a space next to a word, when you use the **Thesaurus** command, this box is named **Insert**. You can then type a word in the box and click the **Look Up** command button to look it up.

Replace command button replaces the word in the document with the word in the **Replace with Synonym** text box. If the document is empty when you use the **Thesaurus** command, this button is named **Insert**.

Look Up command button displays synonyms for the word listed in the **Replace with Synonym** text box.

Cancel command button close the dialog box.

Previous command button displays the last word you looked up, its meaning, and its synonyms.

PAL ON-LINE ACTIVITIES CHECKLIST

☐ **2-10 CONCEPTS.** In this concepts section you interactively explore using the thesaurus to find synonyms and antonyms for words in a document.

☐ **2-10 TUTORIAL.** In this tutorial you are introduced to looking up synonyms in a document so you can find the best possible word.

☐ **2-10 DRILL.** A synonym of a word is another word with the same meaning. An antonym of a word is another word that has an opposite meaning. The document used here is a list of words which you look up in Word's thesaurus to find one or more synonyms and antonyms.

LAB ACTIVITIES

EXERCISES

2-1 Entering and Editing a Memo on Training

As the educational director of the Computer Curriculum Center, one of your responsibilities is to coordinate class schedules. Since many of your courses are taken by people in business, they may have to be rescheduled if there is a conflict within the company you are offering them to. Here you have had to reschedule a class and write a memo notifying the instructor that you have done so.

1. Open the *Memo formats* document stored in the *Exercise Documents* folder on the *Word Student Resource Disk*. Enter your name on the FROM line in the heading where it reads *your name*, then click anywhere in the date and press F9 to update it. (Use the **Zoom Control** button on the Standard toolbar to set the document's zoom to **Page Width**.)

2. Enter the rest of the memo shown below, beginning on the second line below the date.

Janie, the program scheduled for March 27 has been scheduled for May 1. Francis Boyle, coordinator, has affirmed that Room 324 will be available for you.

Please examine the empty classroom, making sure that all equipment is available. Let me know about any equipment needed.

your initials

The Memo

3. Edit the body paragraphs by deleting the words shown here struck-through and inserting the ones shown underscored. (Click the **Show/Hide ¶** button on the Standard toolbar to show spaces.)

Janie, the training program scheduled for March 27 has been rescheduled for May 1. Francis Boyle, classroom coordinator, has already affirmed that Room 324 will be available for your class.

Please examine the empty classroom making sure that all equipment you need is available. Please let me know as soon as possible about any additional equipment needed.

The Edited Memo

4. Use the **Edit**, **Replace** command to replace *Janie* with *Jane*.

5. Use the **Spelling** button on the Standard toolbar to spell-check the document.

6. Save, print, and close the document.

2-2 Entering and Editing a Memo on Punctuation Marks

As the educational director of Computer Tutors you are occasionally called upon to settle disagreements among the faculty. Recently, teachers in the Business English course have been offering conflicting advice on the use of spaces following punctuation marks in business memos, letters, and reports. At a faculty meeting, it was decided that each teacher should have the right to choose the approach used in his or her own classes. Once a decision such as this is made, you always send a confirming memo informing the entire staff of the final decision.

N O T E
One Space or Two

The issue discussed here is real. Ask your instructor which style he or she prefers and then use:

☐ One space ☐ Two spaces after a colon
☐ One space ☐ Two spaces at the end of every sentence

1. Open the memo *Spacing rules* stored in the *Exercise Documents* folder on the *Word Student Resource Disk*. Enter your name in the heading where it reads *your name*, then click anywhere in the date and press `F9` to update it. (Use the **Zoom Control** button on the Standard toolbar to set the document's zoom to **Page Width**.)

2. Enter the rest of the memo beginning on the second line below the date. The memo is shown in the figure "The Punctuation Marks Memo." If your AutoFormat command's **Automatic** **Bulleted Lists** check box is on, bullets will replace the hyphens at the beginning of each line. If this happens, don't type the hyphens at the beginning of the second and subsequent line in each of the three lists. When you press `Enter ←` twice at the end of a list, they automatically turn off.

At today's meeting it was tentatively decided that more variety is desired. For that reason, all faculty members have the right to choose which punctuation styles are to be used in their classes. It is important that you inform students of the styles. That way, when they later take a course from another teacher, they will understand.

Leave one or two spaces:
- after a colon
- after a period ending a sentence. Typewritten business letters, memos, and reports always used two spaces. However, publishers of newspapers, books, and magazines always used one. As publishing has moved to the desktop, so have many publishing styles.

Leave one space:
- after a comma
- after a semicolon
- after a period following an abbreviation or initial
- after an exclamation point within a sentence
- after a question mark within a sentence

Leave no spaces:
- after a period within an abbreviation
- before or after a hyphen
- before or after a dash (two hyphens or an em dash)
  between any word and the punctuation following it
- between parentheses and the enclosed matter
- between quotation marks and the enclosed matter

Also, do not separate punctuation from the word it follows--for instance, allowing a dash to begin a new line.

The Punctuation Marks Memo

3. Use the **Cut** and **Paste** buttons on the Standard toolbar to reverse the order of the two paragraphs after the heading *Leave one or two spaces*. (If automatic bullets are on, you can't click to the left of them, so click to the right when pasting.)

4. In the first body paragraph shown in the figure "The Edited Punctuation Marks Memo," delete the words struck-through and insert the ones shown underscored.

At today's <u>faculty</u> meeting it was ~~tentatively~~ decided that ~~more~~ variety is ~~desired~~ <u>the spice of life</u>. For that reason, all <u>members of the</u> faculty ~~members~~ have the right to choose which punctuation styles are to be used in their classes. ~~It is~~ <u>It's</u> important that you inform students of the <u>different</u> styles<u> and explain why you have picked the one you have</u>. That way, when they later take a course from another teacher <u>using a different set of rules</u>, they will understand <u>the issues involved</u>.

The Edited Punctuation Marks Memo

5. Use the **Spelling** button on the Standard toolbar to spell-check the finished memo.

6. Save, print, and close the document.

2-3 Entering and Editing a Business Letter on Training

As the educational director of a computer training firm, one of your responsibilities is to recruit new students. Frequently, people write in and ask for specific information about your program. Today, a Ms. Carraway from the Department of Transportation did just that. She inquired about courses on Word for Windows, including when they were offered and how much they cost. In your response you provided her with that information but also told her how to enroll and mentioned that your firm was certified to train state employees.

1. Open the document *Letter formats* stored in the *Exercise Documents* folder on the *Word Student Resource Disk*. (Use the **Zoom Control** button on the Standard toolbar to set the document's zoom to **Page Width**.)

2. Enter the letter shown in the figure "The Training Letter" beginning with the current date in the format *January 12, 1996*. Enter your own name at the end of the document above the line *Educational Director*.

3. In the body paragraphs shown in the figure "The Edited Training Letter," delete the words shown struck-through and insert the ones shown underscored.

4. Use drag and drop to move the paragraph that begins *As you may know* above the paragraph that begins *To enroll in this training program*. Make sure there is one blank line between each of the body paragraphs.

5. Use the **Spelling** button on the Standard toolbar to spell-check the finished letter.

6. Save, print, and then close the document.

Current date

Ms. Karen Kay Carraway
32773 Newport Drive
Browning, OH 34526

Dear Ms. Carraway:

The Computer Curriculum Center offers training programs on a variety of software programs. The date for the next scheduled program on Word for Windows is April 3.

To enroll in this program, please call (456) 385-2578, extension 327. The full tuition for the course is $75, which includes a textbook and the instruction.

As you may know, the Computer Center has been officially certified by the State of Ohio to provide training for all employees. We are confident you will be pleased with our program.

Please call to reserve your position in the next training session.

Sincerely yours,

your name
Educational Director

your initials

The Training Letter

The Computer Curriculum Center offers <u>numerous</u> training programs on a variety of ~~software~~ <u>application</u> programs. The date for the <u>beginning of the</u> next scheduled program on Word for Windows is April 3.

To enroll in this <u>training</u> program, please call (456) 385-2578, extension 327. The ~~full~~ tuition for the course is $75, which includes a textbook ~~and the instruction~~.

As you may know, the Computer <u>Curriculum</u> Center has been ~~officially~~ certified by the State of Ohio to provide training for all <u>state</u> employees. We are confident you will be pleased with our program.

Please call <u>soon</u> to reserve your position in the next training session.

The Edited Training Letter

2-4 Entering and Editing an Announcement

Each semester, the educational director publishes a list of the course offerings. This announcement is sent to all staff members and to all people who write in requesting information. It is also used as the basis for advertisements, catalogs, and press releases designed to attract students to the classes.

1. Open the document *Announcement* stored in the *Exercise Documents* folder on the *Word Student Resource Disk*. (Use the **Zoom Control** button on the Standard toolbar to set the document's zoom to **Page Width**.)

2. Enter the rest of the announcement beginning on the second line below the letterhead. When you are entering a course name, press `Tab⇆` after typing the course name and before typing the day it is offered. (The dots that appear when you do this are called dot leaders, and they only appear because we made a tab setting that you will learn about later in the course.)

The Computer Center is pleased to announce its fall schedule of courses on Windows and Windows applications. All classes are lab-oriented, with lots of hands-on experience. Each class begins at 6 p.m. and lasts two hours.

Windows Courses
Introduction to Computers . . . . .Mon
Introduction to Windows 95 . . . . .Tue
Introduction to OLE . . . . .Wed

Word Processing Courses
WordPerfect for Windows . . . . .Mon
Word for Windows . . . . .Tue
Word Pro . . . . .Wed

Spreadsheet Courses
Excel . . . . .Thur
Lotus 1-2-3 for Windows . . . . .Fri
Quatro Pro for Windows . . . . .Sat

Database Courses
Paradox for Windows . . . . .Tue
Access . . . . .Thur
FoxPro . . . . .Fri

Graphics Courses
CorelDRAW . . . . .Sat
Adobe Illustrator . . . . .Fri

Desktop Publishing Courses
QuarkXpress for Windows . . . . .Sat
PageMaker for Windows . . . . .Fri

your initials

The Announcement Document

3. In the first body paragraph, where it reads *Computer Center*, insert the word *Curriculum* between *Computer* and *Center*. Also check capitalization. Word might lowercase the first letter in one or more of the words. If it does, just correct the error.

4. Change the heading for word processing courses that now reads *Word Courses* to read *Word Processing Courses*.

5. Use the **Cut** and **Paste** buttons on the Standard toolbar to arrange the courses in each section in alphabetical order.

6. Use the **Edit**, **Find** command to see if there is a word spelled *Quatro* in the document. If you find one, change it to *Quattro*.

7. Use the **Edit**, **Replace** command to change all of the day-of-the-week abbreviations (Mon, Tue, and so on) to full spellings (Monday, Tuesday, and so on).

8. Use the <u>Tools</u>, <u>Thesaurus</u> command to find a synonym for the word *pleased* in the opening paragraph.

9. Use the **Spelling** button on the Standard toolbar to spell-check the document.

10. Save, print, and then close the document.

2-5 Writing and Editing a Personal Letter Home for Money

Every college student needs money. Many students must earn it, but some have comparatively rich aunts, uncles, or parents to whom they can appeal for funds. Here you take the role of an eighteen-year-old freshman who has overspent and needs a new infusion of cash.

1. Open a new document and enter the letter shown here, using the customized information in places where it is indicated. Use Tab↹ to indent each new body paragraph in the letter. Use one of the suggestions for customizing the letter from the lists below or make up your own.

Today's Date

Dear Mom and Dad,

    This year is progressing extremely well, and I'm working harder than ever (really!). All I do is work, but it's paying off. For example, I've written this letter on a state-of-the-art (*enter the name of your computer*) computer using Word for Windows. I am mastering word processing in half the time it is taking the others in the class. The only glitch is that I'm out of money. To raise the lousy (*fill in the amount needed—make it big!*) I need, I am considering taking a job as a (*choose a job from the jobs list*).

    I realize that this will detract from my studies and jeopardize the thousands of dollars you have already invested in my education, but I really have no other choice. I have overspent on textbooks, reference books, seminars on (*choose a seminar from the seminars list*), computer supplies, and other things needed to ensure the quality of my education. I guess working as a (*enter the job you used above*) for a few months is a small price to pay. Although it will result in my being less well educated, it at least makes it possible to muddle through. Your dreams of my becoming a (*choose a profession from the professions list*) will probably not now be realized, but there are plenty of lower paying and less fulfilling jobs that I will be qualified for.

    Sorry to share my minor problem with you, but other than this, everything is going VERY well! Don't worry—be happy.

Love,

Your Name

The Letter Home Document

Customer Choices		
Jobs List	**Seminars List**	**Professions List**
soldier of fortune	space science	lawyer
sponge diver	nuclear physics	business executive
blast-furnace operator	computer programming	doctor
dynamite detonator	environmental studies	teacher

2. Using what you have learned, locate and correct any mistakes you might have made.

3. Use the **Tools**, **Thesaurus** command to look up the following words and substitute synonyms.

   ▸ extremely

   ▸ realized

   ▸ minor

4. Use the **Spelling** button on the Standard toolbar to spell-check the document.

5. Save the document as *Letter home* in the *Exercise Documents* folder of the *Word Student Resource Disk*.

6. Print the document and then close it.

2-6 Editing and Printing the Job Search Document

In the Projects that follow, you are introduced to a job-search kit that you will be working on throughout this text. This kit has three parts: a cover letter, a résumé, and a followup letter. Each of these documents is explained in the document *Job search kit*. Here you edit and print out a copy.

1. Open the *Job search kit* document stored in the *Exercise Documents* folder on the *Word Student Resource Disk*, use the **Zoom Control** button on the Standard toolbar to set the document's zoom to **Page Width**, then enter your name in the letterhead line COPY BELONGING TO YOUR NAME in place of YOUR NAME.

2. In the first paragraph under the heading *The Cover Letter* shown in the figure "The Edited Cover Letter," delete the words shown struck-through and insert the ones shown underscored.

You will need a <u>cover</u> letter whenever you send a resume <u>or application form</u> to a <u>potential</u> employer. Your cover letter should capture the ~~recipients~~ <u>employer's</u> attention, show why you are ~~contacting them~~ <u>writing</u>, indicate why your employment will ~~add to~~ <u>benefit</u> the company, and ~~beg for~~ <u>suggest</u> an interview. The kind of specific information that must be included in a letter means that each must be written individually. Each letter must also be typed <u>perfectly</u>, so word processing helps. Frequently, only the address, first paragraph, and specifics concerning an interview will vary. These items are easily changed on a ~~typewriter~~ <u>word processor</u>.

The Edited Cover Letter

3. Drag and drop items in the first list so they match the order shown in the figure "The Reorganized Cover Letter."

- Address your letter to a specific person, if possible (use city directories or other sources).
- State exactly the kind of position you are seeking and why you are applying to a particular firm.
- Use care in sentence structure, spelling, and punctuation.
- Be clear, brief, and businesslike.
- Use a good grade of letter-sized white bond paper for the final printout.
- Enclose a resume.

The Reorganized Cover Letter

4. Save the document, print the first page, and then close the document.

2-7 Editing the Computers and Careers Document

In this exercise you edit a document that describes various career opportunities in computing and information processing.

1. Open the *Computers and careers* document stored in the *Exercise Documents* folder on the *Word Student Resource Disk*, use the **Zoom Control** button on the Standard toolbar to set the document's zoom to **Page Width**, and then enter your name following the word *By* just below the letterhead.

2. In the opening paragraph shown in the figure "The Edited Careers Document," delete the words shown struck-through and insert the ones shown underscored.

The <u>increased</u> computerization of the ~~business~~ workplace has led to <u>the development of</u> new positions and a change in responsibilities for existing positions. One major company divides its ~~workers~~ <u>employees</u> into two categories—originators and processors. Originators are <u>those</u> people who draft original documents, reports, numeric analysis, and ~~other stuff~~ <u>so on</u>. Processors are those who prepare this material for presentation. For example, an average originator/processor relationship is that of a ~~manager~~ <u>supervisor</u> and secretary. The supervisor writes a letter to a client and the secretary then uses a word ~~processor~~ <u>processing program</u> to print it and the ~~thing~~ <u>envelope</u> in which it is mailed.

The Edited Careers Document

3. Scroll through the document to find the section with the heading *SPECIALIST POSITIONS*. This section begins with an introductory paragraph followed by a series of paragraphs containing job descriptions. Move these paragraphs (other than the introduction) as needed to arrange them in alphabetical order. Make sure the paragraphs remain separated by single blank lines.

4. Use the **Edit**, **Find** command to locate the following words and then use the **Tools**, **Thesaurus** command to look up a suitable synonym to substitute.

   ‣ personnel

   ‣ client

5. Use the **Edit**, **Replace** command to replace *secretary* with *assistant*. Check the words around the replacements and make changes if any are needed.

6. Save the document, print the second page, and close the document.

2-8 Editing the Bill of Rights Document

In this exercise you edit the ten amendments in the Bill of Rights to the United States Constitution.

1. Open the *Bill of Rights* document stored in the *Exercise Documents* folder on the *Word Student Resource Disk* and enter your name, then click anywhere in the date and press F9 to update it.

2. In Clause 2, shown in the figure "The Edited Bill of Rights" delete the words struck-through and insert the ones shown underscored.

Clause 2
Militia and the Right to Bear Arms
A ~~poorly~~ <u>well</u> regulated ~~neighborhood gang~~ <u>Militia</u>, being necessary to the ~~destruction~~ <u>security</u> of a free State, the right of the people to keep and bear ~~automatic weapons~~ <u>Arms</u>, shall not be abridged.

The Edited Bill of Rights

3. Use the **Cut** and **Paste** buttons on the Standard toolbar to reorganize the ten

clauses into the correct numeric order. Make sure the clauses remain separated by single blank lines.

4. Use the **Edit**, **Replace** command to replace the word *Clause* in all the headings with *Amendment*.

5. Save the document, print page 1, and then close the document.

2-9 Editing the Desktop Publishing Document

In this exercise you edit a document describing desktop publishing.

1. Open the *Desktop publishing* document stored in the *Exercise Documents* folder on the *Word Student Resource Disk* and enter your name on the second line following *By*.

2. Display paragraph marks and use them as a guide to locate the second body paragraph in the document.

3. In the second body paragraph shown in the figure "The Edited DTP Document," delete the words shown struck-through and insert the ones shown underscored.

The ~~preparation~~ <u>publication</u> of documents using ~~old-fashioned~~ <u>traditional</u> procedures takes <u>a great deal of time, money, and</u> experience. The popularity of desktop publishing ~~derives~~ <u>stems</u> from the fact that it reduces the time and money required to do a ~~good~~ <u>professional-looking</u> job. However, desktop publishing still requires skill<u>, and a lot of it</u>. In traditional publishing, the ~~chores~~ <u>tasks</u> involved in publishing a document are handled by many separate ~~people~~ <u>specialists</u>. For example, one person will design a ~~document~~ <u>publication</u>, another will indicate on the manuscript how each element is to be treated, a third will set the type, and a fourth will print it. When a document is desktop published, the same person is <u>frequently</u> responsible for all these tasks <u>and any others</u> in the process.

The Edited DTP Document

4. Use the **Tools**, **Thesaurus** command to find appropriate synonyms for the following words in the opening paragraph. (Use the **Edit**, **Find** command to locate them.)

   ▸ device

   ▸ created

   ▸ situation

5. Use the **Edit**, **Replace** command to replace all but the heading and the first occurrence in the body text of the phrase *desktop publishing* with the abbreviation *DTP*.

6. Save, print, and close the document.

PROJECTS

2-1 The Job-Search Kit—The Cover Letter

When looking for a job, it's common to send out résumés to companies you are interested in. If you do so, you must always accompany the résumé with a cover letter. Since this cover letter is usually read first, it must capture the reader's attention or your résumé goes into the circular file. In this project you enter a sample cover letter.

1. Open the *Cover letter* document stored in the *Project Documents* folder on the *Word Student Resource Disk*. Replace YOUR NAME at the top of the letterhead with your own name.

2. Enter the letter shown in the figure "The Cover Letter" so it exactly match-

es the contents shown in the figure, but use a current date and replace *your name* at the bottom with your actual name. Your lines may wrap at different points. Use whatever tools you have to ensure the letter's accuracy.

3. Save, print, and then close the document.

4. Now that you have finished a sample cover letter, write your own, using what you have learned. Save it under its own filename, make a printout, and then close the document.

YOUR NAME
304 AMEN STREET
SAN FRANCISCO, CALIFORNIA 94102

March 14, 1997

Mr. Wilbert R. Wilson
President, XYZ Company
3893 Factory Boulevard
Cleveland, OH 44114

Dear Mr. Wilson:

Recently I learned through Dr. Robert R. Roberts of Atlantic and Pacific University of the expansion of your company's sales operations and your plans to create a new position of sales director. If this position is open, I would appreciate your considering me.

Starting with over-the-counter sales and order service, I have had progressively more responsible and diverse experience in merchandising products similar to yours. In recent years I have carried out a variety of sales promotion and top management assignments.

For your review, I am enclosing a resume of my qualifications. I would appreciate a personal interview with you to discuss my application further.

Very truly yours,

your name

Enclosure

The Cover Letter

2-2 The Job-Search Kit—The Followup Letter

After you have had a job interview, you should immediately send a followup letter to the person who interviewed you. In this project you enter and format such a letter.

1. Open the *Followup letter* document stored in the *Project Documents* folder on the *Word Student Resource Disk*

2. Enter the document shown in the figure "The Followup Letter," entering your name at the bottom of the document in place of *Your Name*.

3. Use all of the tools at your disposal to ensure the document is accurate.

4. Save, print, and close the document.

5. Imagine that you have had a job interview that went fairly well but you want to reinforce a few points you made and cover a few you didn't. Write a letter covering those points. Save the document under its own filename, make a printout, and then close the document.

COMPUTER CURRICULUM CENTER
STUDENT EMPLOYMENT CENTER

123 NORTH MONROE STREET
CLEVELAND, OHIO 65743

PHONE: 456 385-2578
FAX: 456 385-3456

March 14, 1997

Mr. Lionel Train
Consolidated Corporation
45 Switch Street
Roundhouse, IN 12002

Dear Mr. Train:

Thank you for the interview last Friday. I am impressed with the quality of your organization and would like to express my continued interest in pursuing the position. As I mentioned to you, I feel that I could contribute to your company's objectives in a number of ways:

- I am able to work well with coworkers and am very much a team player.
- My previous working experience has given me an understanding of the responsibilities of the position. I hope you will give me the opportunity to share my abilities with your company.

Since the interview, I have given our discussion a great deal of thought and would like to make the following points:

- While working on the school newspaper, I gained interviewing experience that should make me better at completing the surveys you mentioned would be required as part of the position's responsibilities.
- I have earned over 50 percent of my college expenses and in the process have established a solid employment record over the past four years. I have proved my reliability in this position and hope you will call Mr. Jones at 212-555-1212 to hear his opinions of the contributions that I have made.

Again, thank you for your consideration. If there is any additional information I might be able to supply, please let me know. I am eager to hear from you.

Sincerely yours,

Your Name

The Followup Letter

BASIC FORMATTING

After completing this PicTorial, you will be able to:

▶ **Explain the differences between character and paragraph formats**
▶ **Change font faces, styles, and sizes**
▶ **Align text with margins**
▶ **Change line and paragraph spacing**
▶ **Control page breaks**
▶ **Set and use tab stops**
▶ **Indent paragraphs**
▶ **Number and bullet lists**

As a document is being prepared, you can format it to improve its appearance and readability. Until very recently most typed documents looked pretty much alike. They were all typed on typewriters that had the same limited number of choices, some of which took a great deal of skill to use. Today, with word processing programs rivaling the power of desktop publishing programs, it's easy to format documents so they look as if they were prepared by a professional printer. In this PicTorial we explore some of the many formatting options you have at your disposal. We'll look at fonts, text alignment, line and paragraph spacing, bulleted lists, tabs, and indents. As you use these features, you'll also become more aware of how useful Word's WYSIWYG (pronounced "wizzy-wig") display is, because the screen shows you what the formats will look like in the final printout.

Word's preset formats automatically print a document single-spaced in 10 point Times New Roman type on an 8½-by-11-inch page with 1-inch top and bottom margins and 1¼-inch left and right margins. When you want to change these and other default settings, you do so by formatting either characters, paragraphs, or pages. In this PicTorial we concentrate on character and paragraph formatting, and in the next PicTorial we cover page formats such as margins and page numbers.

3-1 TYPES OF FORMATS

When formatting a document it's important to understand the difference between character and paragraph formats and how you apply, remove, and identify them. Taking the time now to understand these differences will make things a great deal easier for you later on.

▶ *Character formats* affect individual characters or groups of selected characters and include such things as boldfacing, italicizing, or superscripting.

▶ *Paragraph formats* affect selected paragraphs and include such things as text alignment and indents, line spacing, spacing between paragraphs, and tab stops. In Word the term *paragraph* means any line or lines that ends with a paragraph mark (¶) entered when you press ⏎ Enter ⏎ . Therefore, a paragraph can be as short as a blank line without any text or as long as the complete document.

The way you format text with character and paragraph formats depends on whether the text is new or already exists.

You will often see the term *Section* in formatting and printing dialog boxes. A section is simply a division of a document into two or more parts. When you open a new document, it is all one section. Therefore, formats such as margins, columns, headers and footers, page numbers, and columns affect all pages in the document. To change these formats within the document, for example to switch from one column to two columns and then back again, you have to create new sections where you want the formats to change. How you do so is discussed in Section 4-8 of this text.

Applying Formats to New Text

To change character or paragraph formats for new text that you are about to type, position the insertion point where you want the change to take effect and then execute the formatting command. Any text you enter from that point on will have the new formats until you change them or turn them off. For example, to italicize a book title in a report, you could click the **Italic** button to turn italic on, type the title, and then click the **Italic** button again to turn italic off.

When typing new text in or near formatted text, the position of the insertion point determines the format of the new text. For example, let's say you have italicized the phrase *remember the Maine*:

- The new text will be italic if you position the insertion point anywhere in the phrase *remember the Maine*, or at the left side of the space following the word *Maine*.

- The new text will not be italic if you press Ctrl+Spacebar before typing it (pressing Ctrl+Spacebar cancels character formatting), or if you position the insertion point at the right side of the space following the word *Maine*.

If you change a paragraph's format, and then press Enter at the end of it and continue to type, the next paragraph will have the same formats as the one you created it from. You could say that the paragraph formats of the new paragraph are inherited from the paragraph from which it was created.

Applying Formats to Existing Text

To change formats in existing text, you first select the characters or paragraphs to be formatted and then use formatting commands to format them. For example, to italicize a book title in a report, you could type it, select it, and click the **Italic** button on the toolbar. Or, to align paragraphs, position the insertion point anywhere in the paragraph if you are formatting a single paragraph, or select all or part of two or more adjacent paragraphs. Selecting part of a paragraph is the same as selecting it all. For example, if you select the last word in one paragraph and the first word in the next, it's the same as selecting both paragraphs in their entirety.

You can also format multiple lines with one paragraph command, such as those used in addresses, tables, or lists. To do so, don't end each line by pressing Enter. Instead, press Shift+Enter to enter a newline character (↵) that ends the line without ending the paragraph. This way a paragraph format applied to one line affects all lines up to where you press Enter to enter a paragraph mark.

When you select text for formatting, its current formats are displayed on the toolbar and in related dialog boxes. However, when you select text that has more than one format, buttons and dialog box elements related to the command may be affected as follows:

- Text boxes are empty
- Check boxes are dimmed
- List boxes have no choice selected
- Toolbar buttons are not highlighted

If you enter a choice in one of these check boxes or click one of the toolbar buttons, you override previous formats, and all the selected text is affected. If you do not make a choice, the previous formats remain unaffected.

TIP
The Repeat Command

The **Repeat** command is especially useful when formatting existing text. You format the first item, immediately select the next one, and then press F4 to repeat the format.

AutoFormatting Documents

Word has an **AutoFormat** command that will quickly format an entire document for you. (It also has an AutoFormat As You Type command discussed in Section 3-8.) This command recognizes common elements such as headings, bulleted lists, and quotation marks and formats them as such.

QUICKSTEPS

AutoFormatting Documents

1. Pull down the **Format** menu and click the **AutoFormat** command to display a dialog box telling you the document will be automatically formatted. (Click the **Options** command button to specify formatting options.)
2. Click the **OK** command button to begin and the status bar keeps you informed of the command's progress. When finished, a dialog box appears offering you the chance to review the changes, accept the changes, or reject the changes.

Removing Character and Paragraph Formats

Sometimes, when you apply a character or paragraph format to text and then press Spacebar or Enter↵, the format continues to affect the text you type when you don't want it to. At other times you format text and then change your mind. In either case, it's easy to return the text to Word's original preset formats. To begin, position the insertion point where you want the change to take affect, or select text you want changed. Then:

▶ To remove character formats, press Ctrl+Spacebar.

▶ To remove paragraph formats, press Ctrl+Q.

LOOKING BACK

Deleting Paragraph Marks

Word stores all paragraph formatting information in the paragraph mark (¶) at the paragraph's end. Deleting the paragraph mark between two paragraphs makes the contents of the second paragraph become part of the first, and it takes on the formatting of that first paragraph. Since paragraph marks are so important, you should always have them displayed when you edit a document. To display them, click the **Show/Hide ¶** button on the toolbar.

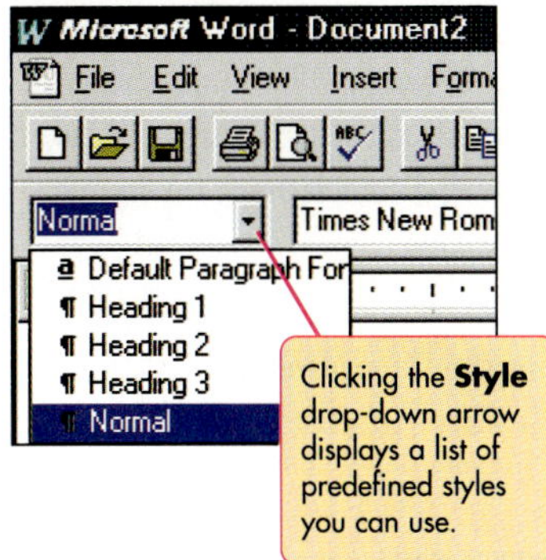

The Style drop-down box

Knowing What Formats Are in Effect

Current formats are indicated on the Formatting toolbar. For example, if the selected text is centered, the **Center** button on the toolbar will be highlighted. (If you select text with more than one format, the affected buttons will not be highlighted.) If you have not selected text, the toolbar shows you what formats will be used for any text you type at the insertion point's position.

The easiest way to determine formats is to click the **Help** button on the toolbar to add a question mark to the mouse pointer. Click the text whose formats you want to check. Each time you do so, a pop-up lists the clicked character's style and direct formats. Direct formats are those you apply by using menu commands or buttons. Paragraph and character style formats listed in the pop-up are applied by picking a stored format from a list. (Styles are beyond the scope of this text; however, you can see currently available styles by clicking the drop-down arrow (▾) next to the **Style** box on the Formatting toolbar.) When finished checking formats, press Esc or click the **Help** button on the toolbar again.

PAL ON-LINE ACTIVITIES CHECKLIST

☐ **3-1 CONCEPTS.** In this concepts section you view movies on applying and removing character and paragraph formats

☐ **3-1 TUTORIAL.** In this tutorial you explore applying, identifying, and removing character and paragraph formats.

☐ **3-1 DRILL.** As you have seen, there are character and paragraph formats. In this drill you explore displaying, applying, and removing these two levels of formatting.

Document Formats	
Number	**Description**
①	
②	
③	
④	
⑤	
⑥	
⑦	
⑧	

3-2 CHANGING FONTS, FONT STYLES, AND FONT SIZES

One of the hallmarks of a professional-looking document is the font used to print it. There are literally thousands of fonts from which to choose, and each has not only its own unique look but also a number of styles and sizes.

Fonts

A font, commonly called a *typeface*, has its own unique design that distinguishes it from all other fonts. Some fonts of a kind known as TrueType fonts are supplied with Windows. They include Arial, Courier New, and Times New Roman and are illustrated in the table "Fonts Supplied with Windows." In addition to these fonts, many others may be added to a system. Some of these fonts are called *serif* and others *sans serif*. Serif fonts, such as Times New Roman, have small cross bars on their bases. Sans serif fonts, such as Arial, do not. In fact, *sans* is French for "without."

Font Styles

Font style refers to variations on a basic font. Font styles supplied by Windows include regular, bold, italic, and bold italic. These styles are illustrated in the table "Windows Font Styles."

WINDOWS FONT STYLES
Arial
Arial Bold
Arial Italic
Arial Bold Italic
Courier New
Courier New Bold
Courier New Italic
Courier New Bold Italic
Times New Roman
Times New Roman Bold
Times New Roman Italic
Times New Roman Bold Italic

T I P
Formatting with Shortcut Keys

You can quickly format characters as you type, using keyboard commands to turn formats on and off as needed. In many cases you will find this much faster than clicking buttons or using menu commands.

To	Press
Boldface text	Ctrl + B
Underline text	Ctrl + U
Italicize text	Ctrl + I
Subscript text	Ctrl + =
Change the font	Ctrl + ⇧ Shift + F
Change the font size	Ctrl + ⇧ Shift + P
Increase the font size	Ctrl + ⇧ Shift + >
Decrease the font size	Ctrl + ⇧ Shift + <
Superscript text	Ctrl + ⇧ Shift + =
Underline single words	Ctrl + ⇧ Shift + W
Double underline words	Ctrl + ⇧ Shift + D
Change the case of letters	⇧ Shift + F3
Remove formatting	Ctrl + ⇧ Shift + Z
Create small caps	Ctrl + ⇧ Shift + K
Create all caps	Ctrl + ⇧ Shift + A

The size of a font is given in a unit of measurement called *points*. A point is about 1/72 of an inch, so 72-point type is 1 inch high, 36-point type is ½ inch high, and 18-point type is ¼ inch high. Normally, body text in books, magazines, and newspapers will be 10 to 12 points in size. The largest and smallest size fonts you can use depend on the capabilities of your printer. Typical sizes are illustrated in the table "Windows Font Sizes."

WINDOWS FONT SIZES

Arial 8 point

Arial 10 point

Arial 12 point

Arial 14 point

Arial 18 point

Arial 24 point

QUICKSTEPS

Changing Font Faces, Styles, and Sizes

Fastest

1. Select the text to be formatted or position the insertion point where you want to type text with a new format.

2. Click the **Font** or **Font Size** drop-down arrows (▼) on the Formatting toolbar to display a list of fonts or font sizes, then click the one you want to use. Or click the **Bold**, **Italic**, or **Underline** buttons on the Formatting toolbar to select a font style.

Menus

1. Select the text to be formatted or position the insertion point where you want to type text with a new format.

2. Pull down the **Format** menu and click the **Font** command to display the Font dialog box.

3. On the **Font** tab, specify the font and its characteristics using the dialog box options described in the box "Understanding The Font Dialog Box," and then click the **OK** command button.

TIP
Changing the Default Font

If you want to change the font for most of your new documents, just select the font in the Font dialog box and then click the **Default** command button. When a dialog box appears asking if you want to change the default font, click the **Yes** command button. All new documents that you open will use the new font.

UNDERSTANDING
The Font Dialog Box

When you display the Font dialog box's **Font** tab, you have a number of options to choose from. As you select from these options, a preview of the resulting font is displayed in the lower-right corner of the screen along with a description.

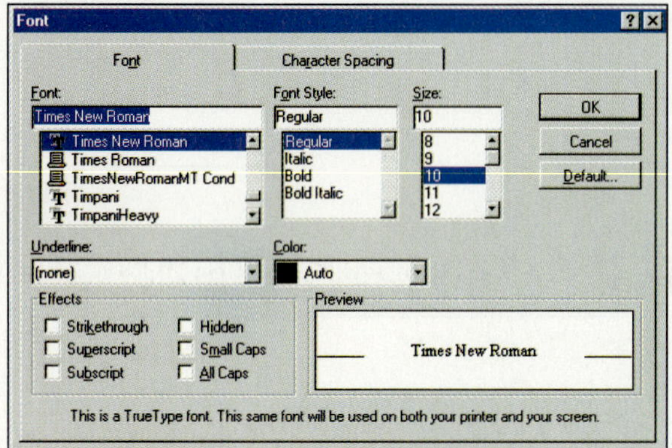

Font lists the fonts from which you can choose.

Font Style lists the styles available for the selected font.

Size lists the sizes available for the selected font.

Underline drop-down arrow (▾) displays a list of underlining styles including none, single, words only, double, and dotted.

Color drop-down arrow (▾) displays a list of colors you can apply to the selected text.

Effects check boxes allow you to specify styles for the selected font. You can turn on or off any or all of the check boxes.

▸ **Strikethrough** strikes through text so you can indicate text proposed for deletion.

▸ **Superscript** prints characters in a smaller size type, raised above the line.

▸ **Subscript** prints characters in a smaller type, sunk below the line.

▸ **Hidden** hides text so it won't be seen on the screen or printed. (To control whether it is displayed or printed, pull down the **Tools** menu and click the **Options** command to display the Options dialog box. Click the **View** or **Print** tabs and click the **Hidden Text** check box on or off.)

▸ **Small Caps** displays and prints lowercase letters in uppercase but in a smaller font.

▸ **All Caps** displays and prints lowercase letters as uppercase.

Default command button makes the currently specified font the default font for all subsequent documents.

TIP
Changing Character Spacing

When the Font dialog box is displayed, you can click the **Character Spacing** tab and use its settings to expand or condense the spaces between selected characters. Normally you use expanded spacing in all-caps headings or special text. You condense it to fit more characters in a given space. You can also use this tab to raise or lower text above or below other text on the line.

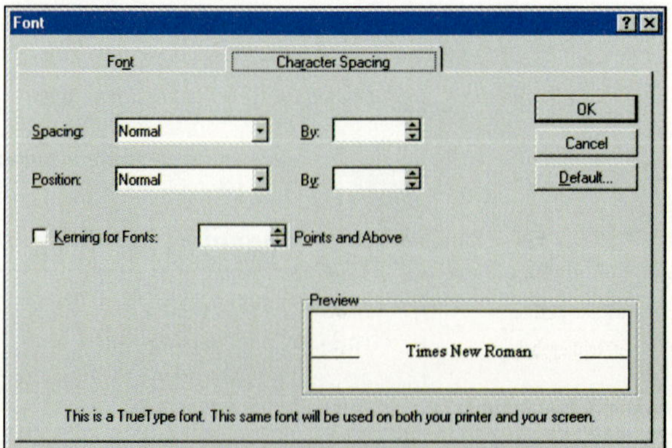

☐ **3-2 CONCEPTS.** In this concepts section you view the concepts of serif and sans serif fonts, font styles, and font sizes.

☐ **3-2 TUTORIAL.** There is no way to change the appearance of a document faster than changing the font used to print it. In this tutorial you explore changing fonts, styles, and sizes using a document you have seen before in finished form.

USING SOFTWARE:
A GUIDE TO THE ETHICAL AND LEGAL USE OF SOFTWARE
FOR MEMBERS OF THE ACADEMIC COMMUNITY

HERE ARE SOME RELEVANT FACTS:
1. UNAUTHORIZED
2. UNAUTHORIZED
3. UNAUTHORIZED
RESPECT
THEREFORE
SOFTWARE AND INTELLECTUAL RIGHTS
QUESTIONS YOU MAY HAVE ABOUT USING SOFTWARE
ALTERNATIVES TO EXPLORE
A FINAL NOTE

The EDUCOM document headings

☐ **3-2 DRILL.** Font styles are used in a wide variety of places. In this drill, you format a number of different documents so you become familiar with the usefulness of these formats.

EXPLORING FONTS	
Font	**Font Size**
Arial	10
Arial	12
Arial	14
Times New Roman	14
Times New Roman	12
Times New Roman	10
Courier New	12

3-3 ALIGNING TEXT

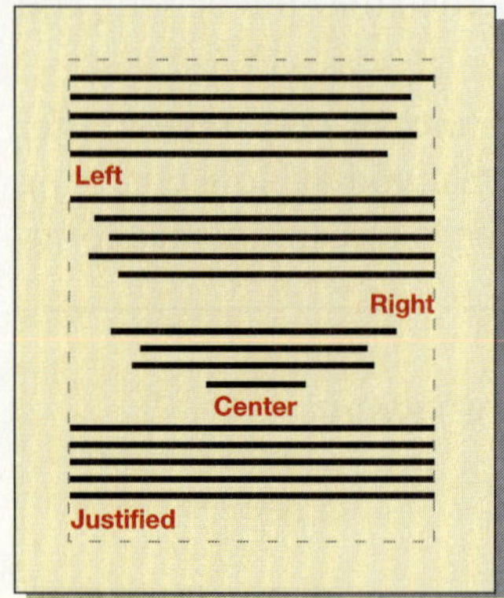

When you first open a new document, text that you type is normally aligned just with the left margin, and the right margin is uneven. If you want, you can change the alignment of your lines and paragraphs so they align in any one of four ways.

▸ *Left Aligned* text is aligned with the left margin, and the right margin is uneven, or *ragged*. This is the default setting for new documents.

▸ *Centered* text is centered between the left and right margins.

▸ *Right Aligned* text is aligned with the right margin, and the left margin is uneven, or ragged.

▸ *Justified* text is aligned with both left and right margins. To make the line exactly fit the space between the margins, Word adds spaces between words. This alignment gives a finished appearance to a document and is therefore often used in publications. However, in short lines or lines with long words, the wide word spaces can make the paragraph harder to read.

QUICKSTEPS

Aligning Lines

1. Position the insertion point in a paragraph or where you want to enter new text with the format, or select a group of paragraphs.

2. Click the **Align Left**, **Center**, **Align Right**, or **Justify** buttons on the toolbar, or pull down the **Format** menu, click the **Paragraph** command, and on the **Indents and Spacing** tab, use the **Alignment** drop-down arrow (▾) to choose an alignment.

PAL ON-LINE ACTIVITIES CHECKLIST

☐ **3-3 CONCEPTS.** In this concepts section you interactively explore the concepts of aligning and justifying text.

☐ **3-3 TUTORIAL.** Normally text is left-aligned, but it just takes a click of a button to align it another way. In this tutorial you practice aligning text in a document.

☐ **3-3 DRILL.** Aligning and justifying paragraphs is as easy as selecting them and clicking a button on the toolbar. In this drill you explore all of the alignments that you can use in your documents.

3-4 CHANGING LINE AND PARAGRAPH SPACING

The spacing between paragraphs and between lines within paragraphs determines how open or dense your document looks. Adding space makes it look more open and easier to read but also makes it longer. Removing space makes it more dense looking, but shorter. Whichever look you choose, you can easily implement it in Word.

Changing Line Spacing

Most documents are single-spaced, but you can easily change this spacing when you want more space between lines of text within paragraphs, as shown in the figure "Variations in line spacing."

SINGLE SPACED

Unauthorized copying of software is illegal. Copyright law protects software authors and publishers, just as patent law protects inventors.

SPACE AND ONE-HALF

Unauthorized copying of software is

illegal. Copyright law protects soft-

ware authors and publishers, just as

patent law protects inventors.

DOUBLE SPACED

Unauthorized copying of software is

illegal. Copyright law protects soft-

ware authors and publishers, just as

patent law protects inventors.

Variations in line spacing

QUICKSTEPS

Changing Line Spacing

1. Position the insertion point in a paragraph or where you want to enter new text with the format, or select a group of paragraphs.
2. Pull down the **Format** menu and click the **Paragraph** command to display the Paragraph dialog box.
3. On the **Indents and Spacing** tab click the **Line Spacing** drop-down arrow (▼) to display a list of settings.
4. Choose any of the settings described in the box "Understanding Line Spacing Choices" and then click the **OK** command button.

UNDERSTANDING
Line Spacing Choices

When you click the **Line Spacing** drop-down arrow (▼) on the **Indents and Spacing** tab of the Paragraph dialog box, a number of spacing choices are listed. Here is what each choice does.

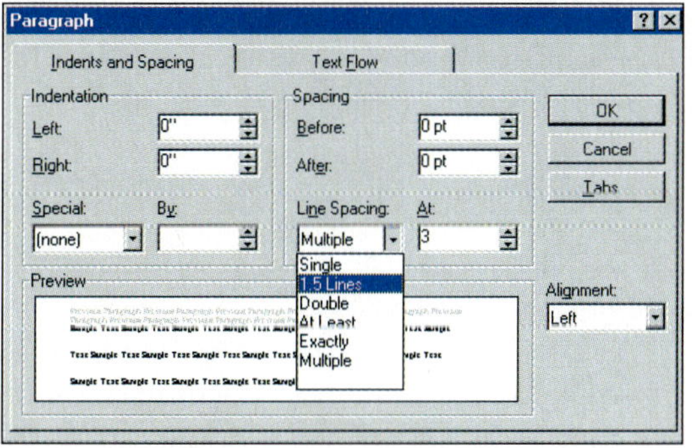

Single sets single spacing.

1.5 Lines sets one and one-half spacing.

Double sets double spacing.

At Least sets a minimum line spacing that Word can then adjust should you format some characters on the line with a larger font.

Exactly sets a fixed line spacing that will not be adjusted should you use larger type on a line.

Multiple is for fine-tuning line spacing. It allows lines to be increased by a specified percentage (or multiple). For example, if **Single** line spacing is too little spacing and **1.5 Lines** is too much, you can set line spacing to 1.2, 1.3, 1.4 or so on using this choice. You specify the multiple by clicking the **At** spin buttons or by typing a number in the text box.

Changing Paragraph Spacing

You can specify space above and below paragraphs to separate body paragraphs from one another without entering a blank line between them (see the figure "Variations in paragraph spacing"). You can also use paragraph spacing to add space above and below headings. Like fonts, paragraph spacing is specified in points. This is a useful command because you can set the space to fractions or multiples of a single line. For example, you can have 12 points above a heading and 6 below it to set it off.

<table>
<tr><td>6 POINTS
This first paragraph has 6 points of space below it.

The first paragraph has 6 points of space below it.</td><td>12 POINTS
This first paragraph has 12 points of space below it.

The first paragraph has 12 points of space below it.</td><td>24 POINTS
This first paragraph has 24 points of space below it.

The first paragraph has 24 points of space below it.</td></tr>
</table>

Variations in paragraph spacing

QUICKSTEPS

Changing Paragraph Spacing

1. Position the insertion point in a paragraph or where you want to enter new text with the format, or select a group of paragraphs.
2. Pull down the **Format** menu and click the **Paragraph** command to display the Paragraph dialog box.
3. On the **Indents and Spacing** tab, click the **Before** or **After** spin buttons (⬍), or type a measurement into the text box.
4. Click the **OK** command button.

PAL ON-LINE ACTIVITIES CHECKLIST

☐ **3-4 CONCETPS.** In this concepts section you interactively explore the concepts of changing line and paragraph spacing.

☐ **3-4 TUTORIAL.** Increasing line and paragraph spacing makes a document look more open and inviting. In this tutorial you explore changing spacing to see the effects it has on a document's appearance.

> HERE ARE SOME RELEVANT FACTS:
> SOFTWARE AND INTELLECTUAL RIGHTS
> QUESTIONS YOU MAY HAVE ABOUT USING SOFTWARE
> ALTERNATIVES TO EXPLORE
> A FINAL NOTE

EDUCOM Headings

☐ **3-4 DRILL.** Most documents are single-spaced, but short documents, and documents you want to edit or write comments on, are better double-spaced. Also, you may want to add space between paragraphs or above and below headings without inserting a blank line to do so. In this drill you practice the procedures you use to change line and paragraph spacing.

3-5 CONTROLLING PAGE BREAKS

A page break is the point at which the printer stops printing lines on the current sheet of paper and resumes printing on the next sheet. You can control where page breaks fall when you print a document. Doing so is important because there are certain places where you want to avoid page breaks and other places where you want them.

▶ Letters should not end with their closing alone at the top of a page.

▶ Tables should be kept together so that they do not break with one part on one page and the rest on the next page.

▶ In finished documents, the first line of a paragraph should not fall by itself at the bottom of a page and the last line of a paragraph should not fall by itself at the top.

▶ Reports, term papers, and other important documents should often have major sections begin at the top of a new page.

Soft Page Breaks

As you edit a document, Word automatically keeps track of how many lines of text will fit on each page when the document is printed. When it determines that a page is full, it inserts a *soft page break* where one page will end and the next will begin. In page layout view, a soft page break causes a new page to be displayed. In normal view a soft page break is displayed as a thin dotted line across the screen. The only way to move one of these soft page breaks is to add or delete lines of text above it. However, there are times when soft page breaks fall at undesirable locations. For example, a soft page break may split a table or put a heading on one page and the paragraph that follows on another. When that happens, you enter a hard page break—see the illustration "Types of Page Breaks."

Hard Page Breaks

To prevent unwanted page breaks, you enter *hard page breaks*. In normal view a hard page break is displayed as a solid line across the document labeled *Page Break*. In page layout view, a hard page break looks just like a soft page break—a new page is displayed. If you add or delete text above a hard page break, it doesn't adjust automatically as a soft page break does. As a result, the page before a hard page break may be too short. (To delete a hard page break, select it and press Del.)

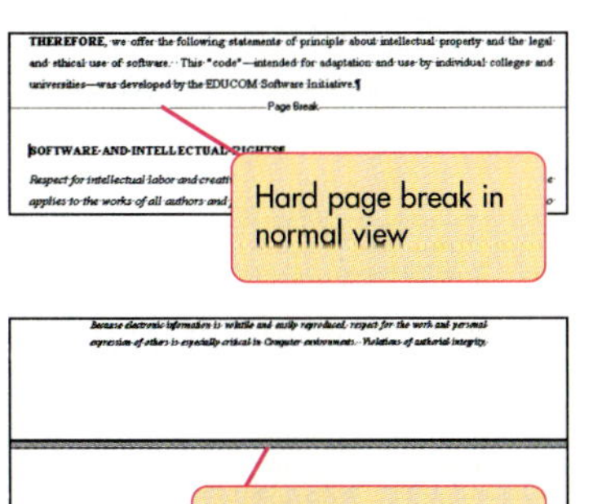

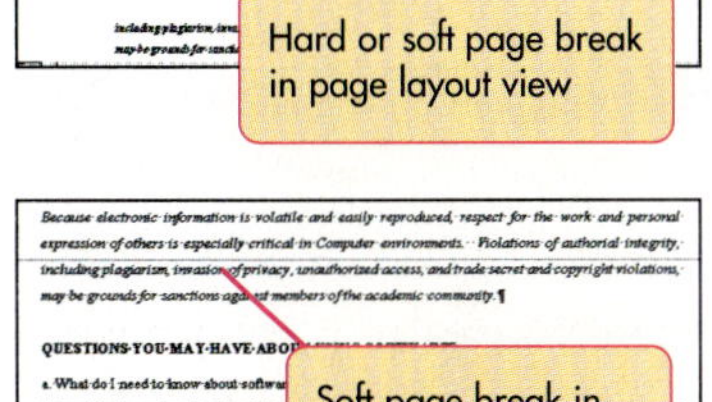

Types of page breaks

Entering Hard Page Breaks

Fastest

▶ With the insertion point where you want to start the new page, press Ctrl + Enter ↵.

Menus

1. Move the insertion point to the beginning of the line that you want to start the new page (or the end of the line you want to be the last on the previous page).

2. Pull down the **Insert** menu, click the **Break** command to display the Break dialog box, click the **Page Break** option button to turn it on, and then click the **OK** command button.

Keeping Text Together

You can prevent soft page breaks from occurring in undesirable places by using widow/orphan control, keeping selected lines together, or keeping one paragraph with the next. These commands are extremely useful when you want to:

▶ Keep the lines of a table on the same page as the table headings

▶ Keep an illustration on the same page as the text that refers to it

▶ Keep a heading and at least the first two lines of the following text on the same page

▶ Avoid widows and orphans. In printing jargon, an orphan is the first line of a paragraph printed by itself at the bottom of a page. A widow is the last line of a paragraph printed by itself at the top of a page—see the margin illustration.

Widows and orphans

Keeping Text Together

1. Position the insertion point in a paragraph or where you want to enter new text with the format, or select a group of paragraphs.

2. Pull down the **Format** menu and click the **Paragraph** command to display the Paragraph dialog box.

3. On the **Text Flow** tab choose any of the settings described in the box "Understanding Pagination Choices" and then click the **OK** command button.

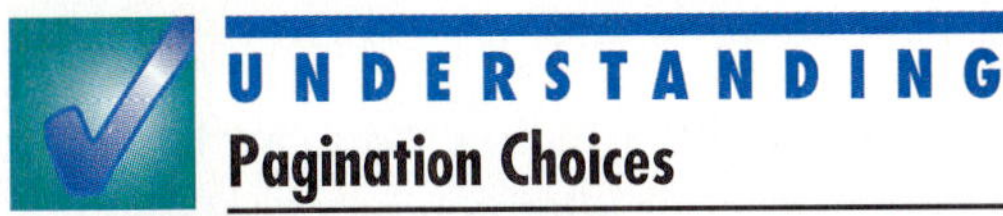

The **Text Flow** tab of the Paragraph dialog box offers three ways to protect sections of your text.

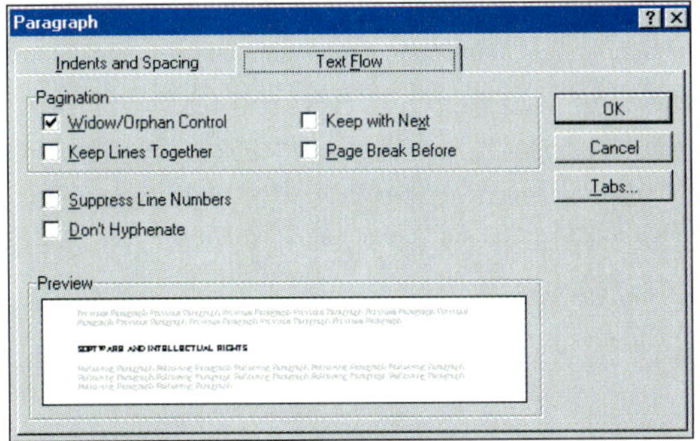

Widow/Orphan Control prevents widows and orphans. (The default setting is on.) If Word calculates that the first or last line of a paragraph will print at the bottom or top of a page by itself, it moves another line to accompany it. Since single lines are prevented, no three-line paragraphs will be split; the entire paragraph will move to the next page if it will not print on the current page.

Keep Lines Together keeps a paragraph from being split by a soft page break.

Keep with Next moves a paragraph to the next page if the paragraph that follows it is moved there. This command is ideal to keep a heading with the paragraph that follows it.

Page Break Before always keeps a paragraph at the top of a page because a page break is inserted before it.

- ☐ **3-5 CONCEPTS.** In this section you interactively explore the concepts of soft and hard page breaks, widows, and orphans.

- ☐ **3-5 TUTORIAL.** Controlling page breaks is sometimes very important. In this tutorial you explore how you do so and see what effects various commands have.

- ☐ **3-5 DRILL.** Word automatically inserts soft page breaks wherever a page is filled. However, there are times when you want to specify where pages should break. In this drill you add hard page breaks to a document so each major heading begins on a new page.

> IDENTIFICATION
> HIGH CLOUDS
> MIDDLE CLOUDS
> LOW CLOUDS
> CLOUDS WITH EXTENSIVE VERTICAL DEVELOPMENT

Clouds Headings

3-6 USING AND SETTING TAB STOPS

To indent the first line of a paragraph or get a column of figures to align properly, you use tab stops rather than regular spaces. Tab stops move text to a specific spot on the page, which is what you need for exact alignment. Pressing the spacebar does not accomplish the same thing. The reason for this is that Word handles spaces differently than other characters. When it wants to squeeze more characters onto a line or expand a line to justify it, it squeezes or expands the spaces on the line. Since spaces can have different widths depending on where they are in a document, they can't be used to align text properly.

Aligning Text with Tab Stops

By default, Word sets left-aligned tab stops every 0.5 inches. You can left-align columns with these tab stops either as you enter it or after you have entered it.

▶ To align a column entry with a tab stop as you enter the text, press [Tab⇆] until the insertion point is in the desired tab stop, and then type the text. (If you type enough text to reach past the right margin, the second and subsequent lines wrap back to and align with the left margin, not with the tab stop.)

▶ To align an entry with a tab stop after you have entered the text, position the insertion point to the left of the first character in the entry to be aligned. When you then press [Tab⇆], the insertion point and all text to its right move to the next tab stop. You must be in insert mode to do this. If you are in overtype mode, pressing [Tab⇆] will delete the character to its right.

Changing Tab Stops

Although Word has left-aligned tab stops set every 0.5 inches, you can change tab stops at any point in the document, and the change affects all selected paragraphs. When you set a tab stop, it automatically turns off all of the default tabs stops set every 0.5 inches between it and the left margin. For example, without changing tab stops, each time you press [Tab⇆] the insertion point moves 0.5 inches to the right. However, if you set a tab stop at 4 inches, pressing [Tab⇆] the first time moves the insertion point 4 inches and then each time you press it, it moves only 0.5 inches. (Default tab stops are not indicated on Word's horizontal ruler, but tabs you set are shown there. We will see how to set tabs from the ruler in PicTorial 4.)

When you set new tab stops, you have the choice of four possible alignments: left, centered, right, and decimal—see the illustration "Types of tabs." You can specify a leader for a tab stop—a dotted, dashed, or solid line that fills the space between tabbed columns. Leaders "lead the eye" from one column of text to the next without getting lost.

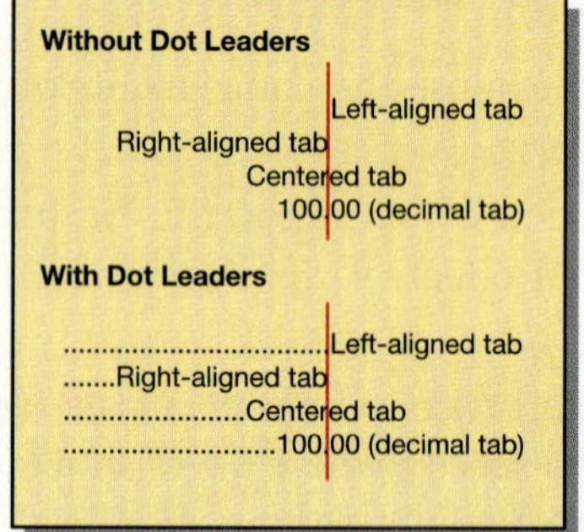

Types of tabs

▶ A left-aligned tab stop aligns columns flush left with the tab stop. Normally you use this type of tab stop to align text.

▶ A centered tab stop centers text on the tab stop's position. This alignment is frequently used for column headings in tables.

▶ A right-aligned tab stop aligns columns of text flush right with the tab stop. This alignment is widely used for numbers without decimal points.

▶ A decimal tab stop aligns columns of numbers containing decimal points. When you press [Tab⇆] to move the insertion point to a decimal tab stop, characters you type align flush right with the stop until you type a decimal point. When you do so, the period remains fixed in the decimal column and additional characters that you type extend out to the right. You can also use decimal tab stops to right-align text with tab stops. Just enter the text without typing a period, or make the period the last character.

▶ Word also has a special kind of tab stop called a bar tab stop that sets a vertical line in the paragraph. You might use this in a series of consecutive paragraphs to visually separate columns of text or numbers aligned with other tab stops.

Table 1. Major U.S. Dams and Reservoirs

Order	Dam Name	River	State	Height	Year
2	Hoover	Colorado	Nevada	725	1936
4	Glen Canyon	Colorado	Arizona	708	1966
5	New Bullards Bar	North Yuba	California	636	1970
8	Mossyrock	Cowilitz	Washington	607	1968
10	Hungry Horse	S Fork Flathead	Montana	564	1953
12	Ross	Skagit	Washington	541	1949
1	Oroville	Feather	California	754	1968
7	Swift	Lewis	Washington	610	1958
3	Dworshak	N Fork Clearwater	Idaho	718	1973
9	Shasta	Sacramento	California	600	1945
11	Grand Coulee	Columbia	Washington	551	1942
6	New Melones	Stanislaus	California	626	1979

When you set tab stops, each type is represented on the horizontal ruler with a unique symbol. These symbols are illustrated in the table "Tab Stop Markers."

TAB STOP MARKERS

Marker	Description
L	Left aligned
⊥	Centered
⌐	Right aligned
⊥	Decimal

QUICKSTEPS

Setting Tab Stops Using the Tab Set Dialog Box

1. Position the insertion point in a paragraph or at the point where you want to set a new tab stop, or select a group of paragraphs.
2. Pull down the **Format** menu and click the **Tabs** command to display the Tabs dialog box.
3. Specify tab stops using any of the settings described in "Understanding the Tabs Dialog Box" and then click the **OK** command button.

UNDERSTANDING

The Tabs Dialog Box

When you pull down the **Format** menu and click the **Tabs** command, the Tabs dialog box appears. You use this dialog box to specify the type and placement of tab stops.

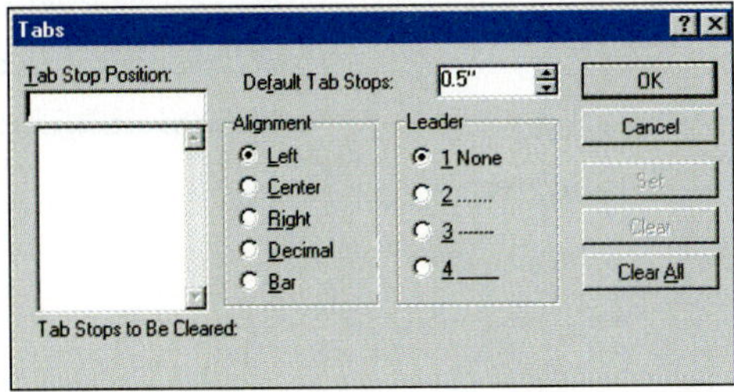

Tab Stop Position text box is where you enter the distance of the tab stop from the left margin. If the paragraph already has any tab stops set, they are listed below the text box. To select one of them and list it in the text box (for example to clear it or add a leader), just click it. If there are some tabs stops that are set in one of the selected paragraphs but not in another, they are displayed dimmed on the ruler and are not shown on this list.

Alignment section contains option buttons where you specify whether the tab stop is **Left**, **Center**, **Right**, **Decimal**, or **Bar**.

Leader section specifies the type of leader, if any, for the tab currently displayed in the **Tab Stop Position** text box.

Command Buttons

Set sets a tab stop at the position currently displayed in the **Tab Stop Position** text box.

Clear clears any tab stop at the position indicated in the **Tab Stop Position** text box.

Clear All clears all existing tab stops, returning the paragraph to the default settings.

If you hold down Alt while dragging, you'll select a rectangular area within the document. You can use this procedure to format, copy, cut, delete, or drag and drop tabbed columns.

PAL ON-LINE ACTIVITIES CHECKLIST

☐ **3-6 CONCEPTS.** In this section you explore the concepts of tab stops and how they are used to align text.

☐ **3-6 TUTORIAL.** Many tables are arranged in columns with each column aligned with a tab stop. In this tutorial you set tab stops to correctly align the columns in a table listing the highest dams in the United States.

☐ **3-6 DRILL.** All computer keyboards have special characters besides the number and letter keys with which you are familiar. These keys are used for a number of purposes when working with the computer. Here you format a table that names each of these special keys.

3-7 INDENTING PARAGRAPHS

Many times, when you want to indicate where a new paragraph starts, you press Tab to indent the first line. However, there are other indents you can use (see the illustration "Types of indents"), especially when you want to set off text in your document so it stands out.

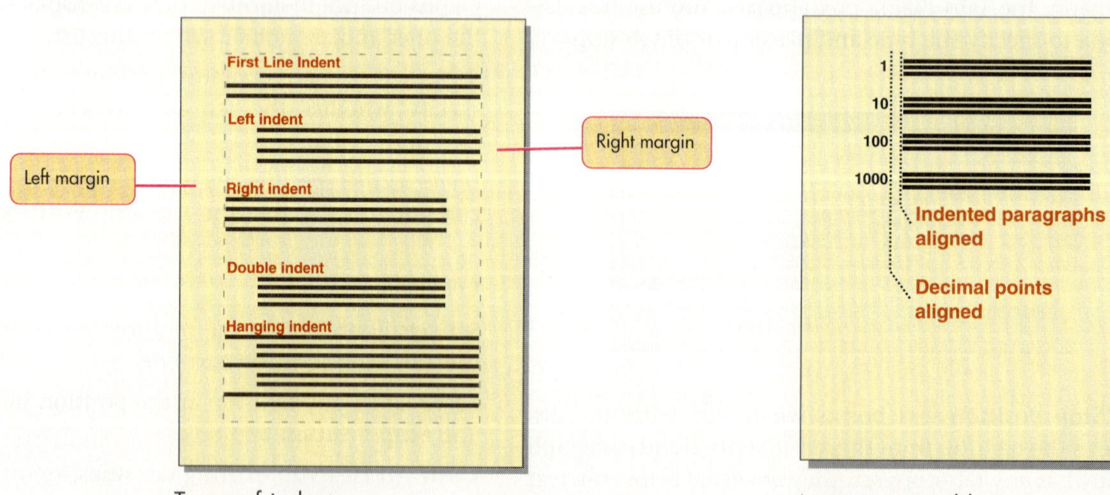

Types of indents

An enumerated list

▶ A paragraph with a *left* or *right indent* has all lines indented from the left or right margin, or from both margins.

▶ A paragraph with a *first line indent* has just the first line indented from the left margin.

▶ A paragraph with a *hanging indent* has the first line indented less than the other lines in the paragraph or not indented at all. This type of indent is frequently used for bibliographies. An enumerated list is a form of hanging indent (see the illustration "An Enumerated List"), but you press Tab⇆ between the number (or bullet) and the first word of the paragraph that follows it. This leaves the number (or bullet) hanging but the text in the paragraph is all aligned at the left indent marker.

QUICKSTEPS

Indenting Paragraphs

Fastest

▶ To left-indent a paragraph, click the **Increase Indent** or **Decrease Indent** buttons on the toolbar. These commands indent the paragraphs to the next or previous tab stop.

Menus

1. Position the insertion point in a paragraph or where you want to enter new text with the format, or select a group of paragraphs.

2. Pull down the **Format** menu, and click the **Paragraph** command to display the Paragraph dialog box, and on the **Indents and Spacing** tab use any of the settings in the *Indentation* section to indent the selected paragraphs. These settings are described in the box "Understanding Indentation Settings."

3. Click the **OK** command to close the dialog box.

UNDERSTANDING
Indentation Settings

When the Paragraph dialog box's **Indents and Spacing** tab is displayed, you can set indents with the commands listed in the *Indentation* section.

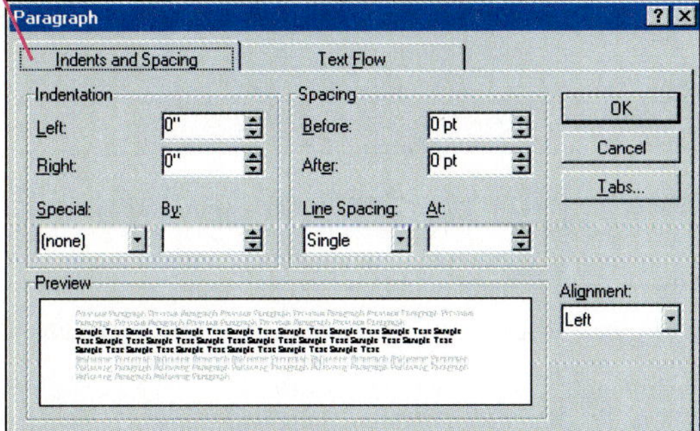

Left specifies the distance the whole paragraph is indented from the left margin.

Right specifies the distance the whole paragraph is indented from the right margin.

Special drop-down arrow (▾) displays the choices **(none)**, **First Line**, and **Hanging** for shifting lines in selected paragraphs.

▶ **(none)** aligns the first line with the rest of the lines in the paragraph.

▶ **First Line** shifts to the right the first line by the distance you enter into the **By** text box.

▶ **Hanging** shifts to the right all lines but the first by the distance you enter into the **By** text box.

By specifies the indent distance for **First Line** and **Hanging** indents. You can type the distance into the text box or use the spin buttons (⬍).

☐ **3-7 CONCEPTS.** In this section you interactively explore the concepts of indenting paragraphs.

☐ **3-7 TUTORIAL.** Indents are a great way to give a professional look to a document. In this tutorial you use hanging indents and left indents to set off enumerated lists and answer paragraphs in the *EDUCOM* document.

☐ **3-7 DRILL.** You use hanging indents to format enumerated lists and bibliographies. In this drill you format a bibliography so you can use the document as a reference when you format bibliographies in your own papers.

3-8 AUTOMATICALLY NUMBERING AND BULLETING LISTS

Many lists are set off from the rest of the text with numbers or bullets. Word makes it easy to create these lists when typing them in, or afterwards.

A Numbered List	A Bulleted List
1. Arizona	• New York
2. California	• California
3. Florida	• Ohio
4. New York	• Texas
5. Ohio	• Florida
6. Texas	• Arizona

Numbering or Bulleting Lists Automatically

Word is set to automatically number or bullet lists as you type unless you turn this feature off. When on, all you have to do to number or bullet the items in a list as you type is to add a number or symbol to the first paragraph. The character in which you enter the first bullet or the form you use for the first number determines the style for the rest of the paragraphs in the list.

▶ To number a list, type **1.** or **(1)** or **1)**, press [Spacebar] or [Tab] and type the first paragraph. When you press [Enter], a **2.** or **(2)** or **2)** will be automatically entered to begin the next paragraph.

▶ To bullet a list, type a **>** (greater-than sign), a lowercase letter **o**, or an asterisk **(*)**, press [Spacebar] or [Tab] and type the first paragraph. When you press [Enter], both the first and second paragraphs are bulleted.

▶ To end automatic numbering or bulleting for a list, press [Enter] twice without entering any text, or press [Enter] and then press [← Bksp].

QUICKSTEPS

Turning Automatic Numbering or Bulleting On or Off

1. Pull down the **Tools** menu and click the **Options** command to display the Options dialog box.

2. On the **AutoFormat** tab click the **Automatic Bulleted Lists** or **Automatic Numbered Lists** check boxes to turn these features on or off.

3. Click the dialog box's **OK** button.

Numbering or Bulleting Lists Manually

If you have already entered a list and then decide to number or bullet it, you can easily do so. The command creates hanging indents—that is, lists in which bullets or numbers align to the left of the text that follows. When numbering or bulleting lists, keep these points in mind.

▸ To renumber a revised list, select the entire list again and repeat the command.

▸ To convert a numbered list to a bulleted list, select the numbered list and click the **Bullets** button on the toolbar.

▸ To convert a bulleted list to a numbered list, select the bulleted list and click the **Numbering** button on the toolbar.

You can tell when bullets or numbers have been added automatically because you cannot select them to delete them. The only way to remove them is to use the same button you used to format them. To remove the bullets or numbers from a list, select the list and click the **Bullets** or **Numbering** button on the toolbar.

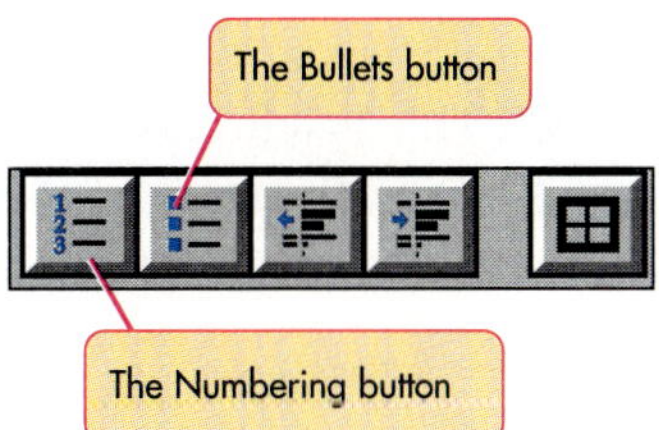

QUICKSTEPS

Numbering or Bulleting Lists Manually

Fastest

1. Position the insertion point in a paragraph or where you want to enter new text with the format, or select a group of paragraphs.
2. Click the **Numbering** or **Bullets** button on the Formatting toolbar.

Menus

1. Position the insertion point in a paragraph or where you want to enter new text with the format, or select a group of paragraphs.
2. Pull down the **Format** menu and click the **Bullets and Numbering** command to display the Bullets and Numbering dialog box.
3. On the **Bulleted**, **Numbered**, or **Multilevel** tab, select your choice and click the **OK** command button. To have the bullets or numbers left hanging so they stand out, be sure the **Hanging Indent** check box is on (☑).

Word allows you to change bullet and number formats. For example, you can add text before numbers, select different bullet numbering styles, specify a font or color, change the number a list starts at, and even control the lists indents.

QUICKSTEPS

Customizing Bullets and Numbers

1. Select the list to be formatted, then pull down the **Format** menu and click the **Bullets and Numbering** command to display the Bullets and Numbering dialog box.
2. Click the **Bulleted**, **Numbered**, or **Multilevel** tab.
3. Click the **Modify** button to display the Modify dialog box.
4. Make any changes to the format and then click the **OK** button to apply the format.

☐ **3-8 CONCEPTS.** In this section you interactively explore the concepts of numbering and bulleting lists.

☐ **3-8 TUTORIAL.** Many lists are either bulleted or numbered. Word makes it possible to achieve these styles with the click of a button, as you will see in this tutorial.

☐ **3-8 DRILL.** Bullets are frequently used to set off the items in a list. Here you add bullets to listings in two separate documents so you can easily distinguish the contents of their lists.

PICTORIAL 3

LAB ACTIVITIES

EXERCISES

3-1 Formatting a Description of Memo Formats

The format for interoffice memorandums varies in details, but the standard parts include a heading with a TO:, FROM:, DATE:, and SUBJECT:. This heading is then followed by the body text, and then by identification. Additional memo parts such as enclosure notations, attachment notations, and copy notations are included when necessary.

1. Open the *Memo layout rules* document stored in the *Exercise Documents* folder on the *Word Student Resource Disk* and enter your name, then click anywhere in the date and press F9 to update it.

2. Select the entire document and use the **Font Size** button on the Formatting toolbar to change the font size to 10 points.

3. Select each of the headings *Margins*, *Heading*, *Body Text*, *Identification*, and *Page Numbers* and use the **Format**, **Font** command to format them as bold with small caps. After formatting the first you can use F4 to repeat the format for the others.

4. Select all paragraphs except the 3-line heading and use the **Format**, **Paragraph** command to change their **Line Spacing** on the **Indents and Spacing** tab to a **Multiple** of 1.25.

5. Select all paragraphs except the 3-line heading and use the **Justify** button on the toolbar to change their alignment.

6. Use the **Bullets** button on the toolbar to add bullets to each of the entries under the headings. (The bullets will be the same kind that were last selected with the **Format**, **Bullets and Numbering** command.)

7. Select the last four indented entries in the document and click the **Increase Indent** button on the Formatting toolbar to indent them under the bullet above.

8. Select all paragraphs except the 3-line heading. Use the **Format**, **Paragraph** command, and on the **Indents and Spacing** tab add 6 points **After**.

9. Save, print, and close the document.

 Formatting a Description of Block-Style Letter Formats

Most business firms have prepared strict guidelines that specify the way business letters should be formatted. Company employees are expected to follow these guidelines so that the firm presents a unified style to all people receiving letters. Letter formats vary from firm to firm; however, many use the block-style format or a variation of it.

1. Open the *Letter layout rules* document stored in the *Exercise Documents* folder on the *Word Student Resource Disk* and enter your name, then click anywhere in the date and press `F9` to update it.

2. Select the entire document and use the **Font** and **Font Size** buttons on the Formatting toolbar to change the font to Arial 10 point.

3. Select each of the headings *Margins*, *Letterhead*, *Dateline*, *Letter Address*, *Salutation*, *Body Text*, *Closing*, *Signature Line*, *Identification*, *Page Numbers*, and *Open versus Mixed Punctuation* and use the **Fo̱rmat**, **F̱ont** command to format them as bold, with small caps, and dotted underlines. After formatting the first, you can use `F4` to repeat the format for the others.

4. Select all paragraphs except the 3-line heading and use the **Fo̱rmat**, **P̱aragraph** command to change their **Li̱ne Spacing** on the **I̱ndents and Spacing** tab to a **Multiple** of 1.1.

5. Select all paragraphs except the 3-line heading and use the **Justify** button on the toolbar to change their alignment.

6. Use the **Fo̱rmat**, **Bullets and Ṉumbering** command to add diamond-shaped bullets to each of the entries under the headings.

7. Select the last four entries under the *Page Numbers* heading and click the **Increase Indent** button on the Formatting toolbar to indent them under the bullet above. Then use the **Fo̱rmat**, **Bullets and Ṉumbering** command to change the diamond-shaped bullets to circles.

8. Select all paragraphs except the 3-line heading. Use the **Fo̱rmat**, **P̱aragraph** command, and on the **I̱ndents and Spacing** tab add 3 points **Afte̱r**.

9. Click the **Show/Hide ¶** button on the toolbar to display paragraph marks and delete all blank lines except the one below the 3-line heading at the top of the document.

10. Save the document, print the first page, and then close the document.

 Formatting the Job Search Document

You often read articles in the paper about people who have sent out thousands, perhaps even tens of thousands, of résumés without any response. When reading such articles, don't you sometimes wonder why these people wouldn't have stopped after a hundred or so and reevaluated their approach? Obviously, people aren't being turned on by what they are sending. It's probably so general in nature or so badly prepared that it goes immediately into the circular file. In this exercise you begin to format a report on how to prepare a successful job-search kit.

1. Open the *Job search kit* document stored in the *Exercise Documents* folder on the *Word Student Resource Disk*.

2. Select all body paragraphs below the letterhead and use the **Fo̱rmat**, **Ṯabs** command to clear all tabs and set a new tab stop .25" from the left margin. Notice how the indents for all of the paragraphs change.

3. Select all body paragraphs and use the **Justify** button on the toolbar to change their alignments.

4. Select all paragraphs except the letterhead, and use the **Format, Paragraph** command to change their **Line Spacing** on the **Indents and Spacing** tab to a **Multiple** of 1.2.

5. Select all paragraphs except the letterhead and use the **Font Size** button on the Formatting toolbar to change the font to 10 points.

6. Select each of the headings *The Cover Letter, The Resume,* and *The Followup Letter* and use the **Format, Font** command to format them as bold with small caps. After formatting the first you can use [F4] to repeat the format for the others.

7. Select each of the headings *The Cover Letter, The Resume,* and *The Followup Letter* and use the **Format, Paragraph** command to set spacing on the **Indents and Spacing** tab to 18 points **Before** and 2 points **After**. After formatting the first you can use [F4] to repeat the format for the others.

8. Select each of the four run-in heads (the first word in a paragraph) *Salutation, Opening, Body,* and *Closing* and use the **Bold** button on the Formatting toolbar to boldface them.

9. There are three lists located throughout the document that use hyphens to set off the paragraphs in the lists. Select each list and use the **Bullets** button on the Formatting toolbar to add bullets to them. Then delete each hyphen and the space that follows it.

10. Select each of the three bulleted lists and use the **Format, Paragraph** command to set a **Right** indent of 0.5" on the **Indents and Spacing** tab. Then use the **Increase Indent** button on the toolbar to increase the left indent.

11. Click the **Show/Hide ¶** button on the toolbar to display paragraph marks and delete all blank lines except the one below the letterhead at the top of the document.

12. Replace all forms of the word *resume* with *résumé.* To do so, locate the first occurrence of the word *resume* and use the **Insert, Symbol** command to replace the two letter *es* in the word with *és* from the **Font** *(normal text).* Copy the entire word *résumé* to the Clipboard and then display the Replace dialog box. Type **resume** in the **Find What** text box and press ⟨⇧Shift⟩+⟨Ins⟩ with the insertion point in the **Replace With** text box.

13. Save the document, print the first page, then close the document.

3-4   **Formatting the Computers and Careers Document**

In this exercise, you format the document on careers in the computer field. As you do so, you make it more attractive and more inviting to read.

1. Open the *Computers and careers* document stored in the *Exercise Documents* folder on the *Word Student Resource Disk.*

2. Select each body paragraph (not the headings) and use the **Format, Paragraph** command to change their first line indent to .25".

3. Select the heading *Careers in Information Processing* and the line below it with your name and use the **Center** button on the Formatting toolbar to align it.

4. Select all body paragraphs and headings and use the **Justify** button on the toolbar to change their alignments.

5. Select all body paragraphs and headings and use the **Format, Paragraph** command to change their **Line Spacing** on the **Indents and Spacing** tab to a **Multiple** of 1.1.

6. Select the title *Careers in Information Processing* and use the **Format, Font** command to format it as 14 points with small caps.

7. Select the line with your name on it and use the **Italic** button on the Formatting toolbar to format it.

8. Select the entire document below the title and use the **Font Size** button on the Formatting toolbar to change the font to 10 points.

9. Boldface all uppercase headings using the **Bold** button on the toolbar. After formatting the first you can use F4 to repeat the format for the others.

10. Select the subheads *Formal Training* and *Informal Training* under the heading *TRAINING AND SUPPORT* and use the **Format, Font** command to format them as small caps. After formatting the first you can use F4 to repeat the format for the other.

11. Under the heading *PROCESSOR POSITIONS*, there is an introductory paragraph and then three paragraphs describing specific positions. Use the **Bullets** button on the Formatting toolbar to add bullets to these three paragraphs and then delete the blank lines between them. Insert space following each of the bullets.

12. Under the heading *SPECIALIST POSITIONS*, there is an introductory paragraph and then a series of paragraphs describing specific positions. Use the **Bullets** button on the Formatting toolbar to add bullets to these later paragraphs and then delete the blank lines between them, and insert a space following each of the bullets.

13. Select the first uppercase heading, ORIGINATOR POSITIONS. Use the **Format, Paragraph** command, and on the **Indents and Spacing** tab add 12 points **Before**. Immediately use F4 to repeat the command for all other headings, including the *Formal Training* and *Informal Training* subheads.

14. Select the first body paragraph (it begins *The increased computerization of the workplace...*) and use the **Format, Paragraph** command to add 6 points **After** on the **Indents and Spacing** tab. Immediately use F4 to repeat the command for all other body paragraphs but not headings or bulleted lists.

15. Select the last paragraph in the first bulleted list. Then use the **Format, Paragraph** command, and on the **Indents and Spacing** tab, add 6 points **After**. Immediately use F4 to repeat the command for the last paragraphs in the other bulleted list.

16. Use the **Edit, Find** command to locate the first occurrence of the words *originators* and *processors*, and boldface them.

17. Use the **Edit, Replace** command to locate double hyphens (--) and replace any you find with em dashes. (See the Tip box "En and Em Dashes.") To insert an em dash in the **Replace With** text box, click the **Special** button, then click **Em Dash**.

18. Click the **Show/Hide ¶** button on the toolbar to display paragraph marks and delete all blank lines except the one below the letterhead and below your name at the top of the document.

19. Save the document, print the first page, and close the document.

Dashes are used to separate phrases—often to indicate an interruption in thought. Typists indicate dashes with two hyphens, but in desktop publishing a long dash called an *em dash* performs this function. Desktop publishing also uses the *en dash*, which is shorter than the em dash, to join ranges of numbers such as *13–151* or to join single words to phrases that contain two or more words, such as *London–New York.*

3-5 Formatting the Bill of Rights Document

In this exercise you format the Bill of Rights so it looks like it has been desktop published.

1. Open the *Bill of Rights* document stored in the *Exercise Documents* folder on the *Word Student Resource Disk*. Click anywhere in the date and press F9 to update it.

2. Insert a blank line above the first amendment, click the **Center** button on the toolbar, type the title **Bill of Rights** and press Enter↵.

3. Each of the ten amendments has a 2-line heading with the number and title of the amendment. Select each heading and use the **Center** button on the toolbar to center it.

4. Select the entire document except the 3-line heading and use the **Font Size** button on the Formatting toolbar to change the font to 18 points.

5. Select the centered title and use the **Font Size** button on the Formatting toolbar to change the font to 48 points.

6. Scroll down the document looking for an amendment split by a page break or a heading split by a page break from the amendment that follows. If you find one, move the insertion point anywhere in the split paragraph or heading, use the **Format, Paragraph** command to display the Paragraph dialog box, and display the **Text Flow** tab. Then:

   ▶ For a paragraph split by a page break, turn on the **Keep Lines Together** check box and then click the **OK** command button.

   ▶ For a heading separated from the paragraph that follows it, turn on the **Keep with Next** check box and then click the **OK** command button.

7. Save the document, print the first page, and then close the document.

3-6 Formatting the End User's Newsletter Document

In this exercise you format a newsletter so it looks as if it has been desktop published.

1. Open the *End User's Newsletter* document stored in the *Exercise Documents* folder on the *Word Student Resource Disk* and enter your name following *Publisher* in the masthead at the top of the document.

2. Select all paragraphs below the *Volume 1 Number 1* line and use the **Format, Tabs** command to set a new tab stop .25" from the left margin. Notice how the indents for all of the tabbed paragraphs change.

3. With the insertion point on the line that gives the volume and number, use the **Format, Tabs** command to clear all tab stops, and set a right-aligned tab stop at the right margin. (You can tell where the right margin is by looking

at the ruler.) Delete the space that separates *Number 1* from *Volume I*, and press ⌨Tab to separate the columns. The number should become right-aligned with the right margin.

4. Select the title *THE END USER'S NEWSLETTER*, and use the **F**ormat, **F**ont command to change **S**pacing on the **C**haracter Spacing tab to **Expanded** and set **B**y to 10 pts. The title should now almost fill the width of the page. If it wraps to a second line, repeat the command setting **B**y to 9, 8, 7 and so on until it just fits. When it's right, click the **Center** button on the toolbar to center it.

5. Select everything below the *ERGONOMICS AND HEALTH* heading and use the **Justify** button on the Formatting toolbar to change its alignment.

6. Select everything below the title and use the **Font Size** button on the toolbar to change its size to 10 points.

7. Select each of the four headings in the body that are all caps and use the **Bold** button on the toolbar to boldface them.

8. Select each of the two headings that begin *Checklist* and use the **F**ormat, **F**ont command to format them on the **Fonts** tab as small caps. After formatting the first you can use ⌨F4 to repeat the format for the other.

9. Under the heading *END-USER SURVEY REPORT* use the **Italic** button on the toolbar to italicize the two run-in heads that read *Microcomputer Applications Survey* and *Benefits of Microcomputer Use*.

10. There are two lists in the document where each item begins with a hyphen. Use the **Bullets** button on the Formatting toolbar to add bullets to the lists, then delete the hyphens and the spaces that follow them. (Be careful because the top three bulleted paragraphs are separated from the rest by a single paragraph.)

11. There are two lists in the document below headings that begin *Checklist* where each item begins with an asterisk. Use the **Bullets** button on the Formatting toolbar to add bullets to the lists, then delete the asterisks and the spaces that follow them.

12. Use the **E**dit, **R**eplace command to locate double hyphens (--) and replace any you find with em dashes. (See the Tip box "En and Em Dashes.") To insert an em dash in the **Re**place With text box, click the **S**pecial button, then click **E**m **Dash**.

13. Save the document, print the first page, and close the document.

3-7 Formatting the Desktop Publishing Document

In this exercise, you desktop-publish the article on desktop publishing.

1. Open the *Desktop publishing* document stored in the *Exercise Documents* folder on the *Word Student Resource Disk*.

2. Select the title *Desktop Publishing* and use the **Center** button on the Formatting toolbar to center it. Then use the **Font Size** drop-down arrow (⏷) on the Formatting toolbar to change it to 48 points.

3. Select the line with your name, use the **Center** button on the Formatting toolbar to center it, then use the **F**ormat, **F**ont command to format it as 14-point italic.

4. Use the **Bold** button on the toolbar to boldface the following headings:

   ▶ The Creation Phase

▸ The Production Phase

▸ The Manufacturing Phase

5. Use the **Italic** button on the toolbar to italicize the following headings:

   ▸ Design

   ▸ Copyediting

   ▸ Typemarking

   ▸ Art Preparation

   ▸ Typesetting

   ▸ Proofreading

   ▸ Pasteup

   ▸ Printing and Binding

6. Format all body paragraphs—not including the headings you have formatted—as follows:

   ▸ Use the **Format**, **Paragraph** command to change their first line indent on the **Indents and Spacing** tab to .25″ and **Line Spacing** to a **Multiple** of 1.1.

   ▸ Use the **Justify** button on the toolbar to change their alignments.

   ▸ Use the **Font Size** button on the toolbar to change the font size to 10-points.

7. Use the **Edit**, **Find** command to locate the first occurrence of the phrase *desktop publishing* in the body of the document, change it to *desktop publishing (DTP)*, and use the **Bold** button on the toolbar to boldface it.

8. Save the document, print the first page, and close the document.

3-8 **Formatting the Menu from Alyce's Restaurant**

In this exercise you format a menu so it looks like it has been desktop published. When finished formatting, your document should look like the figure "The Alyce's Restaurant document."

1. Open the *Alyce's Restaurant* document stored in the *Exercise Documents* folder on the *Word Student Resource Disk* and enter your name, then click anywhere in the date and press [F9] to update it.

2. With all lines below the heading selected starting with the line that reads *Alyce's Restaurant*, use the **Format**, **Tabs** command to clear all existing tab stops and set new center tab stops 1.5″, 3.5″, and 5.5″ from the left margin.

3. Columns are now separated by one or two asterisks. Delete those asterisks and press [Tab⇥] in place of each one that you delete. (Tip: Press [Ins] so *OVR* is displayed on the status bar. When you then click to the left of an asterisk and press [Tab⇥] you insert a tab stop and delete the asterisk at the same time. When finished, be sure to press [Ins] so *OVR* is no longer displayed on the status bar.)

4. Format *Alyce's Restaurant* as 18 point type, small caps, bold.

5. Format *Famous Homemade Ice Cream* as 14 point type.

6. Format *Flavors* as 18 point.

7. Format all text beginning with the line *Open All Year* as 18 point type.

8. Save, print, and close the document.

Name:
Filename: ALYCES.WPD
Date:

ALYCE'S RESTAURANT
Famous Homemade Ice Cream

| Sundaes | Ice Cream Sandwiches (any flavor) | Frappes |
| Ice Cream Sodas | Milk Shakes | Floats & Malteds |

Flavors

Vanilla	Rocky Road	Pistachio
Chocolate	Chocolate Chip	Coffee Almond
Coffee	Chocolate Chocolate Chip	Oreo
Strawberry	Mint Chip	Butter Crunch
Chocolate Almond Fudge	Mocha Chip	Reeses
Banana	Grape Nut	M&M
Bubble Gum	Maple Walnut	Almond Joy
Peppermint Stick	Black Raspberry	Strawberry Cheese
Frozen Pudding	Milky Way	Snickers
Almond Joy	Coffee Almond Fudge	Orange Sherbet
Raspberry Sherbet	Watermelon	Rainbow

Open All Year

Serving You For Over 60 Years
Indoor Seating Available
SEE OUR FOOD MENU ON REVERSE SIDE

The Alyce's Restaurant document

PROJECTS

3-1   The Research Paper

Many courses in college require the preparation of a research paper. To prepare such a paper, you must select a topic, research it, and then prepare a written document. The computer can greatly ease the process of writing, editing, and formatting the paper. You may also find computers in the library that allow you to search for information on specific subjects, easing the research task as well. In this project, you'll be glad to know we have done the research for you. All you have to do is format the document.

As Lynn Quitman Troyka puts it in *Simon & Schuster Handbook for Writers,* 4th ed. (Upper Saddle River: Prentice, 1996): "Because of the differences among disciplines, different formats are expected in each for presentation of material. These special formats have evolved to communicate a writer's purpose, to emphasize contents by eliminating distracting variations in format, and to make the reader's work easier. Writing in the humanities is less often subject to set formats although your writing is expected to be well organized, and accepted documentation formats are expected. Writing in the social sciences and natural sciences often calls for using fixed special formats for specific types of writing. For example, if you are writing a case study or a laboratory report, you are expected to use the formats always used for such writings."

The paper on which you work in this project is based on the style of the Modern Language Association.

1. Open the *Research paper* document stored in the *Project Documents* folder on the *Word Student Resource Disk*.

2. Enter your name, your instructor's name, the course number, and today's date, replacing the copy at the top of the document.

3. Change the font for the entire document to 10 points.

4. Change line spacing to double for all paragraphs below the title.

5. Format the headings *Microcomputer Hardware: The Early Years* and *Microcomputer Software: The Early Years* as follows:

   ▸ Boldface them.

   ▸ Change paragraph spacing before them to 18 points and space after to 6 points.

6. Underline the titles IBM's Early Computers and Popular Electronics in the text. (Use the **Find** command to locate them.)

7. The two paragraphs above the heading *Microcomputer Software: The Early Years* are direct quotations. Indent them a half-inch from the left and right margins.

8. Format the table that begins with the heading *Key Dates in the History of Microcomputers*, as follows:

   ▸ Clear all tab stops and set a new left-aligned tab stop at 1".

   ▸ Delete the blank line between the table's title and the column headings.

   ▸ Boldface the table's title and column headings.

   ▸ Set the line spacing to single.

   ▸ Select the whole table, title, and column heads, except for the very last line and on the **Text Flow** tab of the Paragraph dialog box, specify that lines be kept with next.

9. Enter a hard page break above the *Works Cited* heading, and center the heading on the first line of the new page.

10. Underline the book titles in the *Works Cited* section.

11. Format the list of titles in the *Works Cited* section so they have a hanging indent of 0.5".

12. Save the document, print the first page, then close the document.

3-2   The Flier's Rights Booklet

It feels at times as if we are a herd of cattle as we head for the boarding gate at the airport. However, every air traveler has rights, and the U.S. Department of Transportation has published a guide to inform you of them when flying on an American airline in the United States. (The rules are different in other countries.) In this project, you begin formatting this document as a booklet.

1. Open the *Flier's rights* document stored in the *Project Documents* folder on the *Word Student Resource Disk* and enter your name.

2. Spell-check the document.

3. Format the entire document as follows:

   ▶ Change the font to 8 points.

   ▶ Change the alignment to justified.

   ▶ Change line spacing to 1.1.

   ▶ Set a tab stop at .25".

4. Format all headings as follows:

   ▶ Select all uppercase headings, and format them as 10 points, bold.

   ▶ Select all headings with only the first character uppercased, and format them as 10 points, italic.

   ▶ Change space before all headings to 12 points before and 2 points after.

5. Format all lists that currently are formatted as paragraphs with beginning asterisks: Add bullets to the list and eliminate the asterisks.

6. Format all body paragraphs other than headings and lists so they have 6 points after.

7. Format all body paragraphs other than headings and lists so they have a .25" first line indent.

8. Delete all blank lines in the document.

9. Format the title so it looks as much like the figure "The Flier's-Rights Title" as you can make it.

10. Save the document, print the first page, then close the document.

Flier's Rights

A GUIDE TO AIR TRAVEL IN THE U.S.

U.S. Department of Transportation

your name

The Flier's-Rights Title

ADVANCED FORMATTING

After completing this PicTorial, you will be able to:

▶ **Format text using the horizontal ruler**
▶ **Copy formats and find and replace them**
▶ **Add headers, footers, and page numbers**
▶ **Add footnotes and endnotes**
▶ **Change, margins, paper size, and page orientation**
▶ **Enter section breaks**
▶ **Sort documents**

ONCE you have learned how to enter, edit, and format a document, you are ready to move onto more advanced formatting procedures. In this PicTorial you are introduced to many of these procedures, including formatting text from the ruler; adding headers, footers, page numbers, and footnotes; changing paper size, margins, and orientation; breaking your document into sections; and sorting paragraphs and tabbed material. Mastering these procedures will allow you to prepare almost any kind of document.

Word's rulers not only show you margins and a paragraph's tab stops and indents—they allow you to change them by dragging markers with the mouse.

Displaying the Rulers

The vertical and horizontal rulers reflect settings in the paragraph containing the insertion point. You can change the selected paragraph's margins by dragging margin boundaries, set tab stops by clicking, and set indents by dragging markers.

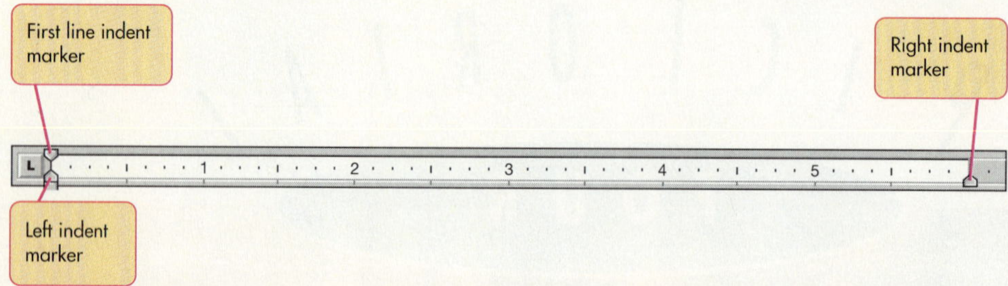

Displaying and Hiding the Rulers

▶ To display or hide the horizontal ruler, pull down the **View** menu and click the **Ruler** command to turn it on or off.

▶ To display the vertical ruler, click the **Page Layout View** button in the lower left corner of the window.

Changing Margins

You change left or right margins for selected paragraphs or top and bottom margins for the document by dragging the margin boundaries on the rulers. These boundaries are the gray part of the ruler just to the left or right of the white area on the horizontal ruler or above or below the white area on the vertical ruler. When you point to this boundary area in page layout view or in print preview, the mouse pointer turns into a double-headed arrow. (↔). You cannot drag these margin boundaries in normal view.

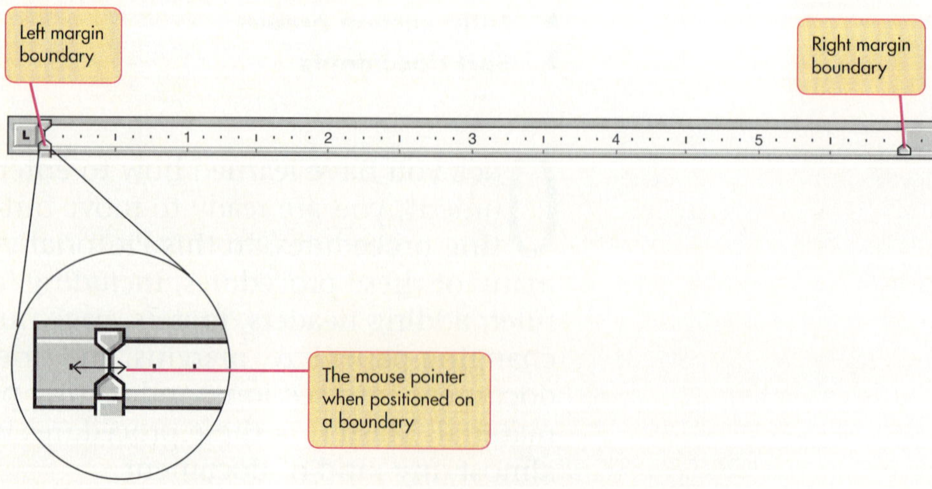

Positioning Markers Accurately

As you drag markers or margin boundaries, hold down $\boxed{\text{Alt}}$ so their current position is displayed on the ruler. Keep your eye on this readout when you want to position a marker accurately.

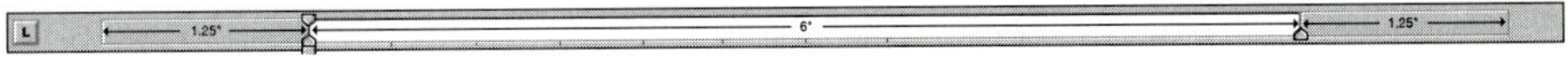

Changing Indents

To change indents, you can drag any one of the three paragraph indent markers. The way you arrange them determines whether you get a first line indent, an entire paragraph indent, or a hanging indent. Dragging the right indent marker is straightforward. However, when dragging the left, there is a little trick involved. If you drag it by either triangle, the markers move independently. If you drag it by the square bottom half, the two indent markers move together.

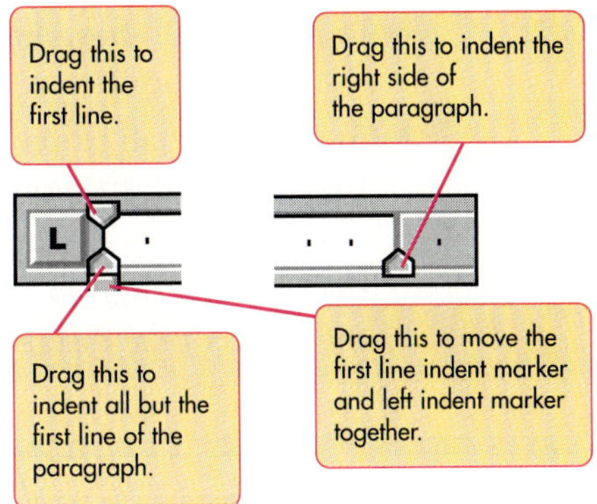

To indent the first line of a paragraph, drag the first line indent marker (the upper triangle) to the right of the left indent marker.

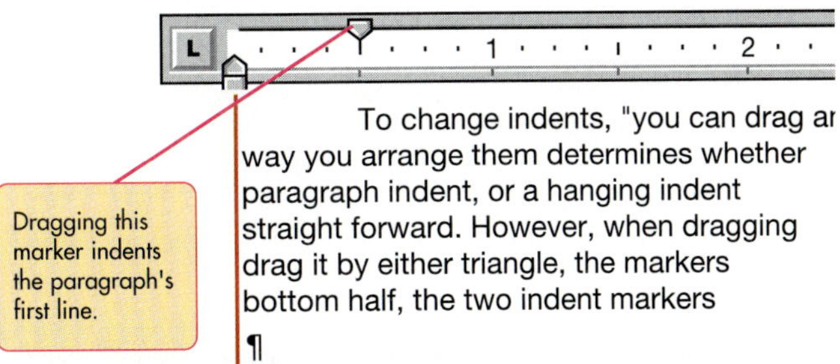

To indent the entire paragraph, drag the square left indent marker or the right indent marker.

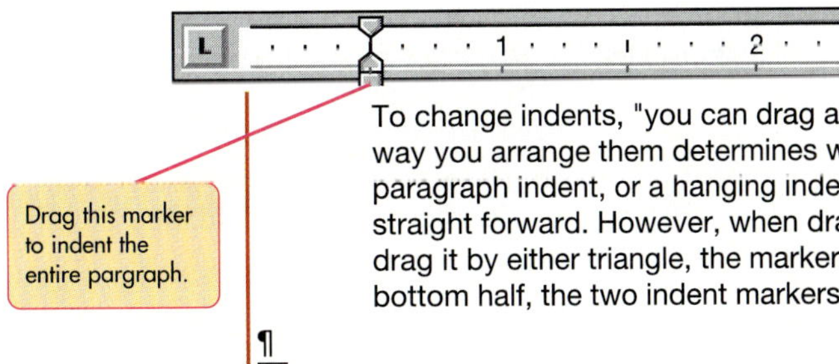

To create a hanging indent, drag the triangular left indent marker to the right of the first line indent marker.

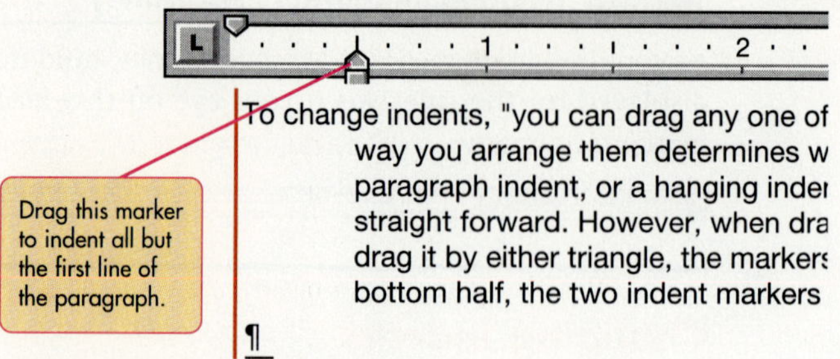

Changing Tab Stops

To change tab stops, you just point and click on the horizontal ruler to insert new tab stops, or drag existing tab stops to new positions. The changed tabs only appear in the selected paragraphs. If there are some tabs stops that are not common to all of the selected paragraphs, they are displayed dimmed on the ruler.

▶ To move a tab stop, drag its marker to a new position and release it. To display the current position as you do so, hold down [Alt] while you drag.

▶ To set a new tab stop of the type displayed on the **Tab Alignment** button (see the margin illustration), click on the ruler.

The **Tab Alignment** button

▶ To set a new tab stop of a different type, click the **Tab Alignment** button until the type is displayed. Each time you click it, a new tab type is displayed. With the correct type displayed, click on the ruler.

The **Tab Alignment** button

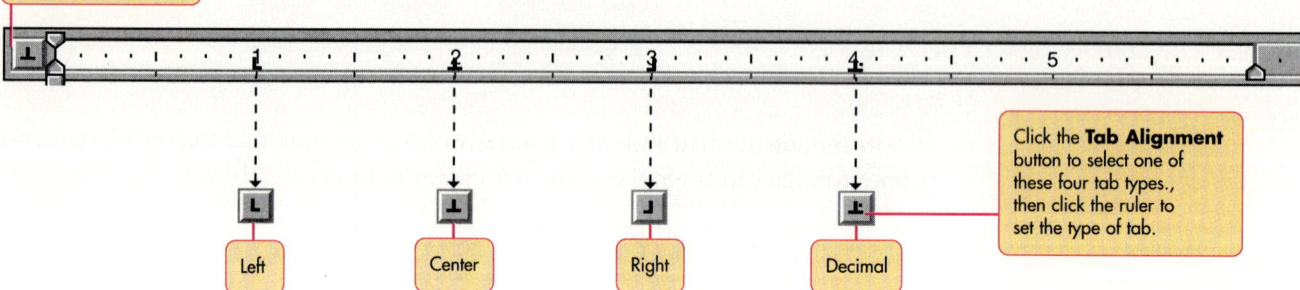

▶ To delete a tab stop, drag its marker off the top or bottom of the ruler and release it.

TIP
Displaying Dialog Boxes

You can display appropriate dialog boxes by clicking on the horizontal ruler.

▶ To display the Page Setup menu double-click the margin boundaries when the mouse pointer is displayed as a double-headed arrow. This allows you to change margins, page size, or orientation,

▶ To display the Paragraph dialog box at any point, double-click any indent marker. This allows you to change paragraph indents, alignments, and spacing.

▶ To display the Tabs dialog box, double-click any tab stop. This allows you to change tab stops or add leaders in the usual way.

☐ **4-1 CONCEPTS.** In this concepts section you view movies that demonstrate the concepts of using the ruler to change margins and indents and set tab stops.

☐ **4-1 TUTORIAL.** In this tutorial you drag markers on the ruler to format a document designed to illustrate the results you can expect to get. As you do so, you hold down Alt so measurements are displayed on the ruler. You use these measurements to format the text.

☐ **4-1 DRILL.** Dragging markers on the ruler is the fastest way to change margins, indents, and tab stops. It's also the most visual way to do it since you can see the changes immediately. In this drill you practice making changes using the ruler.

TABLE 1 Shark System Board Costs

CPU	Q1	Q2	Q3	Q4
Pentium/100	550	500	475	450
Pentium/150	600	550	525	500
Pentium Pro/200	650	600	575	525

TABLE 2 Microprocessor Pricing

CPU	Q1	Q2	Q3	Q4
Pentium/100	250	250	225	200
Pentium/150	300	275	250	225
Pentium Pro/200	350	325	300	250

System Board Price Tables

4-2 COPYING FORMATS

Once you have formatted some text in a document, there is no reason to use commands and dialog boxes to format something else just like it. Word's Format Painter allows you to quickly copy the format from one place to another.

QUICKSTEPS

Copying Formats

1. Select the text that has the format you want to copy. If copying paragraph formats, be sure the paragraph mark at the end of the paragraph is included in the selection.

2. Click the **Format Painter** button on the Standard toolbar, and a paintbrush appears on the mouse pointer. (Double-click it if you want to copy the formats to a number of places.)

3. Select the text you want to apply the copied format to. When you release the mouse button, the paintbrush disappears from the mouse pointer. (If you double-clicked the **Format Painter** button on the toolbar, click it again to turn it off when finished copying the formats.)

☐ **4-2 CONCEPTS.** In this concepts section you view movies that demonstrate the concepts of copying character and paragraph formats.

☐ **4-2 TUTORIAL.** In this tutorial, you use the **Format Painter** button to copy formats from one place to another in a document.

☐ **4-2 DRILL.** Once you have formatted an element the way you like it, you can easily copy the format to other elements in the document. In this drill you practice using Word's Format Painter to do so.

4-3 FINDING AND REPLACING FORMATS

Just as you can Find and Replace text in a document, you can Find and Replace formats. This speeds up formatting when you want to make changes. For example, you can quickly change boldfaced book titles to italic, or find key terms that you have italicized, underlined, or boldfaced.

QUICKSTEPS

Finding and Replacing Formats

1. Pull down the **Edit** menu and click the **Find** or **Replace** command to display the Find or Replace dialog box. (If replacing, move the insertion point into the **Find What** or **Replace With** text boxes.)
2. Click the **Format** command button to display a list of formats. (Or click the **No Formatting** command button to remove previously specified formats.)
3. Click the **Font** or **Paragraph** command to display the Font or Paragraph dialog box.
4. Select formats to find or replace just as you would apply them when formatting text, and then click the **OK** command button.
5. Proceed with the operation just as you would normally.

☐ **4-3 CONCEPTS.** In this concepts section you view movies that demonstrate the concepts of finding and replacing formats.

☐ **4-3 TUTORIAL.** In this tutorial you are introduced to finding and replacing formats in a document.

☐ **4-3 DRILL.** When you receive e-mail or other text files over electronic distribution networks such as the Internet or CompuServe, they are frequently is a very simple format called ASCII. These files have no bold, italic, or other familiar formats. In addition, all lines end in hard returns—making them very hard to edit or format. To make these file more editable, you have to remove these hard returns. This drill shows how many people convert ASCII text files to normal document files.

Headers are lines of text that print in the top margin of pages, and *footers* are lines of text that print in the bottom margin. If they print on more than one page in a sequence, they are called running heads and running feet. They frequently include dates, names, and chapter or part titles that indicate a page's position in a document. To see them on the screen when you aren't entering or editing them, you must be in page layout view.

QUICKSTEPS
Creating and Editing Headers and Footers

1. Pull down the **View** menu and click the **Header and Footer** command to display the insertion point in the header area (a nonprinting dashed-line box labeled *Header* at the top of the page). The Header and Footer toolbar is also displayed. Text in the document is dimmed. (To edit an existing header or footer in page layout view you can also double-click it.)

2. Type the header or footer text, edit and format it using any of the commands you use to format your document, or use any of the commands described in the box "Understanding the Header and Footer Toolbar."

3. Click the Header and Footer toolbar's **Close** command button to remove the toolbar and return to the document.

UNDERSTANDING
The Header and Footer Toolbar

When you use the command to enter a header or footer in a document, the Header and Footer toolbar is displayed. Here is a brief description of each of the buttons on the toolbar.

Switch Between Header and Footer switches the insertion point between the boxes at the top and bottom of the document.

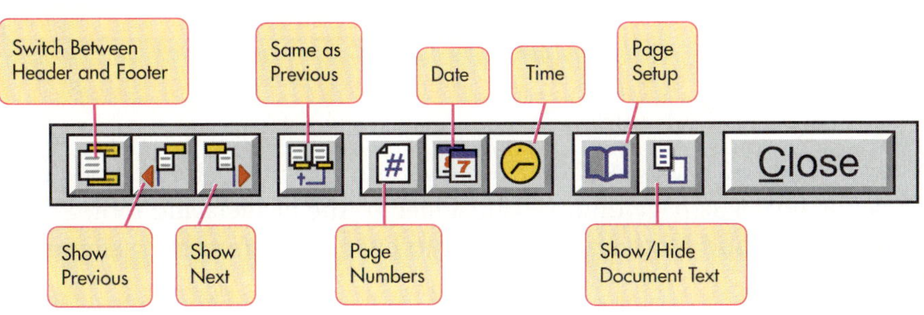

Show Previous displays the previous header or footer, if any.

Show Next displays the next header or footer, if any.

Same as Previous is used when you want to print different headers or footers in the same document. To do so, you must add sections as described in Section 4-8.

Page Numbers inserts page numbers in the header and footer.

Date inserts the current date into the header and footer.

Time inserts the current time into the header and footer.

Page Setup displays the Page Setup dialog box. On the **Margins** tab you can set the distance between the edge of the page and the header or footer in the **Header** and **Footer** text boxes. On the **Layout** tab you can then turn on or off the **Different Odd and Even** and **Different First Page** commands.

- **Different Odd and Even** specifies if you want different headers or footers on odd and even pages.

- **Different First Page** specifies if you want a different header or footer on the first page.

Show/Hide Document Text displays or hides the document text (which is displayed dim when shown).

Close returns you to the document and removes the toolbar.

☐ **4-4 CONCEPTS.** In this section you interactively explore the concepts of entering headers and footers.

☐ **4-4 TUTORIAL.** Headers and footers are used in almost all published documents and college research papers. In this tutorial you explore entering headers and footers into the *EDUCOM* document.

☐ **4-4 DRILL.** Headers and footers can be used to list names, page numbers, chapter or part titles, or anything else that would help you know where you are in a document. In this drill you add headers and footers to a document that discusses when to use headers and footers and what to put in them.

4-5 ADDING AND REMOVING PAGE NUMBERS

Word does not normally print page numbers, but you can have them automatically printed on any or all pages. You can also specify that they be printed as Arabic numbers (1, 2, 3), Roman numerals (i, ii, iii or I, II, III) or letters (a, b, c or A, B, C), and print them in a variety of positions on the page, as shown here:

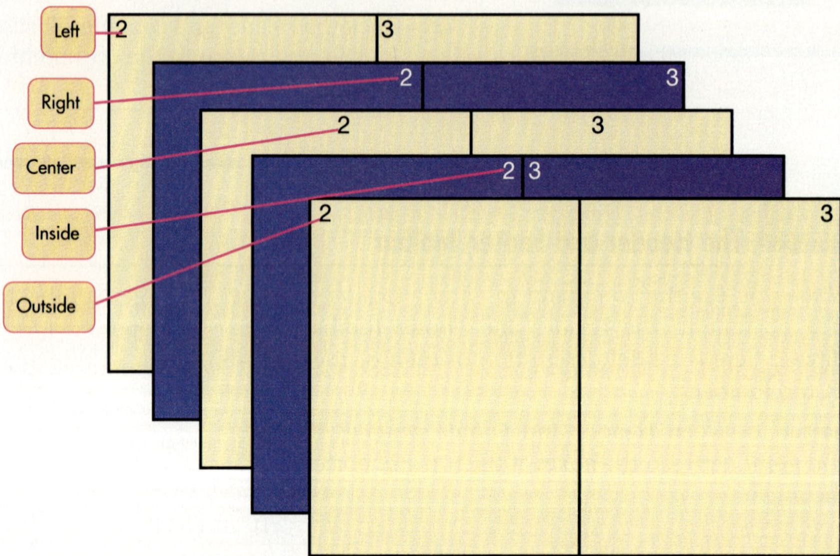

Adding Page Numbers

To add page numbers, you select their position and alignment from drop-down lists in a dialog box. The page numbers are added to the headers and footers. You can display headers and footers at any point to change the format or alignment of the page numbers.

Adding Page Numbers

1. Pull down the **Insert** menu and click the **Page Numbers** command to display the Page Numbers dialog box.
2. Make any of the choices described in the box "Understanding the Page Numbers Dialog Box."
3. Click the **OK** command button.

UNDERSTANDING
The Page Numbers Dialog Box

When you use the **Insert**, **Page Numbers** command, the Page Numbers dialog box is displayed. When you make changes in this dialog box, the results of those changes are shown in the Preview area so you can preview your choices before clicking the **OK** command button.

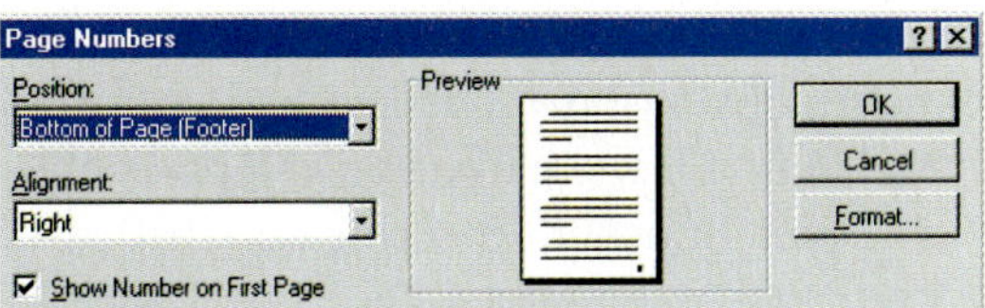

Position drop-down list (▼) lets you specify if page numbers are printed at the top of bottom of the page.

Alignment drop-down list (▼) lets you specify one of the following positions:

- ▶ **Left**, **Center**, **Right** aligns the page number relative to the left and right margins.
- ▶ **Inside** or **Outside** prints the page numbers on alternating left and right pages so they appear aligned with the inside or outside margins when pages are printed or copied back to back and bound.

Show Number on First Page check box prints a page number on the first page when on, and doesn't when off.

Format command button displays a dialog box you use to specify a **Number Format** (1,2, 3; a, b, c; i, ii, iii, and so on), include chapter numbers, or specify how numbering continues from the previous section (see Section 4-8).

Removing Page Numbers

Once you have inserted page numbers, you can delete them if you no longer want them.

Removing Page Numbers

1. Pull down the **View** menu and click the **Header and Footer** command to display the header area of the document. If the page number is in a footer, click the **Switch Between Header and Footer** button on the Header and Footer toolbar.
2. Select the page number and then press [Del] to delete it.
3. Click the Header and Footer toolbar's **Close** command button to close the toolbar.

☐ **4-5 CONCEPTS.** In this section you interactively explore the concepts of adding page numbers.

☐ **4-5 TUTORIAL.** In this tutorial you remove existing page numbers from the footer of the *Software rights and responsibilities* document and then insert new ones in the header.

☐ **4-5 DRILL.** Unless you specify otherwise, none of your documents will be printed with page numbers. This isn't a problem with very short documents, but it is with longer documents. In this drill you practice the procedures you use to add page numbers to a document and change their format.

4-6 ENTERING FOOTNOTES AND ENDNOTES

Word automates the insertion of footnotes and endnotes into a document. Footnotes are notes or comments or references placed at the foot (bottom) of a page and keyed to the body text with a reference mark (see the figure "Footnotes"). Endnotes are like footnotes, but they appear at the end of the document. Most academic disciplines have conventional practices for the use of footnotes and endnotes in research papers, and it is there that you will probably make the greatest use of this Word feature. A major benefit of the feature is that whenever you add or delete a note it automatically renumbers the notes that follow.

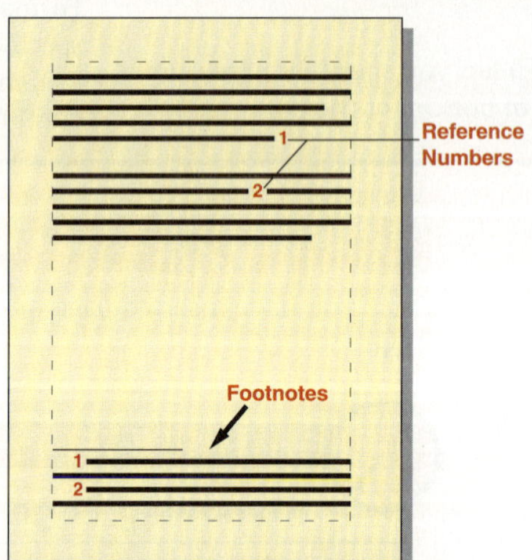

Footnotes

Entering Footnotes and Endnotes

You can enter a footnote or endnote anywhere in a document and view the result in page layout view.

Entering a Footnote or Endnote

1. Position the insertion point where you want to enter a footnote or endnote reference number.

2. Pull down the **Insert** menu and click the **Footnote** command to display the Footnote and Endnote dialog box.

3. Click the **AutoNumber** option button if you want notes numbered (the default) or click the **Symbol** command button and select a symbol instead. When you click a symbol and then click the **OK** command button, the symbol is displayed in the **Custom Mark** text box and that command's option button is on.

4. Click the **Footnote** or **Endnote** option button to turn it on (◉) and then click the **OK** command button. The insertion point moves to a window displaying footnotes or endnotes, or in page layout view to the end of the page or document. If there are any footnotes or endnotes already entered, they are listed. If you move the insertion point into one of them to edit it, the document scrolls so you can see the reference number and its context.

5. Type in the text of the footnote or endnote or edit and format it.

6. Click back in the document to return there.

Editing Footnotes and Endnotes

After entering footnotes or endnotes, you can edit them. During editing, they are displayed the same way as when you enter them.

Editing a Footnote or Endnote

1. With the insertion point anywhere in the document, pull down the **View** menu and click the **Footnotes** command to display existing footnotes or endnotes. (In normal view all are shown in their own window. In page layout view only those on the same page are shown in position on the page.)

2. When you move the insertion point into one of them to edit it, the document scrolls so you can see the reference number and its context.

3. Edit the footnote or endnote and then click back in the document to return there.

Changing Footnote and Endnote Options

Word gives you a great deal of control over how footnotes and endnotes print. The changes you make in these settings affect all footnotes or endnotes in the document.

Changing Footnote and Endnote Options

1. Pull down the **Insert** menu and click the **Footnote** or **Endnote** command to display the Footnote and Endnote dialog box.
2. Click the **Options** command to display the Footnote or Endnote Options dialog box.
3. Change any of the settings described in the box "Understanding the Note Options Dialog Box."
4. Click the **OK** command button.

UNDERSTANDING
The Note Options Dialog Box

When you display the Footnote and Endnote dialog box, you can click the **Options** command button to display the Note Options dialog box. The changes you make in these settings affect all endnotes or footnotes in the document. The commands for them are the same except Endnotes doesn't have the option to restart numbering each page.

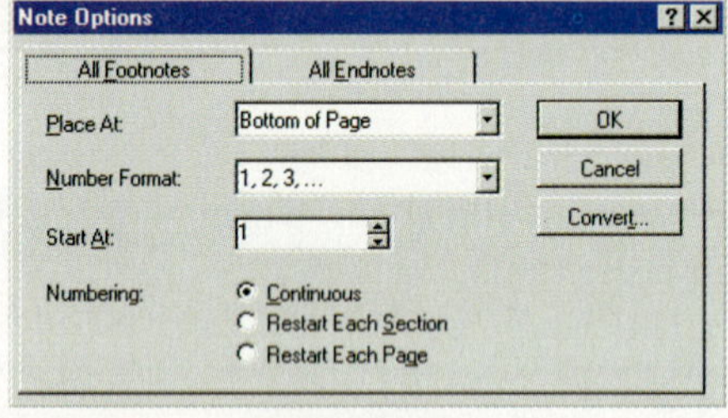

Place At displays a list of positions where footnotes or endnotes can be printed.

Number Format displays a list of number formats you can choose from.

Start At is where you can enter a number that you want the first footnote or endnote to start at.

Numbering section allows you to specify how number sequences run through the document.

▶ **Continuous** numbers footnotes or endnotes continuously through the document.

▶ **Restart Each Section** restarts footnote or endnote numbering for each section. Sections are discussed in Section 4-8.

▶ **Restart Each Page** (footnotes only) restarts footnote numbering on every page.

Convert command button converts endnotes to footnotes or vice versa.

☐ **4-6 CONCEPTS.** In this section you interactively explore the concepts of entering footnotes.

☐ **4-6 TUTORIAL.** In this tutorial you explore adding footnotes to the *EDUCOM* document and then how to edit and delete them. As you do so, you see how they are automatically numbered.

☐ **4-6 DRILL.** In college papers or business reports, footnote references to cited works are often required. In this drill you enter the form of various footnotes so you will have a reference you can later use when entering your own. These forms indicate what information should be provided, how it should be arranged, and how it should be formatted.

	FOOTNOTE FORMS
Number	**Footnote to Enter**
1	First Last, *Title* (City, State: Publisher, copyright date), pages.
2	First Last, First Last, and First Last, *Title* (City, State: Publisher, copyright date), pages.
3	Name of Corporation, *Title* (City, State: Publisher, copyright date), pages.
4	First Last, *Title*, Volume or Part (City, State: Publisher, copyright date), pages.
5	First Last, "Title of Article," in *Title of Publication*, ed. First Last (City, State: Publisher, copyright date), pages.
6	"Title of Section," *Title of Book*, copyright or edition date.
7	First Last, "Title of Article," *Name of Periodical*, date, section, page, column.
8	First Last, "Title of Article," *Name of Newspaper*, date of issue, page.
9	First Last, dir., *Film Title*, with Major Actor, Studio, date of release.
10	Personal interview with First Last, date.

4-7 CHANGING PAGE SETUP

You've seen how to change margins by dragging the margin boundaries on the rulers. However, you can also change them with the Page Setup menu. This not only gives you a few more options but also allows you to change the orientation of the page on the paper from vertical to horizontal.

Margins

Margins are the white area on the page around the printed block of text on the page (see the figure 'Margins"). Word is preset to print documents with 1" top and bottom margins and 1.25" left and right margins. You can change one or all of these margin settings. For example, you may want more room on the left edge so you can punch pages for a binder. A change in margin settings affects the entire document.

When you change margins, you can specify gutter margins. The gutter is the area on the inside or binding edge of a document that is printed on both sides of the page. On page 2, it would be the right margin and on page 3 the left (see the figure "Gutter Margins").

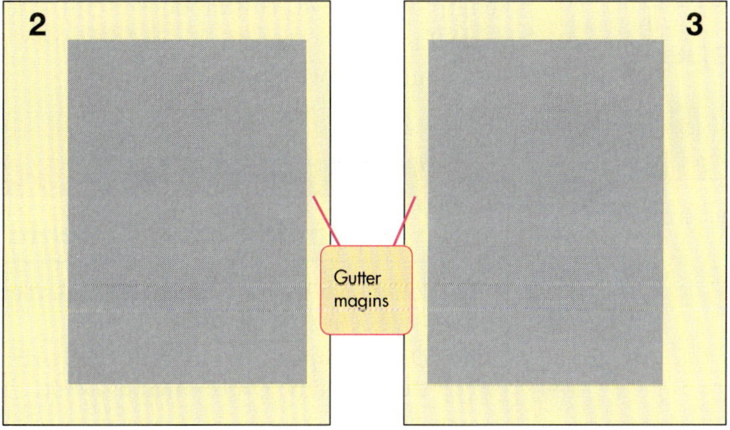

Margins

Gutter margins

Finally, you can also mirror margins. When you do so, you can have matching inside and outside margins, as shown in the figure "Mirror Margins."

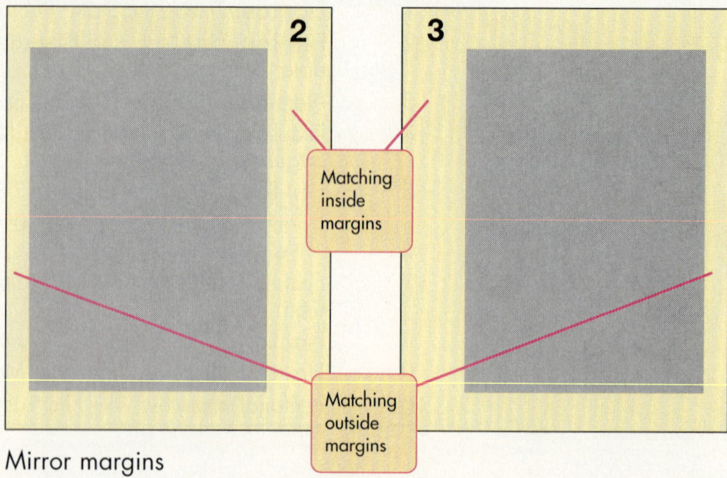

Mirror margins

Paper Size and Page Orientation

With Word it's easy to change the size and type of paper you are printing on. For example, if you print a document on most laser printers, you can print text across the width or length of the page. The direction is called the orientation or mode, and it can be either portrait mode or landscape mode. *Portrait* is the orientation of a normal document, that is, text is printed across the width of the page. *Landscape* orientation rotates the image 90 degrees so that it is printed along the length of the page. This mode is useful when you are printing wide tables, charts, and illustrations that are more horizontal than vertical (see the figure "Portrait and landscape orientations").

Portrait and landscape orientations

□ **4-7 CONCEPTS.** In this section you interactively explore the concepts of changing page setup between portrait and landscape orientations.

□ **4-7 TUTORIAL.** In this tutorial, you change margins and then change a document to landscape orientation and back again using menu commands. Some printers are not capable of printing in landscape orientation or take so long to do so that you wouldn't want to bother. Ask your lab assistant if you should complete this tutorial on printing in landscape mode.

□ **4-7 DRILL.** Often, tables and other documents print better in landscape orientation than in portrait orientation. In this drill, you change the orientation of an existing document and then preview or print it. As you have seen, some printers are not capable of printing in landscape orientation. If you are using such a printer, preview the document but don't print it.

4-8 ENTERING SECTION BREAKS

When you open a new document, it is all one section. *Section formats* such as margins, headers and footers, page numbers, and columns affect all pages in the document. To change section formats, for example to switch from Roman numeral to Arabic page numbers, or to change headers and footers, you have to create a new section where you want the section formats to change. To do so, you move the insertion point to the point at which you want the new section to begin and use the **Insert**, **Break** command. This inserts a dotted double line labeled *End of Section*. This line is simply a visual indicator of where you changed section formats. Until you make any changes, both sections have the same formats. However, when you now change section formats they only apply to the section in which the insertion point is positioned.

Section breaks are similar to paragraph marks in that they store all section formatting information. You can delete a section break by selecting it and pressing [Del]. When you do so, the formats from the lower section are automatically applied to the top section also.

When dividing a document into more than one section, here are some things to keep in mind:

▶ When you enter a header or footer in a document with more than one section, it will print on all pages of all sections. If you revise it in one section it will be revised in all sections. To change a header or footer in only one section you break the link between sections. To do so, you click the **Same As Previous** button on the Header and Footer toolbar to turn it off. Then when you delete or revise the new header or footer the change affects only the current section.

▶ To specify pages when using the **Go To** or **Print** commands, you indicate the section number as well as the page number. For example, to go to or print the first page in the second section, you would specify the page as p1s2. To print pages 1 through 3 of the second section, you would specify p1s2-p3s2.

▶ To use more than one type of page numbering in a document, create a new section and change its number format. For example, to use Roman numerals for the table of contents and Arabic numbers for the rest of the document, enter a section break following the table of contents.

▶ When you change margins or switch from portrait to landscape or back again, you can have the change affect the entire document, just the section, or from the insertion point forward in the document.

QUICKSTEPS

Creating a New Section

1. With the insertion point where you want the new section to begin, pull down the **Insert** menu and click the **Break** command to display the Break dialog box.

2. Make any of the choices described in the box "Understanding Section Break Choices" and click the **OK** button.

UNDERSTANDING

Section Break Choices

When you display the Break dialog box, the section headed *Section Breaks* contains four option buttons from which to choose.

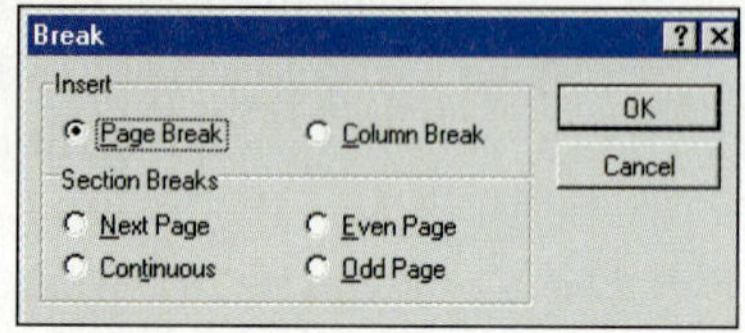

Next Page starts the new section at the top of a new page. The section break acts like a hard page break.

Continuous starts the new section on the same page as the old without inserting its own page break. Some section formats may apply to the top of the page and others at the bottom. For example, margins could be changed to accommodate a table.

Even Page starts the new section on the next even-numbered page, and inserts a blank page if needed.

Odd Page starts the new section on the next odd-numbered page, and inserts a blank page if needed.

PAL ON-LINE ACTIVITIES CHECKLIST

☐ **4-8 CONCEPTS.** In this section you interactively explore the concepts of section breaks.

☐ **4-8 TUTORIAL.** In this tutorial you insert a section break into a document to separate the title page and body text. You then use this section break to add different headers and footers.

☐ **4-8 DRILL.** In this drill you enter two different types of section breaks in a document. You then use these section breaks when going to or printing specific pages in the document.

Word allows you to sort all or part of a document into ascending or descending order. All you have to do is make a few choices from a dialog box and the job is done.

When you sort, you can do so by paragraphs or by fields. Paragraphs are any lines that end with paragraph marks. Fields are tabbed columns, or text separated by commas or other characters, and are counted from left to right. When you sort using fields, you must specify which fields are to be used as the basis of the sort. For example, if you want to sort a table that has three columns—name, department, and extension—you can sort it by any column—called a field. Perhaps you want the names in alphabetic order to use as a phone directory or the phone extensions in numeric order for the maintenance department. When you sort, you must tell the program which field you want to sort by. When you specify a field and sort the document, the sort is based on that field, and all lines are rearranged, not just the column you specified.

QUICKSTEPS

Sorting Documents

1. Select the data that you want to sort.
2. Pull down the **Table** menu and click the **Sort Text** command to display the Sort Text dialog box.
3. Make any of the settings described in the box "Understanding the Sort Text Dialog Box."
4. Click the **OK** command button.

UNDERSTANDING

The Sort Text Dialog Box

When you pull down the **Table** menu and click the **Sort Text** command, the Sort Text dialog box is displayed. It contains three identical sections, **Sort By**, **Then By**, and **Then By**. The choices in each of these sections work exactly the same but the last two work only when sorting by fields and not paragraphs.

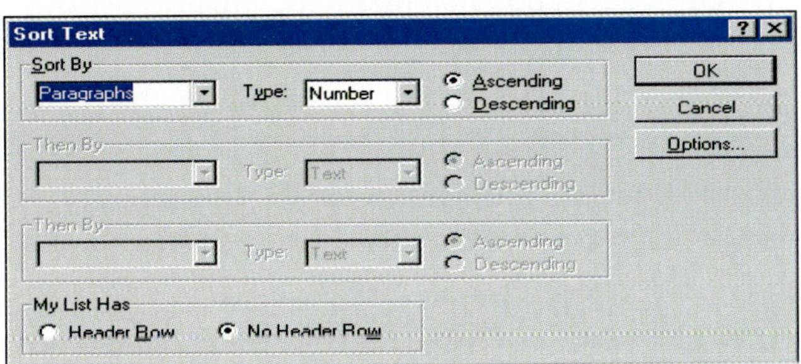

Sort By specifies whether the selected text is to be sorted by **Paragraphs** or **Fields**. Fields are specified when sorting tabbed columns of data or when sorting data separated by commas or other characters.

▸ **Type** specifies whether the data in the field is text, numbers, or dates.

▸ **Ascending** (A to Z and 0 to 9) and **Descending** (Z to A and 9 to 0) specify the order of the sort. In an ascending sort, items beginning with punctuation marks or symbols are sorted first, followed by numbers, then by letters. In a descending sort this order is reversed.

Then By and **Then By** allow you to break ties in the original sort when sorting by fields. For example, should you sort tabbed columns by last names, you can use the first one of these section to sort then by first names so they are also in order. The **Type**, **Ascending**, and **Descending** options work the same here as they do in the **Sort By** section.

Header Row and **No Header Row** specifies if the selected text includes a header such as column headings. Turning on the **Header Row** keeps this header row from being sorted along with the rows that follow it.

Options command button lets you specify if fields (columns) are separated by tabs, commas, or other characters. It also allows you to make the sort case sensitive and to sort a column by itself without including other entries on the row.

☐ **4-9 CONCEPTS.** In this section you interactively explore the concepts of sorting documents.

☐ **4-9 TUTORIAL.** In this tutorial you sort a document in both ascending and descending orders based both on paragraphs and fields.

☐ **4-9 DRILL.** In this drill you sort a long list of films in which Bugs Bunny stared. This allows you to quickly see films grouped by director and studio, and arranged in the order in which they were released.

PICTORIAL 4

LAB ACTIVITIES

EXERCISES

4-1   Formatting the Job Search Document

In this exercise you change indents and add footers and footnotes to the document describing how you prepare a job-search kit.

1. Open the *Job search kit* document stored in the *Exercise Documents* folder on the *Word Student Resource Disk*.

2. Use the **File**, **Page Setup** command to change the left margin to 1.5" on the **Margins** tab.

3. Select the two lines in the letterhead with the address and phone numbers and drag the tab marker so it overlaps the right margin.

4. Use the **View**, **Header and Footer** command to display the Header and Footer toolbar.

   ▸ Click the **Switch Between Header and Footer** button on the Header and Footer toolbar to move the insertion point to the footer box.

   ▸ Click the **Page Setup** button on the Header and Footer toolbar, then click the **Different Odd and Even** check box to turn it on.

   ▸ Click the **Show Next** and **Show Previous** buttons on the Header and Footer toolbar to move between the *Even Page Footer* and *Odd Page Footer* boxes.

   ▸ In the *Odd Page Footer* box, enter a footer that prints your last name flush right in all uppercase letters.

   ▸ In the *Even Page Footer* box, enter a footer that prints your last name flush left in all uppercase letters.

5. Use the **Insert**, **Page Numbers** command to add page numbers that print in the top outside corner of every page but the first.

6. Use the **Insert**, **Foot_note** command to enter a footnote at the end of the first body paragraph that reads **These recommendations have been adapted from a government publication.** (including the period).

7. At the end of the sentence that begins *Let's go through a typical letter point by point*: just above the *Salutation* section on the first page, use the **Insert**, **Foot_note** command enter a footnote that reads **These letter formats are also discussed in the *Letter layout rules* document in the *Exercise Documents* folder of the *Word Student Resource Disk*.** (including the period and using italics where shown).

8. Use print preview to see how page numbers, footers, and footnotes look. Your name should appear on the outside (right) edge of odd-numbered pages and on the inside (left) edge of even-numbered pages.

9. Save, print, and then close the document.

4-2   Formatting the Computers and Careers Document

In this exercise you indent body paragraphs, add headers and footers, and add a footnote to the document describing careers in the computer field.

1. Open the *Computers and careers* document stored in the *Exercise Documents* folder on the *Word Student Resource Disk*.

2. Use the **File**, **Page Setup** command to change the left margin to 1.5 inches on the **Margins** tab.

3. Select the two lines in the letterhead with the address and phone numbers and drag the tab marker so it overlaps the right margin.

4. Use the **View**, **Header and Footer** command to add a flush-right header on every page but the first with your last name in uppercase letters.

5. Use the **View**, **Header and Footer** command to add a flush-right footer on every page but the first that prints today's date. (To insert a date, click the **Date** button on the Header and Footer toolbar.)

6. Immediately after the phrase *One major company* in the first paragraph, use the **Insert**, **Foot_note** command to add the footnote **Federal Express Corporation**.

7. Use the **Insert**, **Page Num_bers** command to add pages numbers so that they print in the bottom center of every page but the first.

8. Save, print, and then close the document.

4-3   Formatting the Bill of Rights Document

In this exercise you enter footers and footnotes in the Bill of Rights.

1. Open the *Bill of Rights* document stored in the *Exercise Documents* folder on the *Word Student Resource Disk* and click anywhere in the date and press `F9` to update it.

2. Use the **View**, **Header and Footer** command to display the Header and Footer toolbar.

   ▸ Click the **Page Setup** button on the Headers and Footers toolbar, then click the **Different O_dd and Even** check box to turn it on.

   ▸ Click the **Switch Between Header and Footer** and then the **Show Next** and **Show Previous** buttons on the Headers and Footers toolbar to move between the *Even Page Footer* and *Odd Page Footer* boxes.

▶ In the *Odd Page Footer* box, enter a footer that prints *Bill of Rights* flush right.

▶ In the *Even Page Footer* box use the **Date** button on the Header and Footer toolbar to enter the date flush left.

3. Use the **Insert**, **Page Numbers** command to add page numbers that print in the upper-outside corner of every page.

4. Following the centered title at the top of the document, use the **Insert**, **Footnote** command to enter a footnote that states *All amendments passed unanimously* and use the **Options** command button to change the footnote numbering method to symbols.

5. Save and then print the document. Notice where the page numbers, footer, and footnote print.

4-4 Formatting the End User's Newsletter Document

In this exercise you indent body paragraphs and add page numbers to the newsletter.

1. Open the *End User's Newsletter* document stored in the *Exercise Documents* folder on the *Word Student Resource Disk*.

2. Use the **File**, **Page Setup** command to change all four margins to .75" on the **Margins** tab.

3. Use the **Insert**, **Page Numbers** command to add pages numbers so that they print centered at the bottom of every page but the first.

4. Save and then print the document.

4-5 Formatting the Desktop Publishing Document

In this exercise you indent body paragraphs and add headers, footers, and footnotes to the desktop publishing document.

1. Open the *Desktop publishing* document stored in the *Exercise Documents* folder on the *Word Student Resource Disk*.

2. Use the **File**, **Page Setup** command to change all four margins to .75" on the **Margins** tab.

3. Use the **View**, **Header and Footer** command to display the header box:

▶ Add a flush-right header on every page with your last name in uppercase letters followed by a space and then a page number entered by clicking the **Page Numbers** button on the Header and Footer toolbar.

▶ Add a flush-right footer on every page with today's date entered by clicking the **Date** button on the Header and Footer toolbar.

5. After the phrase *dedicated solely to DTP* at the end of the first body paragraph use the **Insert**, **Footnote** command to enter the footnote **Including a more recent program, QuarkXpress**.

6. Use the **Insert**, **Page Numbers** command to add page numbers that print in the bottom center of every page.

7. Save the document, print the first page, and then close the document.

4-1 **The Research Paper—Continued**

In this project you continue working on the research paper about the history of computing.

1. Open the *Research paper* document stored in the *Project Documents* folder on the *Word Student Resource Disk*.

2. Enter a right-aligned header that prints your last name flush-right in all uppercase letters on all pages but the first.

3. Enter a right-aligned footer that prints PAGE followed by the page number on all pages but the first.

4. At the end of the phrase *companies that supplied its components* enter the endnote shown here:

> Though the MITS system is no longer manufactured, its method for connecting peripherals and the main computer has become an industry standard. Within three years after it was introduced, Radio Shack, Apple, and Commodore had entered the market.

5. At the end of the phrase *VisiCalc did that for them* enter the endnote shown here:

> The introduction of VisiCalc is usually credited with making the Apple II the fastest selling computer of its time and with making the microcomputer acceptable in business offices.

6. Insert a hard page break at the end of the document. Then on the first line of the new page enter the heading **Notes**. Center the heading, and insert two blank lines below it so that the endnotes print starting on the third line.

7. Save, print, and close the document.

4-2 **The Flier's Rights Booklet—Continued**

In this project you continue formatting the *Flier's rights* document as a booklet.

1. Open the *Flier's rights* document stored in the *Project Documents* folder on the *Word Student Resource Disk*.

2. Enter the header FLIER'S RIGHTS so it's right-aligned on odd-numbered pages and left-aligned on even-numbered pages. Format it so it prints in 8-point Arial type.

3. Enter the footer PAGE followed by the page number so it's right-aligned on odd-numbered pages and left-aligned on even-numbered pages. Format it so it prints in 8-point Arial type.

4. After the heading *INTRODUCTION*, enter the following footnote:

> We're making every effort to keep *Flier's-Rights* up to date, but during this period of deregulation, airlines are making many changes in the way they do business. So by the time you read this, a few rules we explain may be different. Contact the airline you plan to use if you have any questions.

5. Change all four margins to 0.5".

6. Insert a section break below your name on the title page that begins a new page.

7. Save the document, print the first page of the second section, then close the document.

AUTOMATING PROCEDURES

After completing this PicTorial, you will be able to:

- **Describe the structure and function of main documents and data sources**
- **Merge main documents and data sources to print customized letters and labels**
- **Add input from the keyboard while merging documents**
- **Specify that only selected records are merged**
- **Record, play back, and edit macros**
- **Using AutoText and AutoCorrect to speed things up**

THE true power of a word processing program is best demonstrated when you begin to use it to automate your work. The two most common ways of doing this are with Mail Merge and macros. Mail Merge is a way to automatically print customized letters, labels, or other documents. Macros are a way to automate other procedures so you can execute them quickly. Word also has some automatic features built-in. These include AutoText, which enters text your have previously saved, and AutoCorrect, which corrects common spelling mistakes as you make them.

Most of us have received one of those mailers proclaiming something like **Mr. Steven Johnson of 100 Mill Street, you may have won a million dollars!** Ever wonder how they print your name on the copy you receive and each of your neighbor's names on the ones they receive? It's done with a process called merge-printing, or mail merge, as Word calls it. Instead of individually entering and editing tens, hundreds, or thousands of letters, envelopes, mailing labels, forms, or other documents, Mail Merge combines two documents; a *main document* containing the data that is to appear in each copy and a *data source* that contains the data that personalizes each copy. In our example, the mailer you received would be the main document because it is the same for everyone on your street, in your city, and in the country. The screaming headline that tries to make you think you have won something is from a data source because it personalizes the mailer for you and you alone. As you have seen from the volume of these customized mailers that arrive, Mail Merge can greatly increase your speed in preparing all kinds of documents which are essentially the same, except for minor changes, from copy to copy.

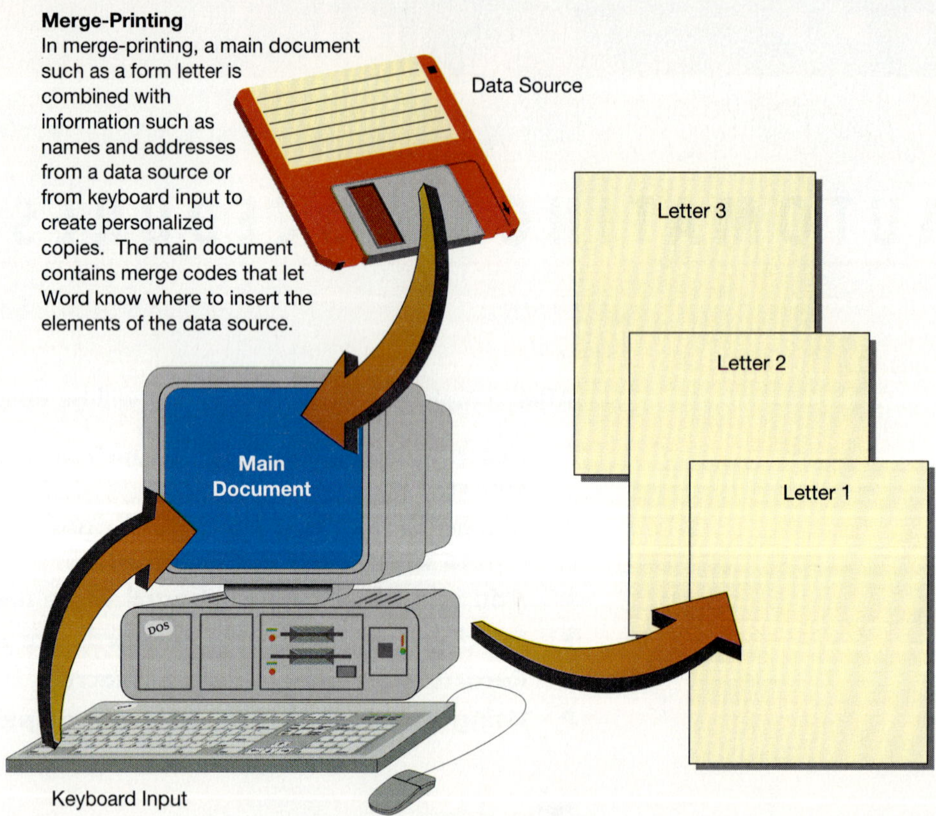

Understanding Data Sources

The information that customizes copies during merge-printing, such as names and addresses, is stored in a data source. A data source is a structured document that has three basic parts: a header row, fields, and records. Think of it as a table, like this:

Salutation	FirstName	LastName	Company	Address1	City	State	PostalCode
Mrs.	Suzanne	Steven	3D Graphics	1 Pierce Street	Saratoga	CA	95070
	Kim	Foley	Virtual Reality	60 Friend Street	Beverly	MA	01915
Mrs.	Debbie	Star		1 Oak Road	Marblehead	MA	01945

- ▶ The header row, the first row in the table, contains the names of all fields in the data source.
- ▶ The table's columns are fields, and each field contains a specific piece of information. For example, fields can store first and last names or postal codes.
- ▶ The table's rows are records, each divided into a number of fields. A typical record would contain a person's name, company, and address.

When merged, each record causes one new document to be printed. For example, the name and address in the first record are used to print the first envelope. Then the name and address in the second record are used to print the second envelope, and so on.

The advantage of storing data in a data source is that the data can be used over and over again to automatically print documents such as letters, envelopes, and mailing labels.

Understanding Main Documents and Merge-Printing

The part of a mail-merged document that stays the same from copy to copy is stored in the main document. However, this document also contains codes—called *merge fields*—that specify what and where data is to be inserted into each copy from the data source during merge-printing. For example, merge fields placed in the heading of the main document might specify where people's first and last names are to be inserted. (See the figure "A main document.")

When the document is merge-printed, its merge fields are replaced with the names taken from the data source. The reason the correct information is inserted is that each merge field refers to a specific field in the data source. It's as if a link is established between a code and the field to which it refers. When merged, as the first copy is being printed, data is sent down that link from the first record in

A main document

the data source. As the second copy is being printed, data is sent down that link from the second record in the data source. This process continues until a document has been printed for each record in the data source. Each copy of the final document contains all of the text from the main document and all of the specified fields from a single record in the data source. Therefore, if the data source contains 10 records, 10 different letters can be merged.

TIP
Displaying Merge Fields

When you enter merge fields in a document, they are enclosed in chevrons. This view is called "field results." To see merge fields in their entirety, you can display them as "field codes." For example, the merge code *«name»* displayed as a field result becomes *{ MERGE-FIELD name * MERGEFORMAT }* when displayed as a field code. To change your view of the codes, right-click them, and then click the shortcut menu's Toggle Field Codes command. This toggles the single code you clicked or the group of codes that you selected. (You can also pull down the **Tools** menu, click the **Options** command to display the Options dialog box, on the **View** tab click the **Field Codes** check box to turn it on (☑) or off (☐), and then click the **OK** command button to return to the document.)

QUICKSTEPS

Using Mail Merge Helper

1. Pull down the **Tools** menu and click the **Mail Merge** command to display the Mail Merge Helper dialog box.

2. Use the **Create** button under the section heading *1 Main Document* to open or create a main document—the document that contains the text that is to appear in each copy and merge fields that will be replaced with personalized data from the data source during merging. When you do so, select the type of document (Form Letters, Mailing Labels, Envelopes, or Catalog) and specify if you want to use the document in the **Active Window** or a **New Main Document**.

3. Use the **Get Data** button under the section heading *2 Data Source* to open or create a data source—the file that contains the data to be inserted into each copy of the main document during merging to personalize it. Once the two files have been opened or created and then saved, they are permanently linked. Whenever you open the main document, it is recognized by Word as a main document linked to the specific data source that you specified.

4. Use the **Merge** button under the section heading *3 Merge the Data with the Document* heading to merge the documents.

Understanding Mail Merge Helper

Word's built-in Mail Merge Helper guides you through the process of creating main documents and data sources and merging them. As you progress through the steps in the sequence, the variations depend on your previous responses. Just carefully read the instructions as you progress and you can create or open a main document and a data source and then merge them.

☐ **5-1 CONCEPTS.** In this section you interactively explore the concepts of mail merge.

☐ **5-1 TUTORIAL.** In this tutorial you are introduced to Mail Merge Helper using two existing documents. The main document contains merge fields that will print names and company information on name tags. The data source is a Word table that contains information on four individuals.

☐ **5-1 DRILL.** Whenever you need to make multiple copies of the same document, Mail Merge is very useful. In this drill you use Word's Mail Merge Helper to merge a data source containing names, departments, and phone numbers with a main document formatted as a name tag.

5-2 MAIL-MERGING FORM LETTERS

One of the most common uses of Mail Merge is the printing of form letters. It's an easy process since Word's Mail Merge Helper is designed to lead you step by step through the preparation of a main document and a data source and then merging the two.

Not all data merged into the main document has to come from the data source. You can insert merge fields that display a prompt during merging that asks you to enter data from the keyboard. For example, the FILLIN field prompts you to type data that is then merged into the document at the place where the FILL-IN field is entered.

QUICKSTEPS

Merging Your Own Documents

1. Open a new document or open an existing document that you want to use as a main document for your form letter.

2. Pull down the **Tools** menu and click the **Mail Merge** command to display the Mail Merge Helper dialog box.

3. Complete each of the three steps **Create**, **Get Data**, and **Merge** in order and follow the instructions that appear on the screen during the procedure. When working on the main document, use the command buttons on the toolbar to insert merge fields or Word fields. These buttons are described in the box "Understanding the Mail Merge Toolbar."

4. Save the finished main document.

When you are working on a main document, the Mail Merge toolbar is displayed. You use the buttons on this bar to enter merge fields into the main document, preview merged data, merge the documents, and find and edit records in the data source.

Check for Errors checks to see if there are any errors in the merge fields and reports any that it finds.

Merge to New Document merges the main document and data source to a new document on the screen so you can check it before printing.

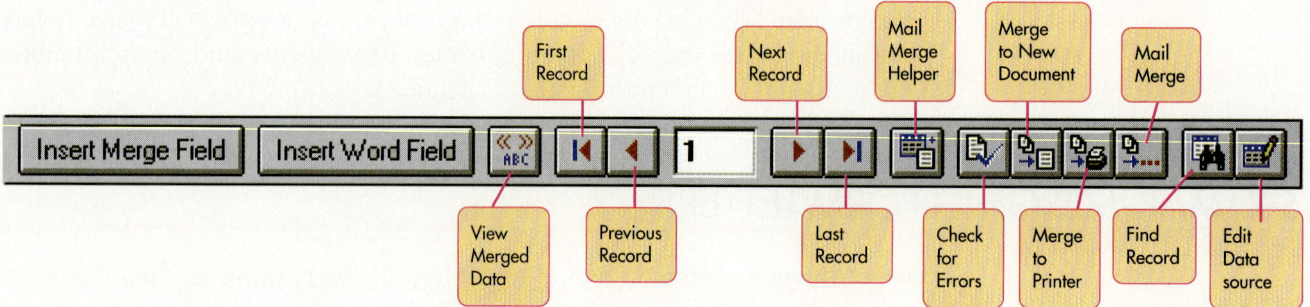

Insert Merge Field displays a list of the field names in the data source which you can insert into the main document. For example, if the data source has a field named *Company*, selecting that name from the list will insert a field «*Company*» in the main document, and data stored in the *Company* field of the data source will be inserted in that location in place of the merge field in each document that is merged.

Insert Word Field displays a list of other fields you can insert into the document. For example, inserting the **Fill-in** field in a main document will display a dialog box into which you can type the requested information which is then inserted into a single copy of the merged document.

View Merged Data replaces merge fields in the main document on screen with data from the first record in the data source. This allows you to preview your results before you merge the documents. You can also use the buttons described below to scroll through the data source record by record.

First Record, **Previous Record**, **Go to Record**, **Next Record**, and **Last Record** buttons scroll you through records in the data source when you are viewing merged data.

Mail Merge Helper displays the Mail Merge Helper dialog box.

Merge to Printer merges the main document and data source directly to the printer.

Mail Merge displays the Merge dialog box where you can specify if the merge is to a new document, the printer, or electronic mail, specify the records in the data source to be merged if you don't want to merge all of them, and specify whether blank lines are printed when a data field on a line by itself is empty.

Find record displays a dialog box in which you specify a field in the **In Field** drop-down list and its contents in the **Find What** text box so you can locate any matching records. The number of any found record is listed on the status bar, and you can click the **Edit Data Source** button on the Mail Merge toolbar to display it. (If you click the **Edit Data Source** button on the Mail Merge toolbar to display the data form, you can also click its **Find** button to locate records.)

Edit Data Source displays the Data Form dialog box listing records in the data source so you can edit, add, or delete records.

PAL ON-LINE ACTIVITIES CHECKLIST

☐ **5-2 CONCEPTS.** In this section you interactively explore the concepts of mail merging form letters.

☐ **5-2 TUTORIAL.** In this tutorial you use Mail Merge Helper to create a data source with four records which you then merge with a form letter confirming appointment times and dates. Since the times and dates vary widely when sending confirmations, that data is not stored in the data source. Instead,

merge fields are inserted into the main document that will prompt you to enter
this information from the keyboard when merging the documents.

Salutation
~~Title~~
FirstName
LastName
~~JobTitle~~
Company
Address1
~~Address2~~
City
State
PostalCode
~~Country~~
~~HomePhone~~
~~WorkPhone~~

Field Names to Delete

Salutation
FirstName
LastName
Company
Address1
City
State
PostalCode

Field Names to Use

Field Names	Record 1	Record 2	Record 3	Record 4
Salutation	Mrs.	Ms.	Mrs.	yours
FirstName	Suzanne	Kim	Debbie	yours
LastName	Steven	Foley	Star	yours
Company	3D Graphics	Virtual Reality		yours
Address1	1 Pierce Street	60 Friend Street	1 Oak Road	yours
City	Saratoga	Beverly	Marblehead	yours
State	CA	MA	MA	yours
PostalCode	95070	01915	01945	yours

Records to Enter

«Salutation» «FirstName» «LastName»
«Company»
«Address1»
«City», «State» «PostalCode»

Dear «Salutation» «LastName»:

I am pleased to confirm your appointment at my office.

Sincerely yours,

your name

The Main Document

Appointment Times and Dates		
Letter	**Time**	**Date**
1	9:00 a.m.	June 1, 1997
2	2:00 p.m.	June 3, 1997
3	10:00 a.m.	June 4, 1997
4	1:00 p.m.	June 5, 1997

☐ **5-2 DRILL.** The most common application of Mail Merge is the printing of form letters. In this drill you use Word's Mail Merge Helper to create a very simple data source and main document and then merge them.

STAFF DATA		
FirstName	**JobTitle**	**WorkPhone**
Betty	Accounting	1002
Bob	Manufacturing	1005
Jose	Sales	1008

Your Name

Name: «FirstName»
Department: «JobTitle»
Extension: «WorkPhone»

The Staff Main Document

5-3 MAIL MERGING LABELS

Once you have created a data source for form letters, you can also use it to print mailing labels or envelopes. To print labels, you create a main document by specifying the type of labels you want to print on and then enter merge fields that print the data you want to appear on the labels. When you then merge the main document, all of the labels are automatically filled in from the associated data source.

PAL ON-LINE ACTIVITIES CHECKLIST

☐ **5-3 CONCEPTS.** In this section you interactively explore the concepts of mail merging labels.

☐ **5-3 TUTORIAL.** In this tutorial you use Word's Mail Merge Helper to create a main document to print mailing labels. The data source is a list of some of the leading companies on the Fortune 500 list. The names and addresses of the companies are already stored in a data source file on the disk.

«SAL» «FIRST» «LAST»
«COMPANY»
«STREET»
«CITY», «ST» «ZIP»

The Label Fields

5-3 DRILL. Printing labels is one of the leading applications of Mail Merge. In this drill you create a main document that prints labels using an existing data source already on the *Word Student Resource Disk*.

```
Your Name
«COMPANY»
«STREET»
«CITY», «ST» «ZIP»
```

Sample Label

5-4 SELECTING SPECIFIC RECORDS TO MERGE

There are times when you do not want to merge all of the records in the data source. You may want to merge letters just to people in New York, or to those that owe over $100. In these cases, you merge as you normally would but when the Mail Merge Helper dialog box is displayed, you click the **Query Options** command button and then specify conditions to filter or sort records to be merged. The choices you can make when querying a data source are described in the box "Understanding The Query Options Dialog Box."

UNDERSTANDING
The Query Options Dialog Box

When you click the **Query Options** command button in the Mail Merge Helper dialog box, the Query Options dialog box is displayed. You can then click the **Filter Records** or **Sort Records** tabs to make them active.

The Filter Records Tab

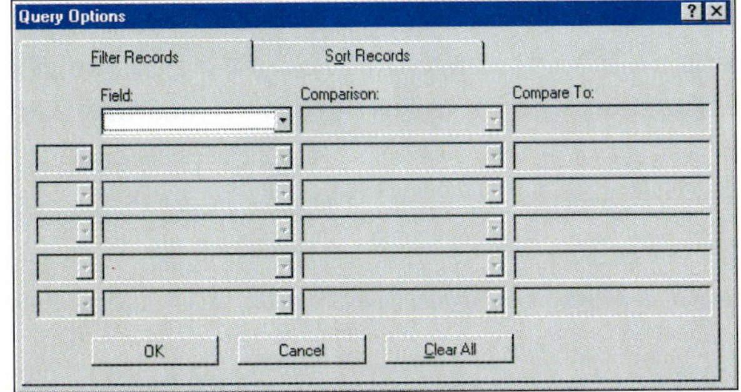

Field drop-down arrows (▼) display the names of fields in the data source so you can select one.

Comparison drop-down arrows (▼) displays a list of comparison operators that compare one value to another. For example, **Equal to** will print all records that match the entry in the **Compare** text box next to it. **Greater than** will print records with larger numbers or that appear alphabetically later.

Compare text boxes are where you enter what the field is being searched for. For example, if the **Field** is *State* and

the **Comparison** is *Equal to*, entering **NY** here will merge only records with NY is the State field.

The Sort Records Tab

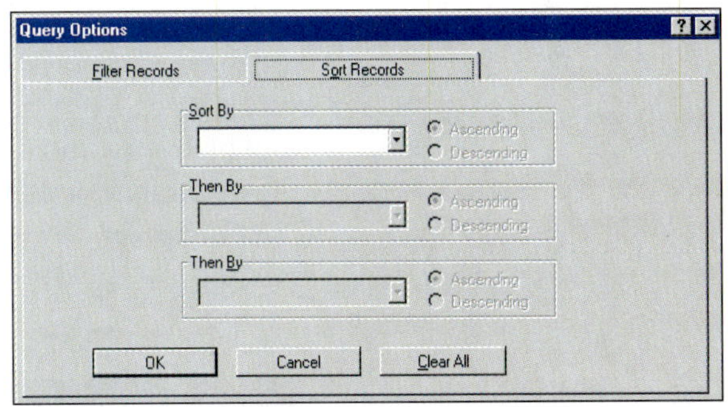

Sort By specifies the first field to sort by. Click the **Ascending** or **Descending** option button to specify the order of the sort.

Then By specifies the second field to sort by. This field will break any ties in the first sort by subsorting the list based on the contents of this field. Click the **Ascending** or **Descending** option button to specify the order of the sort.

Then By specifies the third field to sort by. Click the **Ascending** or **Descending** option button to specify the order of the sort.

☐**5-4 CONCEPTS**. In this section you interactively explore the concepts of mail merging selected records.

☐**5-4 TUTORIAL**. In this tutorial you use the *Labels* main document that you created in Section 5-3 to merge just selected labels from the *Fortune 500 companies* data source.

☐**5-4 DRILL**. As you have seen, it isn't necessary to merge all of the names in a data source. In this drill you merge only those records with Massachusetts addresses.

5-5 AUTOMATING WITH MACROS

Since many of the tasks you perform while working at a computer are repetitive, you often find yourself pressing the same sequence of keys to format text or complete some other complex series of commands. Programs such as Word allow you to create macros that automate these repetitive tasks. Macros are simply a way to record keystrokes so that they can be played back later. Creating a macro is like making a piano into a player piano; the only difference is that the computer's keys do not move up and down—it is all done electronically.

There are two steps to using macros: recording them and then running them. You can record and then run any sequence of keystrokes, including entering text and executing commands. Doing so is easy and can save you a lot of time if you use the same long sequence of commands over and over again.

Recording Macros

To create a macro, you turn on the program's record mode, enter the keystrokes you want to record, and then turn off record mode. In the process you can assign the macro to keys on the keyboard, a menu, or the toolbar so you can quickly execute it later. Keep in mind that a macro is not saved until you save the template in which it is stored. You will be prompted to save the template when you close the document or exit Word. You can also save it using the **Save All** command on the **File** menu.

T I P
Understanding Templates

A *template* is like a plan for a particular type of document. It controls how text, graphics, and formatting are handled and stores specific styles, macros, AutoText entries, toolbar buttons, and customized menu and shortcut key settings. When you open a new document it uses the *Normal* document template unless you specify otherwise. When you record a macro you can specify which document template it is saved to using the **Save Changes In** drop-down list. Normally it is saved to the *Normal* document template so it's available whenever you open a new document using that template.

1. Pull down the **Tools** menu and click the **Macro** command to display the Macro dialog box.

2. Click the **Record** command button to display the Record Macro dialog box.

3. Type a name for the macro in the **Macro Name** text box. The name must begin with a letter and can only contain letters and numbers. (If the name isn't valid, the **OK** button remains dimmed.) If you plan to assign the macro to a menu or the toolbar, enter text in the **Description** text box that will be displayed on the status bar when you highlight the menu command or point to the button on the toolbar.

4. Click **OK** if you don't want to assign the macro and skip to 7 below, or click **Keyboard** in the *Assign Macro To* section (**Toolbars** and **Menus** are not covered in this text) to display the Customize dialog box. **Current Keys** lists the keys already assigned to macros during earlier sessions.

5. With the insertion point in the **Press New Shortcut Key** text box, hold down Alt, Ctrl, or ⇧ Shift and press the key you want to assign the macro to. The area below the text box displays information about whether this key combination is currently assigned to another function. Click the **Assign** button to assign the shortcut key.

6. Click the **Close** command button to close the Customize dialog box. The mouse pointer has the recorder graphic added to it when in the text area to indicate that you are in record mode. Also, the Macro Record toolbar is displayed.

7. Type the text and/or execute the commands you want to record. (When recording a macro, you must use the keyboard to move the insertion point in the document. The mouse pointer has a recorder graphic attached to it when in the text area to indicate that you can't use it to position the insertion point although you can use it to select menu commands and click buttons on the toolbar.) The **Pause** button temporarily pauses it so you can enter commands you don't want recorded. Click the **Pause** button again to resume recording.

8. When finished, click the **Stop** button on the Macro Record toolbar.

Running Macros

Once you have recorded a macro, it is available in all existing and new documents that you create. The way you run it depends on whether or not you added it to a toolbar, menu, or keyboard.

▶ If you did not add the macro to a toolbar, menu, or keyboard, pull down the **Tools** menu and click the **Macro** command to display the Macro dialog box. Click the name of the macro in the **Macro Name** text box and then click the **Run** command button to run the macro.

▶ If you assigned the macro to the keyboard, press the keys you assigned it to.

Editing Macros

Word allows you to edit macros so that you can correct mistakes or add procedures without having to rerecord the text or commands.

Editing a Macro

1. Pull down the **Tools** menu and click the **Macro** command to display the Macro dialog box.

2. Click the name of the macro in the **Macro Name** text box and then click the **Edit** command button to open the macro just as if it were a document.

3. Edit the macro and then save and close it as you'd save or close any document.

☐ **5-5 CONCEPTS.** In this section you interactively explore the concept of using macros.

☐ **5-5 TUTORIAL.** In this tutorial you are introduced to recording a macro and then running it to play back the text and commands it recorded.

☐ **5-5 DRILL.** Macros can take much of the repetition out of word processing. In this drill you record a macro that automatically enters a heading for memos into a document.

INTEROFFICE MEMORANDUM

Date

TO:

FROM:

SUBJECT:

Recorded Memo Heading

5-6 USING AUTOTEXT

When you find yourself entering the same text over and over again, you can store it as AutoText and enter it with a few clicks of the mouse. This is great not only for text, but also for symbols and special characters.

Storing AutoText

1. Select the text you want to store as AutoText, then pull down the **Edit** menu and click the **AutoText** command to display the AutoText dialog box.

2. Type the name you want to store the AutoText entry under into the **Name** text box and click the **Add** button.

Inserting AutoText into a Document

Fastest

▶ Type the name of the AutoText and press F3.

Menus

1. With the insertion point where you want to insert AutoText, pull down the **Edit** menu and click the **AutoText** command to display the AutoText dialog box.

2. Click the name of the AutoText you want to enter in the **Name** list, and click the **Insert** button.

PAL ON-LINE ACTIVITIES CHECKLIST

☐ **5-6 CONCEPTS.** In this section you interactively explore the concept of using AutoText.

☐ **5-6 TUTORIAL.** In this tutorial you add an entry to AutoText and then copy it back into the document.

Sincerely yours, [Enter ↵]
[Enter ↵]
[Enter ↵]
[Enter ↵]
Your Name [Enter ↵]

Letter close

☐ **5-6 DRILL.** Using a macro to store text isn't the only way to automate that procedure. You can also use Word's AutoText command to store any amount of text and then insert it into any document you choose. In this drill you store the memo heading you created in Drill 5-5 as AutoText and then insert it into a new document.

Word's AutoCorrect fixes typing mistakes as you make them. For example, it will automatically change *i* to *I*, *teh* to *the*, and *adn* to *and*. You can also have AutoCorrect convert quote marks and check capitalization. AutoCorrect is normally on and corrects a limited number of preassigned words. However, you can add words to correct or turn AutoCorrect off. You can even add words such as *asap* so they are automatically expanded into *as soon as possible* when you type them and press Spacebar.

QUICKSTEPS

Using AutoCorrect Options

1. Pull down the **Tools** menu and click the **AutoCorrect** command to display the AutoCorrect dialog box.

2. Change any of the settings described in the box "Understanding the AutoCorrect Dialog Box" and then click the command button.

UNDERSTANDING

The AutoCorrect Dialog Box

When you pull down the **Tools** menu and click the **AutoCorrect** command, the AutoCorrect dialog box is displayed. Here are the settings you can change.

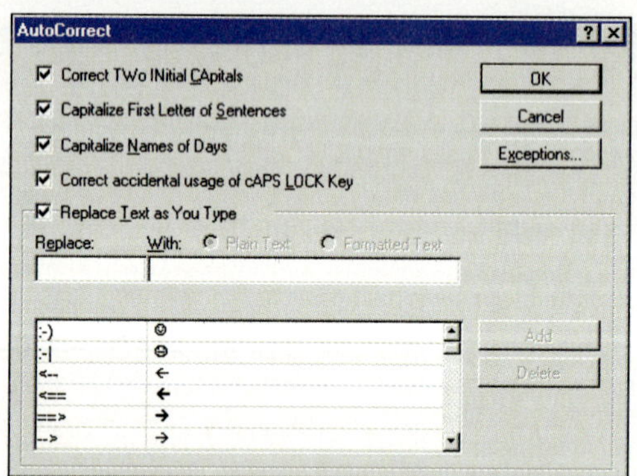

Correct TWo INitial CApitals check box changes the case of the second letter should you type two capital letters to begin a word.

Capitalize First Letter of Sentences check box corrects the case of the first character in a sentence.

Capitalize Names of Days check box corrects the first character in names of days.

Correct accidental usage of cAPS LOCK Key corrects the case of letters when you inadvertently have CapsLock on when typing.

Replace Text as You Type check box turns AutoCorrect on and off.

Replace and **With** text boxes are where you enter the text you type incorrectly and the text you want it changed to.

Add command button adds any entries currently in the **Replace** and **With** text boxes.

Delete command button deletes the highlighted entry in the **Replace** and **With** lists.

TIP

Adding Words to AutoCorrect During Spell-Checking

When spell-checking a document, you can add word pairs to the **Replace** and **With** lists by clicking the **AutoCorrect** command button in the Spelling dialog box. Only click the button when the incorrectly spelled word is displayed in the **Not in Dictionary** text box and the correct spelling is displayed in the **Change To** text box.

☐ **5-7 CONCEPTS**. In this section you interactively explore the concept of using AutoCorrect.

☐ **5-7 TUTORIAL**. In this tutorial you explore how AutoCorrect corrects certain entries as you type them.

AutoCorrect Pairs	
If You Enter	**It is Changed To**
_________	__________
_________	__________
_________	__________
_________	__________
_________	__________
_________	__________
_________	__________

☐ **5-7 DRILL**. Word's AutoCorrect will automatically correct a number of common mistypings and provide other services for you as you type. In this drill you explore how this command works.

> word's AutoCorrect command automatically fixes a lower-case letter beginning a sentence and corrects misspellings such as "teh" and "adn" as soon as you press the spacebar. It also corrects two initial capital letters in a word such as MAine and changes the case of text you typed with Caps Lock on. Finally, it will automatically uppercase the first letter in days of the week such as monday, tuesday, and so on.
>
> your name

The AutoCorrect Document

PicTorial 5
LAB ACTIVITIES

EXERCISES

5-1   Merge-Printing a Form Letter to Computer Companies

In this exercise you use Word's Mail Merge Helper to create a form letter main document and a data source containing names and addresses. You then merge the two files to create letters requesting catalogs from leading computer mail order businesses. In the following exercise, you create a new main document to print mailing labels for the envelopes used to mail the letters.

1. Open a new document and use the **Tools**, **Mail Merge** command to display the Mail Merge Helper.

2. Click the **Create** button under the *Main Document* heading, then specify first **Form Letters** and then **Active Window**.

3. Click the **Get Data** button under the *Data Source* heading and then click **Create Data Source** to display the Create Data Source dialog box. Create a data source containing the five field names: Company, Address1, City, State, and PostalCode by removing all other field names. Save the document as *Computer company list* in the *Exercise Documents* folder on the *Word Student Resource Disk*. Then, click the **Edit Data Source** button and enter the four records shown in the table "Computer Companies." When finished, the main document appears.

Computer Companies				
Company	**Address1**	**City**	**State**	**PostalCode**
PC Connection	6 Mill Street	Marlow	NH	03456
Gateway 2000	610 Gateway Drive	North Sioux City	SD	57049
Dell Computer Corporation	9505 Arboretum Blvd.	Austin	TX	78759
Zeos International, Ltd.	530 5th Avenue N.W.	St. Paul	MN	55112

4. Enter the text shown in the figure "Form Letter to Computer Companies" and use the **Insert Merge Field** button on the Mail Merge toolbar to enter the merge fields shown. Save the main document as *Computer company letter* in the *Exercise Documents* folder on the *Word Student Resource Disk*.

Your Name
Your Street
Your City, State ZIP

Today's date

Catalog Department
«Company»
«Address1»
«City», «State» «PostalCode»

Dear Sir or Madam:

Please send me a catalog of your current computer offerings.

Sincerely yours,

Your name

Form Letter to Computer Companies

5. Click the **Merge to New Document** button on the Mail Merge toolbar to merge the *Computer company list* main document and the *Computer company letter* data source.

6. Print the first page of the merged document and then close the merged document without saving it.

7. Save *Computer company letter* and then close it. When you do so, you are prompted to save the *Computer company list*. Click the **Yes** button to save your data source.

5-2 Merge-Printing Mailing Labels to Computer Companies

In this exercise you use Word's Mail Merge Helper to create mailing labels for the envelopes used to mail the letters to computer companies.

1. Click the **New** button on the Standard toolbar to open a new document.

2. Use the **Tools**, **Mail Merge** command to display the Mail Merge Helper.

3. Click the **Create** button under the *Main Document* heading, specify first **Mailing Labels** and then **Active Window**.

4. Click the **Get Data** button under the *Data Source* heading, then click the **Open Data Source** button and select the *Computer company list* data source stored in the *Exercise Documents* folder on the *Word Student Resource Disk*. When a dialog box appears, click the **Set Up Main Document** button to display the Label Options dialog box.

5. Select a label for the printer type you are using:

   ▶ If you are using a laser printer, click the **Dot Matrix** option button, choose *4603-Address* from the **Product Number** list, and then click the **OK** command button to display the Create Labels dialog box.

   ▶ If you are using a dot matrix printer, click the **Laser** options button, choose *5160-Address* from the **Product Number** list, and then click the **OK** command button to display the Create Labels dialog box.

6. Type **Catalog Department** in the **Sample Label** window, and then use the **Insert Merge Field** button in the dialog box to enter the merge fields shown in the figure "Labels to Computer Companies." When finished, click the **OK** command button to return to the Mail Merge Helper dialog box.

7. Click the **Merge** button in the Mail Merge Helper dialog box and the **Merge** button in the Merge dialog box to merge to a new document.

8. Print the first page of the merged document and then close the merged document without saving it.

9. Save the new main document with the merge fields as *Computer company labels* in the *Exercise Documents* folder on the *Word Student Resource Disk* and then close it.

Catalog Department
«Company»
«Address1»
«City», «State» «PostalCode»

Labels to Computer Companies

5-3 Keyboarding Data into the Letter to Computer Companies

In this exercise you revise the main document requesting a catalog from computer companies so you can type in information specific to each company during the merge.

1. Open the *Computer company list* document stored in the *Exercise Documents* folder on the *Word Student Resource Disk*. This document is the data source you are going to use.

2. Open the *Computer company letter* document stored in the *Exercise Documents* folder on the *Word Student Resource Disk*. This document is the partially completed main document you are going to use. It contains five merge fields that refer to the data source for the company's name and address.

3. With the insertion point to the left of the period at the end of the body paragraph, type **, especially those** (including the comma at the beginning and

the space at the end) and then use the **Insert Word Field** button on the Mail Merge toolbar to enter a **Fill-in** field. When a dialog box asks you to enter the prompt, type **Enter the type of computer that most interests you** and click the next two **OK** command buttons. (To see or hide the field, use the **Tools**, **Options** command and click the **Field Codes** check box on the **View** tab to turn it on or off.)

4. Click the **Save** button on the Standard toolbar to save your changes to the main document. Then click the **Merge to New Document** button on the Mail Merge toolbar. When prompted *Enter the type of computer that most interests you* type one of the following for each letter:

   ▶ **featuring complete multimedia capability** and click **OK**.

   ▶ **with the most recent Intel microprocessors** and click **OK**.

   ▶ **that are low priced** and click **OK**.

   ▶ **that have only recently been introduced** and click **OK**.

5. Scroll through the document to see how the company names and addresses are taken from the data source but the last phrases in the body paragraphs have been entered from the keyboard.

6. Print the first page of the merged document and then close the merged document and *Computer company list* without saving them. However, save *Computer company letter* and then close it.

5-4 Creating Macros to Enter Symbols

One way to enter symbols you use frequently is with a macro. In this exercise you record a series of macros that enter symbols into a document.

1. Open the *Macros to enter symbols* document stored in the *Exercise Documents* folder on the *Word Student Resource Disk* and enter your name, then click anywhere in the date and press `F9` to update it.

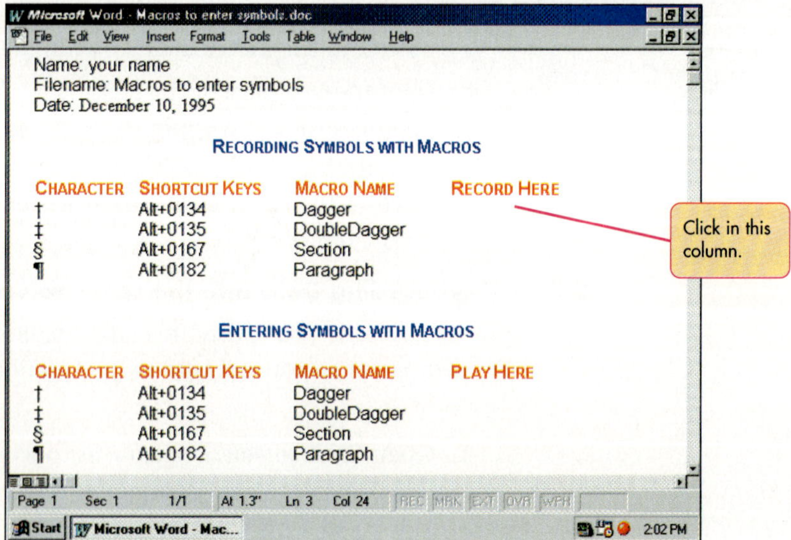

2. Position the insertion point in the column that reads *Record Here* on any row of the table in the top half of the screen, then:

   ▶ Use the **Tools**, **Macro**, **Record** command to display the Macro dialog box.

   ▶ In the **Record Macro Name** text box, enter the name given in the *Macro*

Name column on the same row of the table, then click the **OK** command button to begin recording.

> ▸ Press NumLock to turn it on, then hold down Alt and type the numbers shown in the *Shortcut Keys* column on the same row of the table. You must type them using the numeric keypad.

> ▸ Press NumLock to turn it off, then click the **Stop** button on the Record Macro toolbar to end recording.

> ▸ Repeat this procedure for each of the other characters described in the top half of the screen.

3. Position the insertion point in the column that reads *Play Here* on any row of the table in the lower half of the screen, then use the **Tools**, **Macro** command to run the macro named on the same row of the table.

4. Use the **Tools**, **Macro** command to delete all of the macros that you created.

5. Save, print, and then close the document.

5–1   Mail-Merging the Cover Letter

When you hear stories about people sending out 10,000 résumés to find a job, you hope they are using some form of automation. In this project you convert your cover letter to a main document and then use the *Fortune 500 companies* list of company names to mail merge copies.

1. Open the *Cover letter* document that you are created and saved in the *Project Documents* folder on the *Word Student Resource Disk*.

2. Display Mail Merge Helper and use *Cover letter* as the main document form letter and *Computer company list* in the *Exercise Documents* folder on the *Word Student Resource Disk* as the data source.

3. Edit *Cover letter* to replace the inside address with field names from the *Computer company list* data source. Change the salutation line to read *Dear Sir or Madam*. Save the changes.

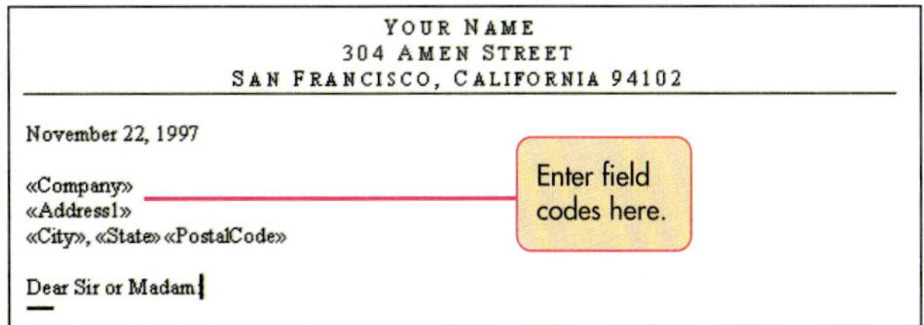

4. Merge the two documents to a new document, then print the first page of the merged document and close it without saving it. Close all other open documents and save any changes when prompted to do so.

DESKTOP PUBLISHING

After completing this PicTorial, you will be able to:

- Add borders and shading to paragraphs
- Generate tables of contents
- Print in two or more columns
- Insert pictures into your documents
- Create and format tables

No course is long enough to introduce you to all of the features of a program as powerful as Word. What you have learned so far are the basic and most frequently used features of the program. In this PicTorial we introduce you to a few of the features used in desktop publishing—preparing documents that look as if they had been printed by a professional printer. Special programs exist for desktop publishing, but today many desktop publishing features have been added to word processing programs such as Word. In this PicTorial you learn about those features including borders and shading, tables of contents, columns, pictures, and tables.

You can add borders and shading to paragraphs to set them off from other elements or to make them look more attractive. You can do so from the toolbar or with menu commands.

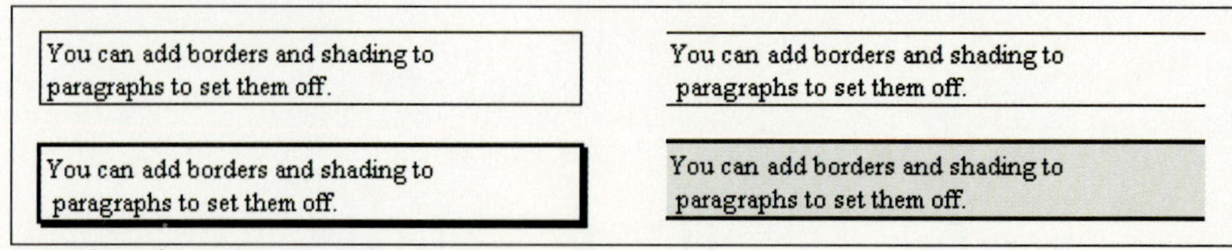

Samples of borders and shading

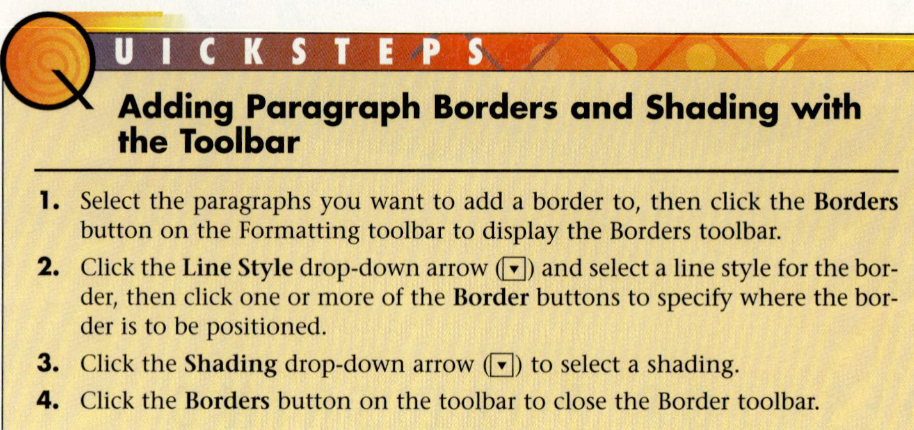

Adding Paragraph Borders and Shading with the Toolbar

1. Select the paragraphs you want to add a border to, then click the **Borders** button on the Formatting toolbar to display the Borders toolbar.
2. Click the **Line Style** drop-down arrow (▾) and select a line style for the border, then click one or more of the **Border** buttons to specify where the border is to be positioned.
3. Click the **Shading** drop-down arrow (▾) to select a shading.
4. Click the **Borders** button on the toolbar to close the Border toolbar.

The Formatting toolbar

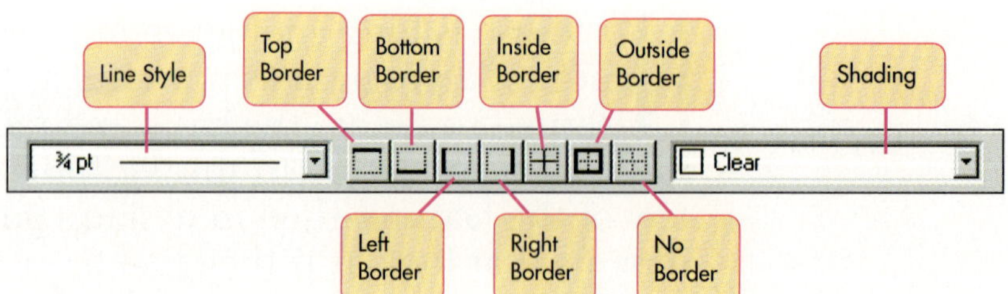

The Borders toolbar

Adding Paragraph Borders and Shading with the Menu

1. Select the paragraphs you want to add a border or shading to, then pull down the **Format** menu and click the **Borders and Shading** command to display the Paragraph Borders and Shading dialog box.

2. Make any of the settings described in the box "Understanding the Paragraph Borders and Shading Dialog Box."

3. Click the **OK** command button to close the dialog box and apply the formats.

UNDERSTANDING
Understanding the Paragraph Borders and Shading Dialog Box

When you pull down the **format** menu and click the **Borders and Shading** command, the Paragraph Borders and Shading dialog box is displayed. Here are the choices.

Line section lets you click a line **Style** to select its width or type, and click the **Color** drop-down arrow (▼) to select a line color. Click the **None** option button on to remove any lines.

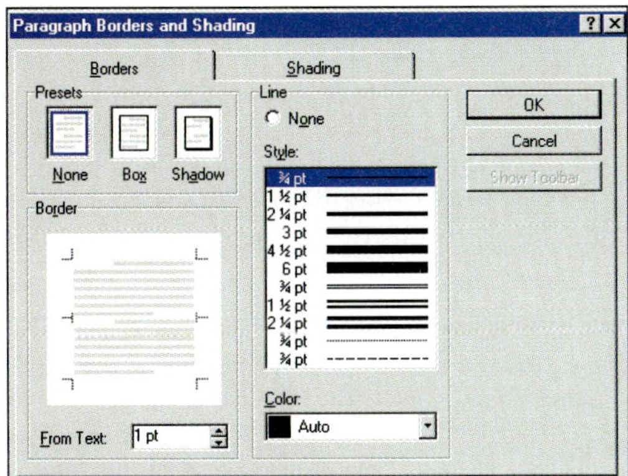

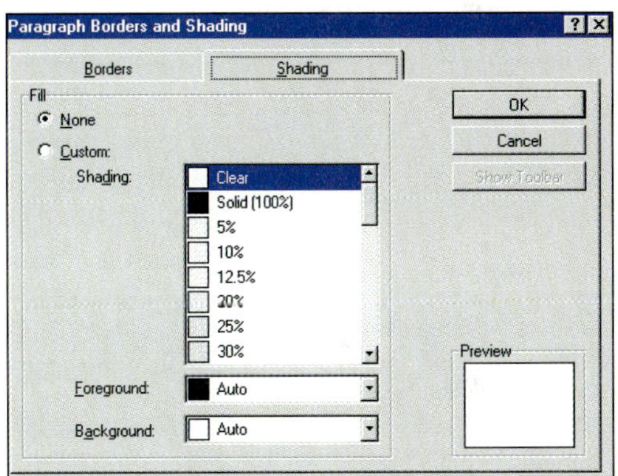

Borders Tab

Presets section lets you click a graphic to select a pre-designed **Box** or **Shadow** border, or click **None** to remove any border you previously applied.

Border model allows you to click various sides of the graphic to place the line currently selected in the *Line* section. You can use this command to make all four sides the same or different. Just select a new line and click a border when you want to change the format. Clicking in the middle of the box adds horizontal lines below each paragraph in the selection. (The four outer sides of the graphic specify the outline around multiple paragraphs.).

From Text spin buttons (▲▼) specify the distance between a border and the text within it.

Shading Tab

None turns off any previously applied shading.

Custom allows you to then specify a color or pattern:

▶ **Shading** adds a gray shading or any color selected in the **Background** box in densities between 5 and 90 percent or one of twelve patterns. **Clear** applies the color shown in the **Background** box and **Solid (100%)** applies the color shown in the **Foreground** box.

▶ **Foreground** specifies the colors used for the dots and lines in the selected pattern. **Auto** usually displays as black.

▶ **Background** specifies the background color used for shading. **Auto** usually displays as white.

Most printers don't print colors even though you can use colors in the document. When you print a document with colors, each of them prints in its own shade of gray.

PAL ON-LINE ACTIVITIES CHECKLIST

☐ **6-1 CONCEPTS.** In this section you interactively explore the concept of adding borders and shading to paragraphs.

☐ **6-1 TUTORIAL.** In this tutorial you explore adding borders and shading to set off the heading in the *EDUCOM* document.

☐ **6-1 DRILL.** Adding borders around paragraphs is a great way to make them stand out from the rest of the document. In this drill you copy a key phrase from the document and enclose it in a border. This kind of box, used in newspaper and magazine articles, is called a "pull quote." It is designed to catch your interest as you browse so you will then read the entire article.

6-2 GENERATING A TABLE OF CONTENTS

When working on a long document with many headings, you often need to prepare a table of contents to help readers find the information they need. Manually preparing a table of contents takes a great deal of time; moreover, if any revisions are made in the document, all page number references might have to be changed. Word has automated the preparation of tables of contents to make it easy for you.

PICTORIAL 6

DESKTOP PUBLISHING

6-1. ADDING PARAGRAPH BORDERS AND SHADING	2
6-2. GENERATING A TABLE OF CONTENTS	5
CREATING A TABLE OF CONTENTS	6
UPDATING A TABLE OF CONTENTS	7
6-3. FORMATTING IN COLUMNS	9
FORMATTING COLUMNS FROM THE TOOLBAR	10
FORMATTING COLUMNS FROM THE MENU	10
6-4. INSERTING PICTURES	13
INSERTING PICTURES	14
MOVING AND SIZING PICTURES	15
6-5. CREATING TABLES	17
6-6. FORMATTING AND EDITING TABLES	20
AUTOFORMATTING TABLES	20
SELECTING CELLS, ROWS, AND COLUMNS	21
CHANGING COLUMN WIDTHS	21
INSERTING CELLS, ROWS, AND COLUMNS	22
DELETING CELLS, ROWS, AND COLUMNS	22
DELETING TABLES	22

An automatically generated table of contents with page numbers

Creating a Table of Contents

To insert a table of contents the first step is to format the entries you want to appear in it with styles. Styles are formats that have been saved for later use. For example, you can create and save a style that formats a main heading (called *Heading 1*) so that it is printed in bold, 14 point type, with more space above it than below it. When you then save this format as a style, you can apply it to any heading just by selecting its name *Heading 1* from a drop-down list on the toolbar. However, to use styles you needn't know how to create them. Word has a number of them already defined for you. To use them you just select the paragraph you want to apply them to and select them from the **Style** drop-down list on the toolbar. It is these predefined styles you use to create a table of contents.

QUICKSTEPS

Applying Heading Styles for Table of Contents Entries

1. Click in each heading that you want listed in the table of contents, click the **Style** drop-down arrow (▼) on the toolbar, and click *Heading 1* through *Heading 3* depending on the level of the entry.

2. Click in the document where you want the table of contents to appear—usually on a line by itself.

3. Pull down the **Insert** menu, click the **Index and Tables** command to display the Index and Tables dialog box, and on the **Table of Contents** tab make any of the settings described in the box "Understanding the Table Of Contents Tab."

4. Click the **OK** command button to insert the table of contents.

UNDERSTANDING
The Table of Contents Tab

When you display the **Table of Contents** tab on the Index and Tables dialog box you use the options to specify the design of your table of contents. The results of the current settings are displayed in the **Preview** box.

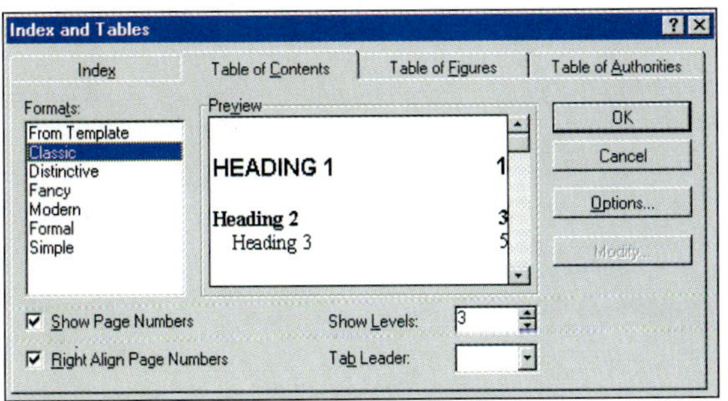

Formats allows you to choose one of seven predefined formats. As you click each format name, its appearance is displayed in the **Preview** box. (If you select the **From Template** choice, you can click the **Modify** button to change its formats using styles which are beyond this text.)

Show Page Numbers check box, when on (☑), adds page numbers to each entry in the table of contents.

Right Align Page Numbers check box, when on (☑), aligns page numbers in the table of contents with the right margin.

Show Levels spin buttons (⬍) set the number of levels to appear in the table of contents. You don't have to list all of the heading levels that you applied styles to.

Tab Leader drop-down arrow (▼) adds leaders of your choice between the entries and the page numbers in the table of contents.

Updating a Table of Contents

When you make changes to a document after you have created a table of contents, you may have to update the table to be sure that it's accurate. A table of contents is a field so you can update it the way you update any field.

QUICKSTEPS

Updating a Table of Contents

Do one of the following:

▶ Click the table of contents, then press F9. Specify if you want to update just the page numbers or the entire table and click the **OK** button.

▶ Right-click the table of contents, and then click the shortcut menu's **Update Field** command. Specify if you want to update just the page numbers or the entire table and click the **OK** button.

PAL ON-LINE ACTIVITIES CHECKLIST

☐ **6-2 CONCEPTS.** In this section you interactively explore the concept of automatically creating a table of contents.

☐ **6-2 TUTORIAL.** In this tutorial you apply heading styles to the *EDUCOM* document and then use those headings to generate a table of contents.

SOFTWARE AND INTELLECTUAL RIGHTS
QUESTIONS YOU MAY HAVE ABOUT USING SOFTWARE
ALTERNATIVES TO EXPLORE
A FINAL NOTE

Site-Licensed and Bulk-Purchased Software
Shareware
Public Domain Software

☐ **6-2 DRILL.** A table of contents makes it easier for the reader to grasp a long document's contents and to locate items of interest. In this drill you insert a table of contents for the document on clouds.

IDENTIFICATION
HIGH CLOUDS
     Cirrus
     Cirrocumulus
     Cirrostratus
MIDDLE CLOUDS
     Altocumulus
     Altostratus
     Altocumulus Castellanus
     Standing Lenticular Altocumulus Clouds
     Nimbostratus
LOW CLOUDS
     Stratus
     Stratocumulus
     Cumulus
     Towering Cumulus
     Cumulonimbus
CLOUDS WITH EXTENSIVE VERTICAL DEVELOPMENT

Table of Contents Headings

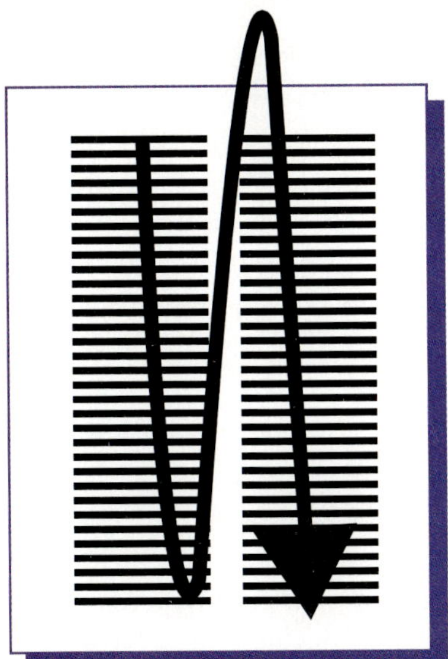

Text flow in newspaper columns

Word makes it easy to format a document in columns. Commonly called *newspaper-style columns* or *snaking columns*, they are just like those you see in newspapers, newsletters, and books. As you enter text, it gradually fills the first column. When that column is full, text flows into the next column. When the last column on the page is full, text starts to fill the first column on the next page. If you add text to or delete text from any of the columns, the following text moves down or up in the columns.

Formatting Columns from the Toolbar

You can format the entire document in columns using the **Columns** button on the toolbar. However, if you select text first and then use the **Columns** button, only the selected section is affected. Word automatically puts section breaks above and below the formatted text.

QUICKSTEPS

Formatting in Columns Using the Toolbar

1. Leave the insertion point anywhere in the document to format it all, or select the text you want to be in columns.
2. Click the **Columns** button on the toolbar, then click the column you want to be the rightmost column in the document. For example, click the second column for a two-column document.
3. Click the **Page Layout View** button to see the columns side by side on the screen. (In normal view they are shown as a long narrow column.)

Formatting Columns from the Menu

When you want more control over how your columns look, you use menu commands and specify options in the Columns dialog box. Using the menu allows you to format the entire document, a selected area of the document, or all of the document from the insertion point forward. This last choice is ideal when you want everything in two or three columns but the heading.

QUICKSTEPS

Formatting in Columns Using the Menu

1. Move the insertion point to where columns are to begin, or select the text you want to be in columns.
2. Pull down the **Format** menu and click the **Columns** command to display the Columns dialog box.
3. Enter any of the settings described in the box "Understanding the Columns Dialog Box."
4. Click the **OK** command button.
5. Click the **Page Layout View** button to see the columns side by side on the screen.

UNDERSTANDING
The Columns Dialog Box

When you use the **Format**, **Columns** command, the Columns dialog box appears. You use the settings in this box to define the way you want your columns laid out on the page. A preview of the current settings is always displayed in the Preview box.

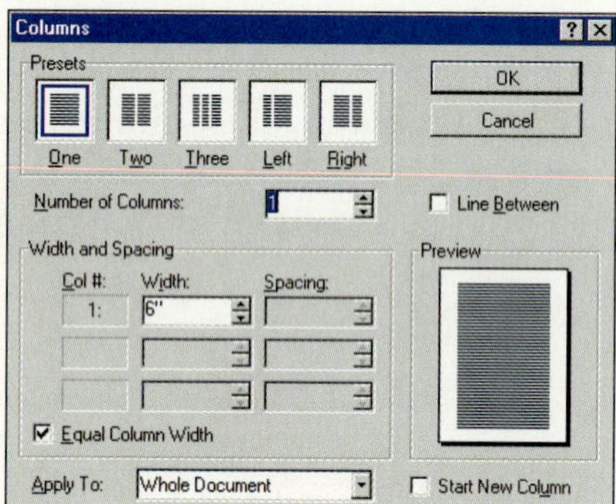

Presets section provides you with five column formats from which to choose.

Number of Columns spin buttons () specify the number of columns and makes them all equal width with equal spacing between them.

Line Between check box, when on (☑), prints a vertical line between columns.

Width and Spacing section displays settings for predefined columns, but you can also enter your own **Width** and **Spacing** for each.

Equal Column Width check box, when on (☑), sets all columns to the same width.

Apply To drop-down arrow (▾) lets you specify if the columns apply to the whole document, selected text, selected sections, or from the insertion point forward.

Start New Column check box, when on (☑), starts a new column at the insertion point.

TIP
Columns and the Ruler Bar

With the insertion point in text formatted in columns, the horizontal ruler looks different than it normally looks. It works the same way it does in normal text, but there is a set of margin borders for each of the columns. This allows you to adjust margins for each column separately.

TIP
Column Breaks

To start a new column when another isn't full, press Ctrl+⇧Shift+Enter↵ or pull down the **Insert** menu, click the **Break** command to display the Break menu, click the **Column Break** option button to turn it on, and then click the **OK** command button.

PAL ON-LINE ACTIVITIES CHECKLIST

☐ **6-3 CONCEPTS.** In this section you interactively explore the concept of formatting in two or more columns.

☐ **6-3 TUTORIAL.** In this tutorial, you format all or part of the *Software rights and responsibilities* document in two and three columns using both the toolbar and the menu.

☐ **6-3 DRILL.** Long documents can often be shortened somewhat and made easier to read by formatting them in multiple columns. In this drill you format the document on clouds in first two and then three columns.

Pictures (also called illustrations or graphics) can add greatly to the interest level of a document. For example, charts, maps, and graphs can provide detail in a compressed form, photographs can show people or places, and line drawings can add decoration. You can also use pictures for such things as letterheads and facsimile signatures.

Inserting Pictures

Word allows you to insert pictures directly into your document and to move and change their size once they are there. Word also comes with many pictures, called clip art, that you can insert into a document. And the Microsoft Office CD contains more clip art in the *valupack\clipart* folder. Any of this art that has been installed on your system is likely to be stored in the folder *c:\msoffice\clipart*.

Sample clip art provided with Word

TIP
Pictures Slowing Down Your System?

Displaying pictures on the screen can bring some systems to a crawl. To hide pictures on the screen (but not the printout) to speed things up, pull down the **Tools** menu, click the **Options** command to display the Options dialog box, and on the **View** tab turn on the **Picture Placeholders** check box. This will display boxes on the screen where the pictures will print.

QUICKSTEPS

Inserting a Picture in a Document

1. Position the insertion point where you want the picture to appear—usually on a line by itself.

2. Pull down the **Insert** menu and click the **Picture** command to display the Insert Picture dialog box.

3. Select the picture's file in the same way you select a document's when you want to open it. (Some clipart is usually located in the *c:\msoffice\clipart* folder.) If you turn on the **Link to File** check box, the picture will be linked to the file instead of being embedded in it. (Linking and embedding are discussed in PicTorial 7.) The **Save Picture in Document** check box is on only when **Link to File** is also. When on, a copy of the linked picture file is saved in the document.

4. Click the **Open** command button to insert the picture in the document.

Moving and Sizing Pictures

When a picture is selected, it has small black squares, called handles, on each corner and each side. You can drag any one of these handles to change the picture's size. To select a picture, click it (to unselect a picture click anywhere in the document outside of it.) When selected, you can format the picture, drag it elsewhere in existing text, and size it with the handles.

6-5 CREATING TABLES

Tables are made up of rows that run horizontally and columns that run vertically. These elements are indicated by dotted gridlines on the screen. The intersections of rows and columns are called cells, and cells are where you enter data into the table. As you type data into a cell, text will wrap when it hits the margin, and the depth of the cell will adjust automatically.

You can either create a table from scratch and enter data into it or you can convert a table with tabbed columns to a Word table. When you create a table from scratch, you specify how many rows and columns it should have, and then Word divides the screen so each column is of equal width. When you select a table with tabbed columns and create a table, the tab stops in the table determine the width of columns in the new table.

Word's Table Wizard makes it easy to create tables of data. Table Wizard guides you through the process of creating the table by asking you questions about column and row headers, cell formats, and other elements. As you answer the questions, it builds and formats the table for you.

When entering data in a table, you can press `Tab` to move the insertion point from cell to cell. If you press `Tab` with the insertion point in the last cell on the last row, you will add a new row to the table. To insert a tab character in a cell, press `Ctrl`+`Tab`.

TIP

Converting Tabbed Columns into a Table

If a tabbed table already exists, you can select it and then click the **Insert Table** button on the toolbar to convert it to a table. The width of all columns in the table, except the last, will be determined by tab stops you have entered. If you haven't entered any, the columns will be of equal width.

TIP

Using Gridlines

When entering data into a table, it helps to know where the cells are. To display them, pull down the Table menu and click the **Gridlines** command. These lines will not print; they are displayed on the screen only.

☐ **6-5 CONCEPTS.** In this section you interactively explore the concept of inserting a table into a document.

☐ **6-5 TUTORIAL.** In this tutorial, you use Word's table feature to create a résumé, a document that is usually very difficult to format.

	YOUR NAME 216 ORCHARD PARK ROAD READING, MASSACHUSETTS 01866 (617) 555-1212
Objective [Tab⇆]	To obtain a teaching position in an Early Childhood Special Needs setting [Tab⇆]
Education [Tab⇆]	Westfield State College (Westfield, MA) [Enter↵] Young Children with Special Needs major (BED) [Enter↵] Expected graduation date, May 1997 [Tab⇆]
Teacher Training Experience [Tab⇆]	■ Brightwood Elementary School, Springfield, MA [Enter↵] Student teacher in an integrated preschool [Enter↵] ■ Woodland Elementary School, Southwick, MA [Enter↵] Practicum in an integrated preschool [Enter↵] ■ Juniper Park Campus Elementary School, Westfield, MA [Enter↵] Pre-practicum in first grade [Tab⇆]
Work Experience [Tab⇆]	■ Cradle Beach Camp, Angola, NY [Enter↵] Summer camp counselor for children who were physically disabled, mentally disabled, and/or disadvantaged [Enter↵] ■ Reading, MA: part-time jobs while in school, at retail stores, food markets, and a nursing home [Tab⇆]
Certifications and Memberships [Tab⇆]	■ Massachusetts Certification in Young Children with Special Needs (Ages 3-7) [Enter↵] ■ Member, Association of Adults with Learning Disabilities

The résumé

TIP
Creating a Table

▶ Press [Tab⇆] to move the insertion point to the next cell (where shown with [Tab⇆] symbols in the figure). When you press [Tab⇆] with the insertion point at the end of any text in a cell in the lower-right column, a new row is added to the table.

▶ Don't press [Enter↵] within a cell when typing a paragraph. The paragraph will automatically wrap within the cell and the cell will expand to accommodate it.

▶ Press [Enter↵] within a cell to start a new line (where shown with [Enter↵] symbols in the figure). The cell will expand for the new line.

▶ To enter the bullets, pull down the **Insert** menu and click the **Symbol** command to display the Symbol dialog box. On the **Symbols** tab, select *Wingdings* from the **Font** drop-down list, click the 6th character from the right on the 3rd row, and then click the **Insert** button. Click the **Close** button to close the Symbol dialog box. (You may want to insert one symbol this way and then copy and paste the rest.)

▶ When you complete the last line, click outside the table.

☐ **6-5 DRILL.** One of the most useful features of tables created with Word's **Table** command is the way text entries will wrap in a cell. When working with tabbed columns, this doesn't happen. In this drill you convert a table laid out in tabbed columns to a Word table.

6-6 FORMATTING AND EDITING TABLES

Once you have created a table, you can easily edit or format it so it looks exactly as you want it to look.

AutoFormatting Tables

Once you have created a table, you can quickly format it using Word's Table AutoFormat command. You can also format part or all of the table using the **Format** menu's **Borders and Shading** command just as you would format regular paragraphs.

AutoFormatting a Table

1. Click anywhere in the table, pull down the **Table** menu, and click the **Table AutoFormat** command to display the Table AutoFormat dialog box.

2. Click any format on the **Formats** list to select it and display a preview in the Preview box.

3. Click any check boxes in the *Formats to Apply* or *Apply Special Formats To* sections to turn them on or off. (Click the dialog box's **Help** button for a description of these options.)

4. Click the **OK** command button to format the table.

Selecting Cells, Rows, and Columns

When editing and formatting tables, you usually begin by selecting the cells, rows, or columns you want to format. You can select cells by putting the insertion point in one of the cells and then holding down the left button as you drag the highlight. You can also click in one cell and then hold down `⇧ Shift` while you click in another to select all cells between the two. Finally, you can select cells using commands on the Table menu or by clicking, as shown in the table "Selecting Cells, Rows, and Columns."

Selecting Cells, Rows, and Columns	
To Select	**Click**
Cell	Click the cell's selection area—the narrow area just to the right of the cell's left border.
Row	Click the row's selection area—the area to the left of the table.
Column	Click the top gridline or border.
Table	Click in the table, then press `Alt`+`5` on the numeric keypad (`NumLock` must be off)

Changing Column Widths

To change a column's width, point to its right boundary gridline, and the mouse pointer turns into a two-headed arrow. With the mouse pointer in this form, hold down the left mouse button and drag the column wider or narrower. As you do so, the other columns to its right change size proportionally and the overall table width remains unchanged. To have the column widths displayed on the ruler, hold down [Alt] as you drag the boundary.

T I P
Changing Table Column Widths

When dragging table column boundaries to change column widths, there are options you can use.

▶ To move just the boundary you are pointing to (and change the width of the columns to the left and right), hold down [⇧ Shift] while dragging.

▶ To change the width of the column to the left of the gridline you point to and leave all other columns the same width, hold down [Ctrl]+[⇧ Shift] while dragging. This changes the overall size of the table.

Inserting Cells, Rows, and Columns

To insert rows or columns in a table, begin by selecting the same number of rows or columns that you want to insert. For example, to insert two new rows, select two rows in the table. New rows will be inserted above the rows you select, and new columns will be inserted to the left of the columns you select.

Once you have selected rows or columns, use commands on the **Table** menu to make the insertion, or click the **Insert Table** button on the toolbar. The name of the button changes to **Insert Rows**, **Insert Cells**, or **Insert Columns** depending on what you have selected.

To insert a row at the bottom of the table, position the insertion point in the lower-right cell and press [Tab↹]. To insert a column on the right side of the table, click to the right of the table and click the **Insert Columns** button on the toolbar.

Deleting Cells, Rows, and Columns

You can easily delete cells, rows, or columns. To do so, select the section of the table you want to delete, pull down the **Table** menu and click the **Delete Rows**, **Delete Columns**, or **Delete Cells** command (The command's name changes depending on what you have selected.) If you delete cells but not entire rows or columns, the Delete Cells dialog box asks you how you want the remaining cells to shift.

Deleting Tables

When you no longer need a table, you can delete its structure, its content, or both.

▶ To delete the structure but not the contents, select the entire table, pull down the **Table** menu and click the **Convert Table to Text** command. You can then specify if you want the cell contents separated by paragraph marks, tabs, commas, or other character of your choice.

▶ To delete the contents but not the structure, select all or part of the table and press `Del`.

▶ To delete both structure and contents, select the table, pull down the **Table** menu and select the **Delete Rows** command. You can also select the table and one paragraph mark outside of it and press `Del`.

☐**6-6 CONCEPTS.** In this section you interactively explore the concepts of editing and formatting tables.

☐**6-6 TUTORIAL.** In this tutorial, you revise and format the table you used to create a résumé. You'll practice inserting rows, entering new text, formatting columns, and changing line spacing.

YOUR NAME
216 ORCHARD PARK ROAD
READING, MASSACHUSETTS 01866
(617) 555-1212

OBJECTIVE	To obtain a teaching position in an Early Childhood Special Needs setting
EDUCATION	*Westfield State College* (Westfield, MA) Young Children with Special Needs major (BED) Expected graduation date, May 1997
TEACHER TRAINING EXPERIENCE	■ *Brightwood Elementary School*, Springfield, MA Student teacher in an integrated preschool ■ *Woodland Elementary School*, Southwick, MA Practicum in an integrated preschool ■ *Juniper Park Campus Elementary School*, Westfield, MA Pre-practicum in first grade
WORK EXPERIENCE	■ *Cradle Beach Camp*, Angola, NY Summer camp counselor for children who were physically disabled, mentally disabled, and/or disadvantaged ■ Reading, MA: part-time jobs while in school, at retail stores, food markets, and a nursing home
VOLUNTEER EXPERIENCE	■ Spinning Wheels, Reading, MA ■ Coach for Special Olympics Track and Field for mentally and physically disabled young adults ■ Co-leader for weekend recreational activities for mentally and physically disabled young adults
CERTIFICATIONS AND MEMBERSHIPS	■ Massachusetts Certification in Young Children with Special Needs (Ages 3-7) ■ Member, Association of Adults with Learning Disabilities

The final résumé

☐**6-6 DRILL.** Tables are not only easy to create; they are easy to format. All you have to do is select one or more rows or columns and then use formatting commands to format all of the entries identically. In this drill you format the table you created listing films in which Bugs Bunny is the star.

LAB ACTIVITIES

6-1 Formatting the Job Search Document

In this exercise you desktop-publish the *Job search kit* document by adding paragraph borders, formatting it in two columns with a line between them, and adding a picture to the first page.

1. Open the *Job search kit* document stored in the *Exercise Documents* folder on the *Word Student Resource Disk* and display it in page layout view.

2. Use the **Format**, **Borders and Shading** command to add a border to each of headings *The Cover Letter*, *The Resume*, and *The Followup Letter* that prints a thin line above and below the heading. (On the **Border** graphic in the dialog box, you have to click on the top and bottom borders to add two separate borders. If you make a mistake, click the **None** icon and try again.)

3. Starting with the first body paragraph below the letterhead, use the **Format**, **Columns** command to format the document in two columns with a line between them. Be sure to apply it only to this point forward.

4. On a blank line above the heading *The Cover Letter*, use the **Insert**, **Picture** command to insert the *mail* picture. (It should be in the *C:\msoffice\clipart* folder.)

5. Save the document and print the first page.

6-2 Formatting the Bill of Rights Document

In this exercise you desktop-publish the *Bill of Rights* document by adding borders, formatting it in two columns with a line between them, adding a table of contents, and inserting a picture.

1. Open the *Bill of Rights* document stored in the *Exercise Documents* folder on the *Word Student Resource Disk* and display it in page layout view.

2. Use the **Format**, **Borders and Shading** command to add a border and shading of your choice around the title *Bill of Rights* at the top of the document.

3. Use the **Style** drop-down arrow (⏷) on the Formatting toolbar to format each of the amendment numbers (but not the titles) as *Heading 1*.

4. On a blank line below the *Bill of Rights* heading, use the **Insert**, **Index and Tables** command to insert a *Classic* table of contents.

5. On a blank line above the heading for the first amendment, use the **Insert**, **Picture** command to insert the *Scales* picture. (It should be in the *C:\msoffice\clipart* folder.)

6. Save the document, print the first page, and then close the document.

6-3 Formatting the End User's Newsletter Document

In this exercise you desktop-publish the newsletter document by adding paragraph borders, formatting it in two columns with a line between them, and adding a table of contents.

1. Open the *End User's Newsletter* document stored in the *Exercise Documents* folder on the *Word Student Resource Disk* and display it in page layout view.

2. Use the **Format**, **Borders and Shading** command to add a border and shading of your choice around the heading *The Staff* and the four lines of names that follow it.

3. Use the **Format**, **Borders and Shading** command to add a border of your choice around the two headings that begin *Checklist* and the bulleted items that follow each heading.

4. Just below the *Volume 1 Number 1* line, use the **Format**, **Columns** command to format the document into two columns with a line between them from that point forward.

5. Use the **Style** drop-down arrow (▾) on the Formatting toolbar to format each of the four all-caps headings as *Heading 1*. (Remember you can use F4 to repeat a format.)

6. Add the boldfaced heading **CONTENTS** so there is a blank line between it and the box listing the staff above it.

7. With the insertion point on a blank line below the *CONTENTS* heading, use the **Insert**, **Index and Tables** command to insert a *Formal* table of contents.

8. Save the document, print the first page, and then close the document.

6-4 Adding Tables to the Sexism Guidelines Document

It's easy to have your writing subtly affect the way others think about themselves. Writing that offends others because of race, sex, or religion should be avoided. In this exercise, you create a table listing examples of biased and unbiased references to women.

1. Open the *Avoiding sexist language* document stored in the *Exercise Documents* folder on the *Word Student Resource Disk* and enter your name. Click anywhere in the date and press F9 to update it.

2. With the insertion point on a blank line under the paragraph of body text in the section headed *Omission*, use the **Table**, **Insert Table** command to insert a table with 2 columns and 4 rows.

3. Enter the table shown in the figure "The Omission Table" and boldface the column headings in the table.

Biased	Unnbiased
The pioneers crossed the desert with their women, children, and possessions.	Pioneer families crossed the desert carrying all their possessions.
Radium was discovered by a woman, Marie Curie.	Marie Curie discovered Radium.
When setting up his experiment, the researcher must always check his sample for error.	When setting up an experiment, a researcher must always check for sampling error.

The Omission Table

4. With the insertion point on a blank line under the paragraph of body text in the section headed *Equal Treatment*, use the **Table**, **Insert Table** command to insert a table with 2 columns and 4 rows.

5. Enter the table shown in the figure "The Equal Treatment Table" and boldface the column headings.

Biased	Unbiased
Though a woman, she ran the business effectively.	She ran the business effectively.
The little girls played with the boys.	The girls played with the boys; the children played; the little girls played with the little boys.
The line manager was angry; and his secretary told him she was upset too.	The line manager and his secretary were both upset by the mistake.

The Equal Treatment Table

6. Select each table in its entirety and use the **Format**, **Borders and Shading** command to format each with a grid. (It's applied with the **Grid** choice in the *Presets* section of the **Borders** tab.)

7. Save, print, and then close the document.

PROJECTS

6-1   Desktop-Publishing a Booklet

In this project you desktop-publish the document describing your rights as an airline passenger. To do so, you'll format the document in four columns, in landscape orientation, and insert a table of contents and a picture.

1. Open the *Flier's rights* document stored in the *Project Documents* folder on the *Word Student Resource Disk*.

2. Format the document so it looks like the one in the figure "The Flier's-Rights Document." The orientation is landscape and the table of contents is *Formal* with only one level of headings. Be sure to apply column and orientation formats to the entire document. You may have to delete an existing section break below the title. Format the table of contents paragraphs so they have no space above or below them. The clip art shown above the table of contents is *jet.wmf*, which you will probably find in the *c:\msoffice\clipart* folder. If it has not been installed on your system, use another piece of art.

3. Go through the document and use what you have learned about formatting to make it look professional. Change paragraph spacing and indents, bullets, headers and footers, and anything else you like. Look for other pictures to insert at appropriate points.

4. When you have finished, save the document, print at least the first page, and then close the document.

Flier's Rights

A Guide to Air Travel in the U.S.

U.S. Department of Transportation
your name

INTRODUCTION

Deregulating the airlines was a statement of faith by the government in the free marketplace.

The elimination of government regulation has resulted in lower air fares for the American public and a wide variety of price/service options. The spectrum of air service available to consumers has ranged from super premium coast-to-coast service where a limousine picks you up at your door, to no-frills, low-cost shuttle service where passengers carry their bags on board.

In this new commercial environment, consumers have had to take a more active role in choosing their air service by learning to ask a number of questions.

- Am I more concerned with price or scheduling? Am I willing to fly at an odd hour if it means saving $25.?
- Will the airline penalize me for changing my reservation?
- What will the airline do for me if it cancels my flight?

This booklet is designed to explain your rights and responsibilities as an air traveler.

resourceful consumer.

AIR FARES

Because of the emphasis on price competition, airlines don't all charge the same fares anymore. Some of them are trying a "back to basics" approach-offering plane rides at bargain basement prices with few if any extras.

For fare information, you can contact a travel agent, other ticket marketer or an airline serving the places you want to visit. Ask them to tell you the names of all airlines flying there. Then you can call each airline to ask about fares they charge and any special low fares they may offer. You can also watch the newspapers where airlines advertise many of their discount plans. Finally, be alert to new companies serving the market. They may offer lower fares or different services than older established airlines.

Here are some tips to help you decide among air fares:

- *Be flexible in your travel plans in order to get the lowest fare. Often there are

must meet to qualify for a discount.

- Plan as far ahead as you can. Some airlines set aside only a few seats on each flight at the lower rates. The real bargains often sell out very quickly.
- Some airlines may have discounts that others don't offer. In a large metropolitan area, the fare could depend on which airport you use.
- Does the air fare include types of service that airlines have traditionally provided, such as meals or free baggage handling? If you are stranded, will the ticket be good on another airline at no extra charge? Will the first airline pay for meals or hotel rooms during the wait?
- Find out what will happen if you decide to switch flights. Will you lose the benefit of your discount fare? Are there any cancellation fees? Is there a cut-off date for making and changing reservations without paying more money?
- *Some airlines will not increase the fare after the

PAGE 1

The Flier's Rights document

EXCHANGING DATA WITH OTHER APPLICATIONS

After completing this PicTorial, you will be able to:

- **Briefly describe the purpose of object linking and embedding (OLE)**
- **Understand the difference between linked and embedded objects**
- **Paste objects into Word documents so they are linked or embedded**
- **Insert new linked or embedded objects**
- **Insert linked or embedded objects created from existing files**
- **Edit linked and embedded objects**
- **Insert an Access database table into a Word document**

ONE of the recent trends in computing has been to make data, rather than applications, the focus of software design. Advances in design make it possible to include data in a document that has been created by other applications. For example, you can create a budget in Excel and then place it in a Word document. You can also use other types of applications to create and paste in line drawings, photographs, sounds, and even video.

Documents built from parts created with a number of different application programs are called *compound documents*. There is more than one technology used to create compound documents. One of the major ones is called *object linking and embedding*, or OLE—sometimes pronounced "olé," as if you were a bullfighter. OLE allows you to insert data from one application into another just as if it were copied. Compound documents created using OLE are called *OLE documents*.

Imagine how complicated a single program would have to be to edit all of these different components. Instead of one large program, you use many different programs, each dedicated to one task. For example, what if you wanted to send a memo discussing sales, and including a table, a chart, and a spoken explanation? To do so with OLE, you would use a word processing program to create the body of the document, a spreadsheet to create the table and chart, and a sound program to record and edit the comments.

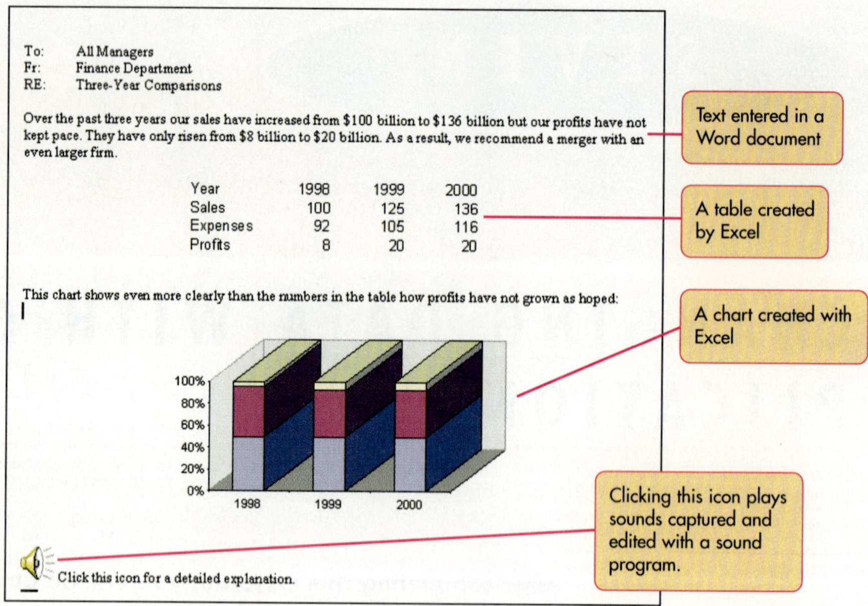

Compound documents are wonderful things. However, the big question is, "How do you get the data from one application into the other?" As you'll now see, Windows gives you more than one way to do so.

Copying Data Between Applications

One of the easiest ways to insert data from one application into another is to cut and paste it. To do so, you just copy some data from one application to the Windows Clipboard and then paste it into another application's document. You can even drag data from one application and drop it into another. It's as if you cut a picture out of a magazine and pasted it into a scrapbook.

As useful as copying data is, it has some drawbacks, the biggest one being that the copied data has no links to the application that created it. If you needed to update the data you pasted into a document, you couldn't do it from the document you copied it to. You'd have to open the application that created it, change the data, cut and paste it again—then delete the old version.

Concepts Behind Object Linking and Embedding

To overcome the shortcomings of copying data, most new Windows applications support OLE so you can insert data from one application into another. When data is placed in an OLE document, you can edit it within the document you placed it in. To better understand this, you have to understand a few new terms that identify the data being copied and the application programs being used.

▶ An *object* is the data you want to copy from one application into another. An object can be any type of data that is recognized by your system. It can include the data from a spreadsheet, paragraphs from a word processing document, a sound from a sound editing program, or a video clip. A *source file* or *source document* is the file on the disk that contains the object.

▶ An *OLE server application* is the application used to create the data that has been embedded. For example, if you paste some data from Excel into Word, Excel is the server application.

▶ An *OLE container* (previously called a *client*) is an application that can contain objects or the document into which you paste an object. For example, if you paste some data from Excel into Word, the Excel data is the object and the Word document is the container.

▶ An *OLE document* (sometimes called a *container document* or *compound document*) is the document created with an OLE application into which objects have been pasted. For example, a Word document containing an object created with another application is an OLE document.

When using OLE, you can often choose between embedding and linking the object. These terms refer to the way the data pasted into an OLE document relates to the server application. Let's take a look at three ways data can be pasted into a container.

▶ *Native data* is the data created by the application into which an object is being pasted. For example, when you copy some data from Excel into Word, any of the accompanying text that hasn't been pasted is Word's native data. If you use the Clipboard to cut and paste data from one application into another, it is converted to native data when you paste it in and is neither linked nor embedded. For example, you can paste Excel data into a Word document and it appears in Word as a table. It has no links whatever to Excel.

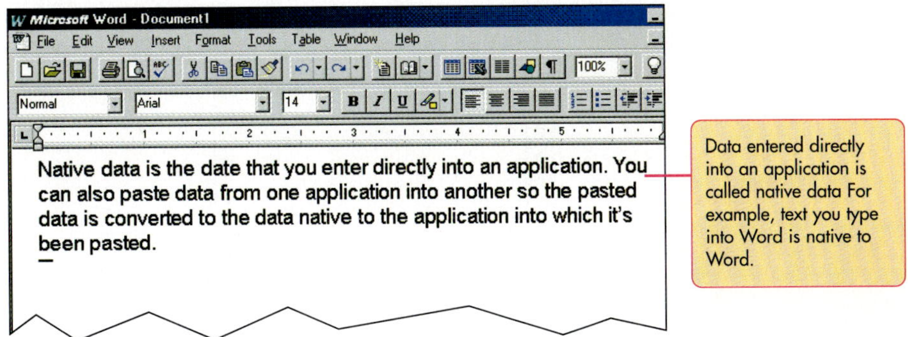

▶ An *OLE embedded object* is a copy of the data created by the OLE server application. When you *embed* an object, a copy of the data in the source document is placed in the OLE document just as if you had copied it. You can just double-click this copy to edit it in the context of its new document. When you do so, a number of things happen. The menu bar and toolbars change to reflect those used to edit the data in the *OLE server application*. In addition, any adornments such as row and column headings and scroll bars appear in the object's window. You can edit the data in the object just as if you had opened the *server application* to do so. However, any changes you make affect only the copy in the OLE document. The copy on the disk that you can open with the server application remains unchanged.

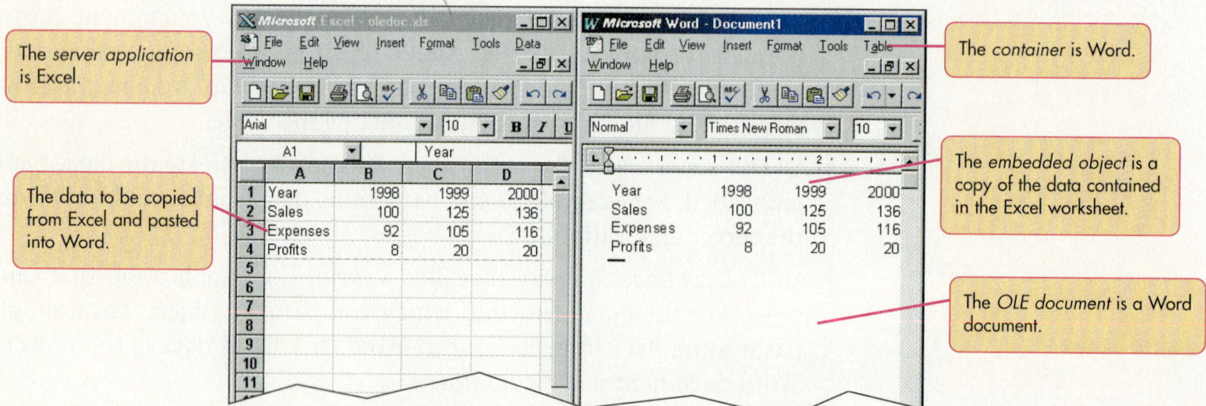

▶ A *linked object* is similar to an embedded object, but there are a few key differences. When you *link* an object, it isn't copied into the destination document—there is only one copy of the object, the original one. Instead, a link is established between the real object and an *image* of it in the OLE document. If you make any changes to the real object, those changes are carried through the link to the image of the object in the OLE document. If you double-click a linked object in a OLE document, the server application opens with the real object displayed. Any changes you make to this object are carried automatically to the object in the OLE document.

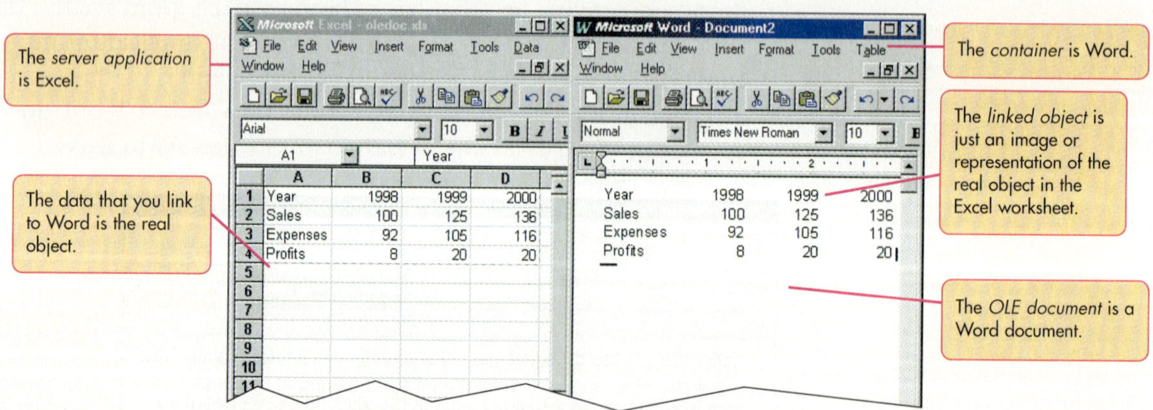

When to Embed and When to Link

When do you link and when do you embed? It depends on a number of issues.

It makes sense to use linking when the same object is used in a number of different OLE documents. With linking, if you edit the object, any changes are immediately reflected in all of the documents to which it is linked. For example, if you prepared a sales report in Excel, you could link the table and chart to a number of memos to different sales manager. Then, if you had to update the data, you would only have to do it once—the changes would be automatically reflected in all of the memos.

One reason to embed is to take advantage of visual editing (discussed in Section 7-3). This allows you to edit the object right in the document in which it's embedded. Linked objects don't offer this ability. Their objects must be edited with the separate application that created them. Another reason to embed is that you want to make changes in the OLE document's object without affecting the original file the object is taken from. For example, if you embed an Excel table in a Word document, you can edit the copy in the Word document without affecting the copy created by Excel.

7-1 PASTING OBJECTS INTO WORD DOCUMENTS

If you have already created data in one application that you want to link or embed into another, you can do so by cutting and pasting.

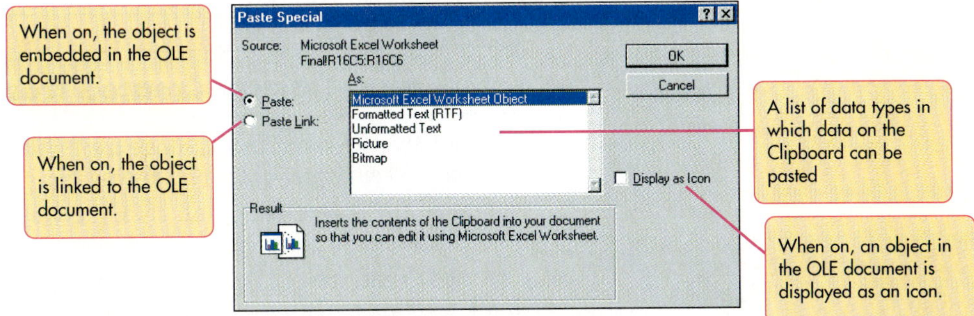

PAL ON-LINE ACTIVITIES CHECKLIST

☐ **7-1 CONCEPTS.** In this section you interactively explore the concepts of cutting data from one document and pasting it into another as an object.

☐ **7-1 TUTORIAL.** In this tutorial you embed and link Excel objects into a Word document. The resulting Word document becomes a compound document.

☐ **7-1 DRILL.** If you have already created a file that you want to link or embed in another application's document as an object, you can copy and paste it in. In this drill you practice these procedures.

If you want to insert a new object in an OLE document, you can do so. You can also insert an existing file on the disk as an object.

Inserting New Objects

When you insert a new object, it can only be embedded and not linked. This is because links can only be established to existing files.

When inserting a new object, you are given the opportunity of selecting an object type from a list. The list contains all OLE data types that are registered for your system. For example, if Excel is on your system, you will be able to create an Excel object. If Excel isn't on your system, you won't be able to.

Inserting New Objects

1. Open the Word document and move the insertion point where you want a new object inserted.

2. Pull down the **Insert** menu and click the **Object** command to display the Object dialog box.

3. On the **Create** New tab, select the type of object from the **Object Type** list and click the OK button. The object you select will be embedded in the document.

Inserting Objects Created from Files

You needn't open an application and a file to cut and paste data from it to create an object in another application. You can create an object directly from an existing file on the disk. When you do so, you can choose between linking and embedding it.

Inserting Objects Created from Files

1. Open the Word document and move the insertion point where you want to insert an object created from an existing file.

2. Pull down the **Insert** menu and click the **Object** command to display the Object dialog box.

3. Click the **Create from File** tab and enter the object's filename in the **File Name** text box or click the **Browse** button to search for it just as you would open an ordinary document. When you find it, click it to select it, then click the **Open** button. Click the **Link to File** check box if you want the object linked instead of embedded.

4. Click the OK button to insert the linked or embedded object.

☐ **7-2 CONCEPTS.** In this section you interactively explore the concept of inserting objects into a document.

☐ **7-2 TUTORIAL.** In this tutorial you insert Excel objects into a Word document. You first insert a new object, and then insert one from an existing file on the disk.

☐ **7-2 DRILL.** If you want to insert a new object or create an object from an existing file on the disk, you can do so. In this drill you practice the procedures used to link and embed objects created from existing files on the disk. Both objects that you insert are animation files similar to movies.

7-3 EDITING LINKED AND EMBEDDED OBJECTS

After embedding or linking an object in a document, you can edit it without leaving the OLE document.

Selecting and Activating Objects

When an object in a document is linked or embedded, you can either select it or activate it. Normally you select an object to move or resize it and activate it to edit it.

▶ To *select* a linked or embedded object in the OLE document, click it. A selected object displays eight handles that you can use to resize it and the mouse pointer turns into a left-pointing arrow when over the object. Also, a message on the status line tells you how to activate it.

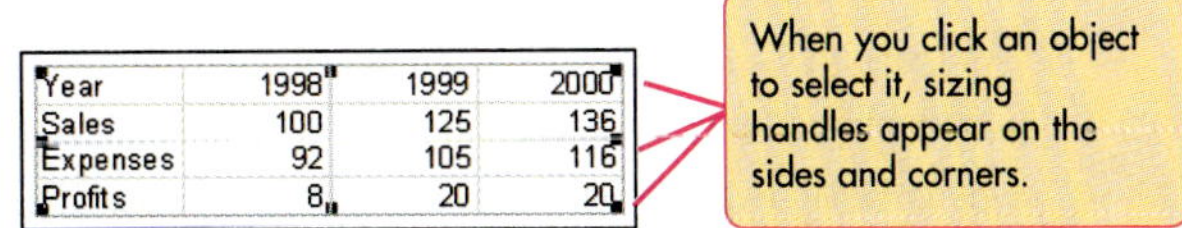

▶ To *activate* a linked or embedded object in the OLE document, double-click it. What happens when you activate it depends on whether it is linked or embedded. If linked, the server application opens with the object displayed for editing or formatting. If embedded, the container application's menu bars and toolbars change to reflect those of the server application.

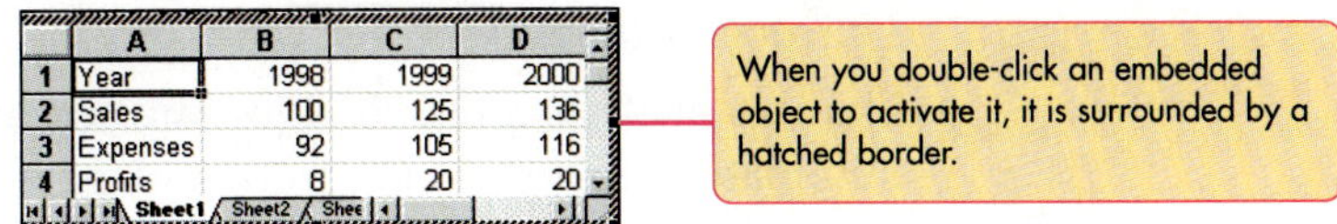

In addition to selecting or activating an embedded object, you can also open it. This displays the object in a separate window so you can see more of the object. When an object is opened, it is displayed in the OLE document with an "open" hatched border that indicates it is open in another window. The easiest way to open an object is to right-click it and select the **Open...** command from the shortcut menu. The window that appears is an alternate window onto the object and a separate application. Any changes you make are immediately and automatically reflected in the object in the OLE document. After making changes to the object, just click the object window's **Close** button to return to the OLE document.

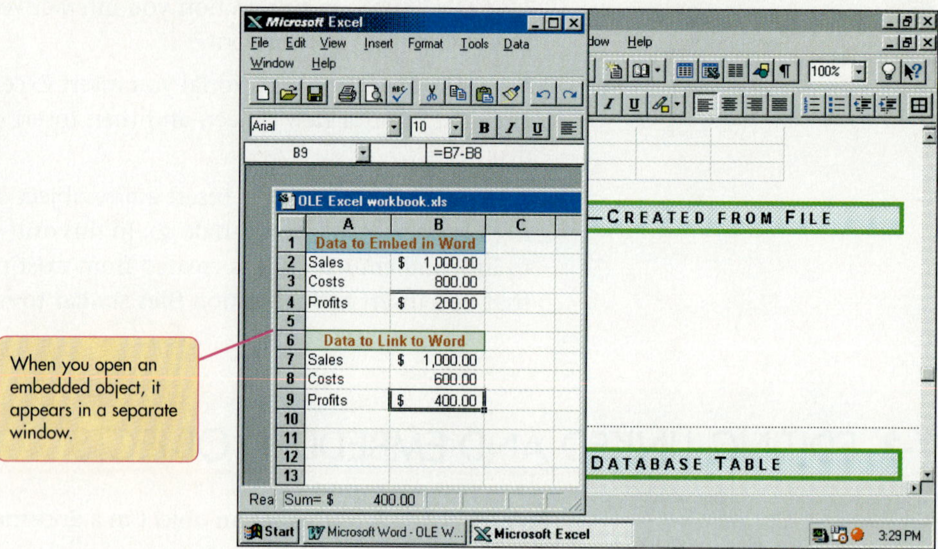

Editing Activated Objects

An object is most commonly activated to edit its contents in its current location.

▶ When you activate an embedded object, it displays a hatched border. This border indicates that the menu commands and toolbar buttons from the object's server application have temporarily taken the place of those normally displayed by the container application. In addition, the object displays its frame *adornments*, the name for such elements as row and column headings and scroll bars. This is called *OLE visual editing* because you edit the object in the visual context of the OLE document in which it is embedded.

▶ When you activate a linked object, the server application opens and displays the object for editing. This is because the object is only a link to another source and is not a real object. It is only a stand-in that allows the source object to be displayed elsewhere, much like a reflection in a mirror. To change the object in the OLE document, you have to change the source object itself.

When you edit an embedded or linked object, the changes take place in the OLE document immediately and automatically. However, there is a difference in how changes affect the source file.

▶ Changes made to an embedded object affect only the copy of the object in the OLE document and are not carried to the original file on the disk.

▶ Changes made to a linked object are actually made in the source file and then automatically carried back to the image of the object in the OLE document.

Editing Embedded Objects

1. Do one of the following to activate the embedded object in the OLE document:

   ▶ To edit the object in place, double-click the embedded object, or click it to select it, pull down the **Edit** menu, click the **x Object** command (where x stands for the type of object) to cascade the menu, then click the **Edit** command.

   ▶ To edit the object in a separate window, click it to select it, then pull down the **Edit** menu, click the **x Object** command (where x stands for the type of object) to cascade the menu, and click the **Open** command.

2. Edit the object using the server application's menu commands and toolbar buttons that appear in the container application.

3. To deactivate the object, do one of the following:

   ▶ If the object is activated within the OLE document, click anywhere else in the document but the object.

   ▶ If the object is open in a separate window, click that window's **Save** button on the toolbar to save the changes, then click that window's **Close** button.

Editing Linked Objects

1. To activate the linked object in the OLE document do one of the following:

   ▶ Double-click the object.

   ▶ Click the object to select it, then pull down the **Edit** menu, click the **x Object** command (where x stands for the type of object) to cascade the menu, and click the **Edit** command.

2. Edit the object using the server application.

3. Click the server application's **Save** button on the toolbar to save the changes, then click that window's **Close** button.

Managing Linked Objects

Linking objects keeps the OLE document's size smaller because the linked object is stored on the disk, not in the document. However, this can occasionally cause problems because the objects must retain links to the source file in which they are stored (the object in the OLE document is just a visual representation, not the real object.)

If you move a linked object's file to another folder on the disk, Windows will keep track of its new location. However, if you delete a linked object's source file and then try to activate it, a message will tell you it can't be edited.

To transfer the OLE document to another system, you must also transfer the file containing the original object if you want to be able to edit it. (You need not do so if you are just going to view the object in the context of the OLE document on the new system.) Even if you include the object's file, then you may have to specify its new location. To do so, select the object, pull down the **Edit** menu, and click the **Lin<u>k</u>s** command. Use the **Cha<u>n</u>ge Source** button to browse for the object's file.

Breaking Links

Sometimes you want to update a linked object without having the change reflected in the document to which it's linked. For example, you have written a memo on monthly sales and linked an Excel chart of June's sales in it. You now want to update the chart to July's sales without affecting the June sales chart in the memo. To do this, you just break the link.

QUICKSTEPS

Breaking a Link

1. Select the object whose link you want to break.
2. Pull down the **<u>E</u>dit** menu and click the **Lin<u>k</u>s** command to display the Links dialog box. The link to the object you selected is highlighted.
3. Click the **<u>B</u>reak Link** button and when asked to confirm the break, click the **<u>Y</u>es** button.
4. Click the **Close** button to close the dialog box.

Deleting Objects

To delete an embedded or linked object from its OLE document, just click it to select it and press `Del`.

Resizing and Moving Linked and Embedded Data

After embedding or linking an object in a document, you can change its size or move it to a new location within the existing text. If there is no existing text, or it is too short, you cannot move the object to a new position.

QUICKSTEPS

Scaling, Moving, and Deleting Linked and Embedded Data

1. Click the object in the OLE document.
2. Do one of the following:
   ▸ To resize the object, drag one of the eight handles.
   ▸ To move the object, point to it, hold down the left mouse button, and drag the mouse pointer to where you want to object moved. When you release the mouse button, the object moves to the new position.
   ▸ To delete the object, press `Del`.

☐ **7-3 CONCEPTS.** In this section you interactively explore the concept of editing linked and embedded objects.

☐ **7-3 TUTORIAL.** In this tutorial you edit both embedded and linked objects to see how the two procedures differ.

☐ **7-3 DRILL.** Once you have embedded or linked objects in a document, you can edit them in place. Here you practice the procedures you use to edit both embedded and linked objects.

7-4 INSERTING AN ACCESS DATABASE TABLE INTO A WORD DOCUMENT

Access database tables can be inserted into Word documents but only in Word's native format. They cannot be linked or embedded.

QUICKSTEPS

Inserting an Access Database Table into a Word Document

1. Open the Word document and move the insertion point where you want a new or existing object inserted.

2. Pull down the **Insert** menu and click the **Database** command to display the Database dialog box.

3. Click the **Get Data** button to display the Open Data Source dialog box.

4. Click the **Files of type** drop-down arrow and click the *MS Access Databases* choice.

5. Search for the database just as you would open an ordinary document. When you find it, click it to select it, then click the **Open** button to display the Microsoft Access dialog box.

6. In the **Tables in OLE Database** list, click the name of the table you want to open and then click the **OK** button display the Database dialog box.

7. Click the **Insert Data** button to display the Insert Data dialog box.

8. Specify the records to be inserted, and click the **OK** button to insert the database table into Word as a Word table. Each field in the table is a column and each record is a row.

☐ **7-4 CONCEPTS.** In this section you interactively explore the concept of inserting an Access database into a document.

☐ **7-4 TUTORIAL.** In this tutorial you insert an Access database table into a Word document.

☐ **7-4 DRILL.** Although you cannot link or embed Access database tables in a Word document, you can insert them as native data—in this case a Word table. Here you practice this procedure.

LAB ACTIVITIES

EXERCISES

7-1 Embedding and Linking Objects

In this exercise, you explore embedding and linking objects on your own. You will work with the same objects you have been working with in tutorials and drills so they will be familiar to you.

1. Use Word to open the *OLE Exercise* document stored in the *OLE Files* folder on the *Word Student Resource Disk*. Use Excel to open the *OLE Excel workbook* stored in the same folder. Arrange the windows side by side.

2. Copy the data in cells A1 through B4 from Excel to the Clipboard and paste it into the Word document below the heading *The Following Item Is Embedded*. Be sure to use the **Paste Special** command on the **Edit** menu to do so.

3. Copy the data in cells A6 through B9 from Excel to the Clipboard and paste it into the Word document below the heading *The Following Item Is Linked*. Be sure to use the **Paste Special** command on the **Edit** menu to do so but this time be sure to click the **Link to File** check box so the object will be linked instead of embedded.

4. Edit the embedded object (the first one) and change the costs in cell B3 to 600.

5. Edit the linked object (the second one) and change the costs in cell B8 to 900. Save the changes and close Excel.

6. Save and print the Word document, then close the application.

PROJECTS

7-1 OLE and the Internet

The Internet is the hottest thing in computing today and it will change the way we all think of computers. New versions of programs such as Word will have Internet access built right into them. Even now, you can access the Internet from within a Word document. Using an Internet browser, the addresses of World Wide Web sites can be saved on a list of favorite sites—much like a phone directory. This way you just click the address the next time you want to visit. However, Windows 95 allows you to drag and drop shortcuts from one place to another. Here some favorites web sites have been dragged and dropped from a list of favorite sites in a Web browser into a Word document. They are clickable shortcuts to these popular sites. If your system is equipped to browse the World Wide Web, click any of the embedded shortcuts to visit a site. Just keep in mind that the Web is changing daily, not all of them may work. To explore this exciting aspect of computing, open the *Internet Hot List* document stored in the *OLE File* folder on the *Word Student Resource Disk*.

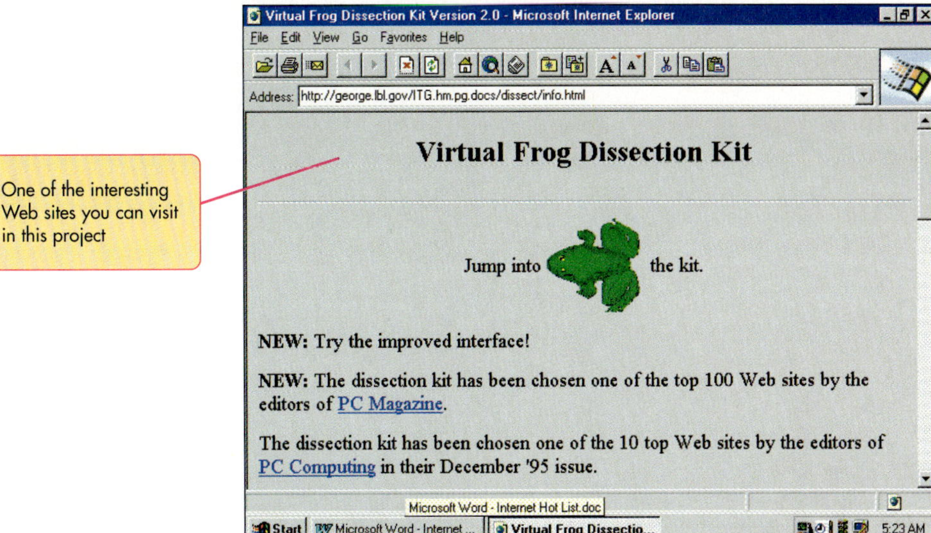

7-2   You're On Your Own

You have now come to the end of the text! At this point, demonstrate your skill with OLE by opening a new Word document and then linking and embedding objects into it in a variety of ways. Label each object and describe the procedure you used to link or embed it. You can use any of the objects that you find in the *OLE Files* folder on the *Word Student Resource Disk*.